Money & Credit in Indian History

From Early Medieval Times

Money & Credit in Indian History

From Early Medieval Times

edited by Amiya Kumar Bagchi

Indian History Congress

Tulika

Published by **Tulika Books**
35 A/1 (ground floor), Shahpur Jat, New Delhi 110 049, India

© Indian History Congress 2002

First edition (hardback) 2002

Second edition (paperback) 2002

Third edition (paperback) 2012

ISBN: 978-93-82381-12-9

Typeset in Minion and Univers at Tulika Print Communication Services, New Delhi, and printed at Chaman
Enterprises, Darya Ganj, Delhi

Contents

CONTENTS

Preface

As Secretary, Indian History Congress, at the time, I had the privilege of organizing on its behalf a panel on Money and Credit in India since Early Medieval Times, at the 61st annual session on 2–4 January 2001, at Kolkata. I was happy that we were able to obtain co-operation from many scholars, so that not only did the deliberations at the panel, chaired by Professor Amiya K. Bagchi, prove most instructive, but the papers received were of such substance that the Indian History Congress decided to publish them in a volume and requested Professor Bagchi to edit it. He kindly agreed and has given us an excellent Introduction, as the reader will see.

The Indian History Congress had decided to organize the panel in order to fill what it felt was a void in Indian economic history in the area of money and credit. The nature of source material did not give us sufficient confidence to begin from a period earlier than the early medieval (or, at one's choice in nomenclature, the late ancient) period; the title of the volume makes clear the modest ambitions of the enterprise in terms of the span of time covered. The reader need not, perhaps be reminded that since the papers are pieces of research in particular aspects, a comprehensive coverage of the subject is not claimed for this volume. However, with both these limitations, it is hoped that the reader will find that the volume distinctly enlarges our knowledge of the field.

The original panel and the present publication have been made possible by generous grants from the Power Finance Corporation, New Delhi, and a leading bank, which, to our regret, asked that its name be not publicized. We also received a subsidy from the United Bank of India, Kolkata. We are highly indebted to Dr Manmohan

Singh and Professor A.M. Khusro for so kindly taking up our cause with the donors.

During the panel and afterwards, I obtained much support from Professor S.P. Verma, the then Treasurer of the Indian History Congress, and from Professor Ramakrishna Chatterjee, the present Secretary of the Indian History Congress. Professor Irfan Habib gave me much guidance and help throughout the time with regard to both the organizing of the panel and the publication of its papers.

Mr Muneeruddin Khan has processed all the authors' contributions; and Mr Arshad Ali helped me most actively with the holding of the panel at Kolkata. Many thanks are owed to both.

I have greatly benefited from the indulgence that Mr Rajendra Prasad and Ms Indira Chandrasekhar of the Tulika Books have always shown me, and if this volume has appeared in time it is entirely due to them.

SHIREEN MOOSVI

Introduction

Money, Banking and Finance in India since Early Medieval Times

Amiya Kumar Bagchi

Media of exchange and credit networks from the first millennium CE to the eighteenth century

Human beings may or may not have a natural tendency to truck or barter, as Adam Smith thought. But in most historical periods in India, for which we have been able to recover the records of our ancestors, many groups of people were engaged in exchanges of their products with their neighbours, and money was extensively used in these exchanges. Families and clans became specialized in these exchanges and in the storing and circulation of money for facilitating these exchanges. These groups were then known as merchants, money-changers, and keepers and lenders of money. There is no point trying to define who exactly were the bankers, or bankers and money-changers, or bankers, merchants and money-changers rolled into one, without specifying the context. It is the function of historians to specify the contexts in which apparently similar institutions functioned in very different ways and thus alert us to the infinite potential of human ingenuity, and, when sufficient evidence accumulates, to tell us something about the way the use of particular institutions has a perceptible influence on the evolution of the larger society.

The anthology of papers presented here arises out of the session on money, banking and finance organized under the auspices of the Indian History Congress held in Kolkata in the year 2000 CE. The first paper in this collection, by K.M. Shrimali, addresses a debate about the way the scarcity of money in the early medieval period may have strengthened the institutions of Indian-style feudalism as conceptualized by major scholars in the area such as D.D. Kosambi and R.S. Sharma. There are at least three different strands of this debate that merit further analysis and research by scholars interested in the subject. First, there is the question of the facts of the case. Did the supply of metals used for coinage decline in India during the early or late medieval period? Connected with that is the further question, 'If the supply of the usual metals declined, did the users of money find substitutes in the form of other substances or in the form of networks of credit?' If the answer is 'Yes', how durable or robust were these credit networks? Is there sufficient evidence of a general decline of trade in India in the first millennium of the Christian era, and in particular between 300 CE and 1200 CE, which is supposed to have been associated with a decline in urban centres, a strengthening of the natural economy of villages, and thereby giving a fillip to the growth of Indian-style feudalism? The second issue is connected with the last question, namely, whether substitutability or innovation in coinage, money substances or credit networks is itself intimately associated with particular modes of production, or more generally with particular state systems and social formations. There is evidence from other lands that shortage of bullion and coins does not necessarily lead to a strengthening of feudal or personalistic ties or authoritarian state formations. For example, it has been claimed that for a hundred years before the beginning of the exploitation of the American silver mines by the Spaniards, Europe lived through a regime of currency shortage (Fossier 1986: 428). But it is difficult to claim that feudal ties were growing stronger, at least in western Europe, during those years. A third issue is the delineation of the conditions under which increased mercantile activity is associated with a strengthening or weakening of feudal ties or ties of personal dependence. Was the 'second serfdom', dating variously from the seventeenth or eighteenth century, also associated with lesser mercantile activity and a monetary shortage? Shrimali's paper prompts us to ask some of these questions again.

Given the variety of conditions in different parts of India and the length of the period covered, the debates will continue for some time and it would appear to be rather unlikely that we should arrive at a scholarly consensus soon. For example, it would be possible that social formations centred around personalistic or vassal-like dependence were growing in the interior of India even as trade across the Indian Ocean was revitalizing old port towns or creating new centres of trade. To take another example, the evidence of extensive use of *cowries* and the relative scarcity of metallic coinage issued in the centuries concerned has been taken as a sign of decline of long-distance trade. But *cowries*, after all, were themselves the product of long-distance trade, and the substitution of coins by *cowries* even in long-distance transactions could have been a sign of monetary innovation rather than one of a reversal to conditions of natural economy. (For a useful summary of the issues involved, see Chakravarti 2001, and the papers and articles assembled in Chakravarti 2001a.)

The next set of papers pertains to the period of Mughal rule and the transition from Mughal to successor Indian states such as the Maratha Confederacy. There is a strong continuity in the institutional basis of the use of money and credit in the domestic economy of India from the late sixteenth century under Mughal rule and the late nineteenth century under British rule. In order to grasp the nature of the continuity we have first of all to recognize that, however integrated the whole economy might appear from the vantage-point of Delhi, Agra or Calcutta, that integration concealed many breaks and differences of intensity of contact within the highly complex network of a commercialized economy which has not got rid of private coercive and discriminatory power in most walks of life. To be more specific, we should recognize that in Mughal India as in British India, there were many circuits of exchange of goods and money, very often (but not always) with different kinds of money being used as the typical medium of exchange in different circuits. Concurrently and overlaying these connected but separate circuits of exchange there were also circuits of credit very often with the same controllers on the lending side operating different circuits with different rules. Even at the top of the hierarchy and circuits of exchange, the royal money or the publicly recognized money might have strict limits within which they might be used and it would be wrong to generalize about the effects, for example, of the effects of changes in the supply of such money without recognizing those limits. To take two examples from the Mughal period and late colonial period, respectively, how many peasants or artisans ever handled a *mohur (muhr)* with the imprint of the reigning Padshah, and how many of them ever handled even a 100-rupee note, let alone a 10,000-rupee note, issued by the colonial government?

The paper by Najaf Haider in this anthology raises a very interesting question that is pertinent beyond the borders of the Mughal economy: 'What dominated the supply of medium of exchange, the supply of metallic coin or the system of credit which often obviated the need for any metallic coin?' That question can rarely be answered with precision under most circumstances. But the question has still to be asked because the meaning of money supply itself may change with changes in political and economic circumstances, and the state of credit is even more susceptible to such influences.

Let me first look at the way metallic money circulated. In many territories, the rulers did not try to impose one single type of coinage on their subjects. In these cases the values of the different types of coins were determined by the intrinsic worth of the metals and their relative values as determined by forces of supply and demand. Demand was, however, very greatly influenced by mercantile usage or by political factors outside the particular realms. In the present anthology, A.R. Kulkarni has vividly brought out the freedom with which coins of very different provenance circulated in the territories ruled by the Marathas. Interestingly, the Ottoman empire, a much more durable and extensive empire than the empire of the Maratha Confederacy, also lived with a multitude of coins (Pamuk 1994, 2000: esp. chapter 11). In such circumstances, the rates of exchange of the different coins were influenced by pulls of supply and demand in the larger macro-region in which the particular territory was located, and ultimately in the global economy. If it happened to be the case that the particular territory ran up a persistently adverse balance of trade with the rest of the world, then it could experience a severe shortage of coin and the realm could suffer economically, unless there were financiers willing and able to lend their resources to the particular state. Even in cases in which there were no long-run problem of balance of trade, the particular territory could suffer because of a shortage of liquidity. A properly organized credit system could take care of the temporary problem of shortage of cash. But in case of persistent balance of trade deficits, only a public credit system which would be supported also by an expanding revenue-raising capacity of the state can prevent depression and contraction of the economic base of the particular territory. Such a public credit system could arise only in states run in the interest of merchants and financiers; thus such a system was first born in the Italian city-oligarchies of Genoa and Venice and found its full maturity in the first industrializing nation, namely, England (Dickson 1968; Dickson and Sperling 1970; O'Brien 1988, 1994; Brewer 1989; Tattara 2002). I shall later explore the implication of the absence of a public credit system in India before the coming of independence.

In the case of Mughal India, it is difficult to disentangle the respective roles of the money supply and the private credit system, precisely because the country enjoyed a persistent balance of trade surplus so that the criticality of credit as a supplement to cash cannot be established by observing a situation in which the Mughal empire experienced a shortage of the liquidity needed to support current economic activities.

Private creditors were, of course, connected by various networks of trust, and these networks could extend even to lending to a person on the basis of security rather than on the basis of personal knowledge. Bearer *hundis* would illustrate this: these *hundis*, however, still bore the name of the original issuer. Most moneylending would take the form of what would be known later as relationship banking (for analysis of relationship banking, see Besanko and Thakor 1993, and Lamoreaux 1994). Within the privileged networks of bankers, cash could often be dispensed with as illustrated by the practice of Gujarati bankers to fix on settlement days and renew the loans on an agreed *anth* or discount for the postponement of the settlement. This kind of transaction could sometimes be unsettling for the rulers since they might not be able to find out whether a banker was preventing an inevitable bankruptcy by continually postponing the day of reckoning, or whether he was simply unwilling to reveal his hand. But the rulers wanted to be certain that public dues would be paid in generally acceptable coin, and would not be snarled up by bankruptcies or non-transparent transactions. So, from the post-Mughal times to the British period, attempts were often made to ban the system of *anth*, but the system seems to have kept alive many transactions or productive economic activities which would have collapsed without it (Ali Muhammad Khan 1761/1965; Habib 1982; Bagchi 1982).

Najaf Haider, Shireen Moosvi and Om Prakash in their papers have discussed the way rates of interest behaved in Mughal India. I only want to add the following remarks to complement their discussion. First, when these authors mention regional differences in rates of interest or changes in rates of interest, and analyse the influence of such factors as differences or changes in money supply, import of bullion or demand for credit as factors causing those differentials or changes in interest rates, their analysis primarily, or even exclusively, bears on what may be called prime lending rates. The capital market, that is, the market for loans and borrowings, are by their very nature highly imperfect, and in every country, and especially in a country that is primarily dependent on the production of primary products, rates of interest and the availability of credit travel a steep gradient along the axis of the degree of creditworthiness: the latter is determined in its turn by a complex of factors among which the size of the collateral or security for the loan, the liquidity or cash flow generated by the project financed by the loan, and enforceability of the explicit or implicit contract, all play an important part. In all these dimensions, the peasants and artisans of a country like India under Mughal or British rule would have faced the steep part of the gradient plotting the terms and availability of credit. We need to know a lot more about the terms of lending to these classes of people before we can decide whether they benefited at all and if so, to what extent, by the fall in the rates of interest in the second part of the seventeenth century.

Secondly, even for the great and the mighty a fall in prime lending rates in the period concerned may not always have meant a better deal for them from their usual creditors. For example, even as rates of interest were easing up for businessmen in England and the Netherlands , the declining empire of Spain and the aspiring kingdom of Louis XIV often found it hard to raise money for their armies and administration except on rather onerous terms. Even Charles II of England was impecunious enough to have to go back on his contract with the goldsmiths of London. This is where the sound construction of a system of public credit – in the Netherlands since the early seventeenth century and in Britain since the early eighteenth century – played their part.

Thirdly, in the differential of prime lending rates as between Bengal or South India and, say, Gujarat in the seventeenth century, the accumulation of bullion and the concentration of bankers in deep pockets interested both in long-distance trade and financing the needs of the Mughal court in Agra and Delhi must have played a part. But can one see two other factors in operation in the two cases in two opposite directions? The long campaigns of Aurangzeb to bring the Sultanates of Bijapur, Golconda and other kingdoms of the south under Mughal dominion must have periodically disrupted the usual channels of communication and thereby raised the cost of credit. In the case of Bengal, it may have been an endogenous factor of the rapidity of growth through the settlement of the Padma–Brahmaputra delta, the trade attendant on that settlement, the gradual shifting of the focus of European trade to Bengal and the remittance of a large tribute to the

Mughal court may have contributed to a rise in the demand for credit: the increase in bullion supplies from European sources or the overland supply of bullion from Yunnan and the Shan territories may not have been enough to counteract that tendency (for evidence of supplies of bullion to Bengal from regions to the northeast of India in an earlier period, see Richards 1983/1994). Our knowledge of the amount of silver entering India has become more complicated by the recent scholarship which stresses the continued importance of the overland trade borne along the Red Sea and Persian Gulf routes during the period in which European trading companies are supposed to have become the main avenues of contact between Europe and India, and India and the countries further east as well (Haider 1996). To that complication we have to add the emerging scholarship on the supply of gold and silver from Japan and other areas to the east and southeast of India during the two hundred years from, say, 1550 to 1750. (For a summary of most of the recent estimates of silver production and trade in the world between the early sixteenth and late eighteenth century, see Frank 1998: 143–50).

The system of public credit and the price paid by Indian states and the subjects of absolutist states without it

I want here to raise an issue which does not seem to have figured in the discourse on the nature of the state and its fate in Turkey, India or China in the face of onslaught by European powers from the eighteenth century. This is the issue of the role public credit played in strengthening a state dominated by capitalists as against absolutist states run basically on patrimonial or dynastic principles.

First of all, the rise of public credit, that is, the rise of a system under which the state borrows money regularly from lenders, many or even all of whom are anonymous, and regularly services that debt according to the contract made at the time the borrowing takes place, requires the state to be a constitutional authority which is answerable to an assembly of common people, aristocrats or moneyed oligarchs. Thus it cannot arise, except perhaps in an attenuated form in special cases such as the French state in the eighteenth century between Louis XIV and the French Revolution, in a state ruled by an absolutist monarch. It is not an accident that public credit in this sense first rose in the Italian city-states, especially in Genoa, Florence and Venice, around the fourteenth and fifteenth centuries. It is also perhaps not accidental that in the long conflict and competition between Genoa and Venice, it was Venice with a cohesive ruling class, with no major feudal interests to cause serious dissension in its ranks, that emerged triumphant and survived to become the longest-lived republic in the history of the world (Bernard 1972; Braudel 1972: esp. pp. 500–04; Lane 1965a, 1965b, 1973: chapters 11 and 16; Procacci 1973: 71–78). The Dutch learned the technique of using banks and private credit to sustain public credit from the Italians. In June 1584, the Venetian Republic set up the Banca della Piazza di Rialto, with three main functions to perform: 'It had to accept and repay deposits, effect transfers between accounts, and credit bills of exchange payable to clients' (Parker 1974: 549). In 1609, the United Provinces of the Netherlands set up a state-regulated Bank of Amsterdam on the model of the Rialto Bank (ibid.).

In India, so long as the Mughal central authority was firmly established, the financiers were subordinated to the ruling power and the state did not have to worry about the way the loyalties of those financiers might waver in moments of crisis. But with the rapid disintegration of the central authority after 1712 and the rise of a number of successor states competing and fighting with one another, the situation changed rapidly. These states had to draw increasingly on the credit extended by particular bankers or sets of bankers for paying their way, especially in situations of war. The European chartered companies used that opportunity of internecine warfare to extend their power and territory. As in Europe, the battle for supremacy was ultimately waged by the forces of England and France, as represented by their chartered companies in India. As the Indian financiers came gradually to perceive that the naval and military organization of the Europeans, and in particular the British, were superior to those of the local rulers, their loyalty shifted: they thought that their future would be better protected if they sided with the victor rather than the power about to be defeated through the might and the wiliness of the *farangis*. The Indian princes opposing the European marauders not only failed to match the European technology of warfare on the sea and land, they could not create a state structure that would depend on the credit of a mass of loyal subjects rather than that of a small group of financiers whose loyalty would shift as they saw the fortunes of their erstwhile patrons seriously threatened, or who would actively conspire, for reasons of short-sighted gain, against their patrons. Thus would the House of

Jagatseth conspire against Siraj-ud-daula and later Mir Kashim in Bengal, and thus would the firm of Nathji Arjunji Travadi side with the British in western India and help them against the Marathas. Indeed, during the Anglo–Maratha wars from the late eighteenth century, the British repeatedly utilized the services of not only the local bankers but also those of the bankers of Banaras for raising funds and transferring subsidies from their richest prize till that date, namely, the Presidency of Bengal (Nightingale 1970; Bagchi 1987: esp. chapters 2, 3 and 12; Torri 1982, 1991; Subramanian 1996). Many of these merchants and collaborators were ruined when the British actually came to be the sovereign power in those kingdoms that they brought under their direct or indirect sway: the objectives of a mercantile conqueror were after all to win more trade and more revenues for itself. Moreover, the profits of the trade were to be remitted abroad season after season and not to be spent in the creation of a large retinue of retainers (Bagchi 1981/2002). Of course, with the onset of British dominion all over India and the ability of the British to mobilize resources without soliciting the help of Indian financiers, those bankers or businessmen who had become too greatly dependent on the overthrown Indian rulers, and failed to extend their business to a larger clientele, were ruined in great numbers. For example, the group of bankers who had earlier financed the operations of the Peshwa's treasury and operated out of Pune were virtually decimated with the onset of British rule after 1818 (Divekar 1982). The general impoverishment of the erstwhile Peshwa's territories as a result of de-industrialization and decline of local public expenditure brought the moneylenders down with the peasants.

State-backed Anglo-Indian banking: birth moment blessed by war-induced monetary stringency

In colonial India, the origin of limited-liability, joint-stock banking lay in state initiatives in the context of availability of sufficient private British capital held by locally resident businessmen. (This section is almost entirely based on Bagchi 1987: chapters 2 and 3.) At different moments of shortage of cash and credit, the two Presidencies of the British East India Company (EIC), in Madras and Bengal, had tried to float a bank under the patronage of the Company or its government, after it had obtained the power to rule over the territory concerned. The Presidency of Bombay was in a special situation. In the first place, until the final defeat of the Peshwa in 1818, it remained an insecure base for the British and the few British capitalists often managed to have a financial stranglehold on the government, so that the latter could not contemplate the setting up of a bank that would loosen that stranglehold. Secondly, for a number of historical factors that I need not go into here (Bagchi 1972: chapter 6; Bagchi 1976, 1987: chapters 2 and 12), Indian capital remained far more prominent in Bombay than in Bengal and Madras, so that the Company's government could not so blatantly discriminate against Indians in the direction of a state-backed bank as it could in the other two Presidencies.

In the late seventeenth century, more specifically, from the 1670s down to 1687, Madras was a more important base for the trading operations of the English East India Company than Bombay and Madras (cf. Chaudhuri 1978: Tables C20, C21 and C22; there is a serious misprint on p. 32 of Bagchi 1987, where the eighteenth century, instead of the seventeenth, is said to be the period when Madras was supposed to have been the biggest source of the East India Company's exports to Europe). But the late seventeenth century was also a period of depression in Europe, so that the Europeans might have found it more difficult to generate enough surpluses of silver to supply the demands of their Asian exporters. There were also frequent commercial and financial crises induced by the depression, often coinciding with wars between the European powers. In the spring of 1683, there was a commercial crisis in the City of London and a number of goldsmith-bankers went bankrupt. In order to allay fears that the EIC would be unable to pay creditors from whom it secured short-term deposits, the Company announced that 'no bullion should be sent out in the Company's ships until all its debts were paid' (Chaudhuri 1978: 170). It is not coincidental that the Council of the Company's Madras Presidency decided to set up a bank which would accept deposits and pay interest on them (Bagchi 1987: 32). But little is known about the functioning of the bank, which must have been wound up at some stage.

In Madras again in 1799, in a situation of acute financial stringency, a Finance Committee set up by the then Governor recommended the establishment of a government-backed bank. But the recommendation could not be implemented, partly because there was a conflict between those policy-makers who wanted a private bank under the patronage of the government, and those who wanted a purely government-controlled bank. In 1806, faced with continued financial difficulties and scornful of the activities of the British traders, who were bent on speculation and extracting as much profit as possible by keeping the rates of interest high on loans to the government, Lord William Bentinck, the then Governor of Madras, founded a bank owned and controlled by the government. The capital of the bank was fixed as 800,000 pagodas and it was empowered to issue notes, subject to the condition that the ratio of notes to specie held by the bank should not exceed 3:1. Interestingly enough, that bank performed creditably until it was superseded by the Bank of Madras in 1843. The latter was constructed on the same lines as the Bank of Bengal – with majority ownership in private hands but under government supervision.

In Bombay, the Council of the Governor set up a bank in 1720, with the apparent objective of extending the Company's trade with the hinterland and supporting it financially. The bank seems to have operated for a number of years, but much of its security, in the nature of lands, orchards and other immovable property, suffered decay and depreciation, and it was wound up at some date subsequent to 1744. In 1770, faced with acute shortage of specie again, the Governor and his Council bruited a scheme of augmenting the money supply with bank notes, but the scheme proved abortive since the specie supply was too meagre to support the credible redemption of bank notes in time. Here again we see that a sustainable scheme of public credit required an assurance of eventual payment in money of broader acceptability.

For the EIC, the Presidency of Bombay long remained primarily an entrepôt for trading with the Malabar coast and with China, the main destination of exports of cotton and opium from India, and a staging-post for launching attacks on the Marathas and other powers the British needed to conquer for bringing the whole of western India under their rule (Nightingale 1970). From the 1790s to the first decade of the nineteenth century, the EIC's government waged almost continuous war against those Indian rulers who refused to submit to their rule. The aggression of the British reached a new peak under the Governor-Generalship of Lord Wellesley. The revenues of the Bombay Presidency were totally inadequate for financing these operations. In the sixteen years from 1792–93 to 1808–09 , the deficit of the Presidency amounted to £18,385,745. Most of this enormous deficit was 'covered by subsidies from Bengal, but in the most critical years such as 1801–04, the Bombay government had to raise loans locally simply in order to survive from day to day' (Bagchi 1987: 41). The subsidies were transferred from Bengal mainly through the network of bankers whose headquarters were in Banaras (Varanasi) (Subramanian 1996: 243–44 cites a letter from Fort William to the Bombay Council of the EIC dated 10 December 1788, which vividly illustrates the dependence of the Company officials on the Banaras bankers for remitting the subsidy from Bengal). But because of their easy access to the Bombay government, of which some of their partners were functionaries till 1806, the British firms, led by Bruce, Crawford and Co. and Forbes and Co., acquired enormous influence on the policies of the government. They, for example, managed to buy the whole exportable crop of cotton from the territories conquered by the Company at prices fixed by them, or even buy up the cotton meant for export by the Company to China at abnormally low prices, to the detriment of the profits of the Company and the ruin of Indian peasants. Under these circumstances, given that the British did not want their Indian financiers to acquire a major voice in a bank supported by the government, there was no serious prospect of success of a privately-owned but government-backed bank.

Let me now turn to Bengal, which served both as the Company's beach-head for the conquest of India and as the richest base of exploitation of the Indian subcontinent. In 1773, faced with continued shortage of coin, caused both by the drain of specie to China for obtaining silk and tea for England on account of the demand for tribute on the part of the EIC directors in London, and by the wars in which the Company's government in India was involved, Warren Hastings, the then Governor of Bengal, sponsored a joint-stock bank in 1773, called the General Bank for Bengal and Bihar, with two leading Indian bankers, Hazari Mal and Dayal Chand, as managers.

> The main objectives of the bank were: (a) to regularize the *batta* or rates of conversion between the different types of coins circulating in the Company's territory; (b) to regulate the *hoondian* or internal rate of exchange for transfer of funds from one place to another; and (c) to limit the extreme seasonal variations of the supply of coin by persuading district Collectors to deposit the revenue in the branch houses of the bank and take out bills on the head office payable in

sicca rupees at a fixed rate of *batta* and *hoondian*. (Bagchi 1987: 45–46)

But the bank was soon wound up, I suspect, mainly because Hastings was not supported by the EIC Directors in London.

The first sustained move to set up a bank with governmental patronage in British India, as in the case of the Bank of England, took place against the background of war. The Marquis of Wellesley (the elder brother of Lord Wellington) who was the Governor-General of India between 1798 and 1805, was continuously engaged in wars against Indian rulers in the north, west and south. At the same time, the EIC demanded a regular tribute to be paid out of Indian tax revenues. This combination strained the finances of the British Indian government and made it increasingly more difficult and more costly to raise loans from private sources. In 1801, Henry St George Tucker, the *de facto* finance minister of the British Indian government, floated a plan of founding a bank with minority government shareholding whose capital resources would be augmented by getting notes issued by it recognized as legal tender for payments to the government. After some vicissitudes and a period of infancy as the Bank of Calcutta, the Tucker plan led to the foundation of the Bank of Bengal in 1809.

In Madras in the south, as we have already noted, the purely government-owned bank set up by Bentinck was abolished in 1843, when the Bank of Madras was founded on more or less the same lines as the Bank of Bengal. In 1840 was founded the Bank of Bombay, again with minority government ownership and with perhaps a stronger representation of private businessmen than in the cases of the Banks of Bengal and Madras. At the time these banks were founded, British or British Indian law did not normally permit the grant of limited liability to shareholders of joint-stock companies. So the British Parliament had to pass laws (in the form of granting a charter in each case) for according the privilege of limited liability to the shareholders of these banks. Alongside these banks there also grew up private joint-stock banks, without limited liability up to 1860 and with limited liability after the passage of the requisite legislation thereafter. However, of all the private joint-stock banks in India or operating in India without a parliamentary charter, only two which were born in the nineteenth century have survived to the present day.

Besides the three so-called Presidency banks, namely, the

Banks of Bengal, Bombay and Madras, another group of banks called the exchange banks began operating in India from the 1850s. The most important of them were banks chartered by the British Parliament or registered in the UK, but they included such banks as the Comptoir d'Escompte de Paris, Yokohama Specie Bank and others from mainly European countries. The British exchange banks came to enjoy the monopoly of the foreign exchange business connected with the foreign trade of India and the immense amount of tribute that had to be sent to Britain from India to maintain the imperial establishment in London and a very large part of British military operations in East Africa and Asia. This monopoly arose because of two major factors: first, the government-backed Presidency banks were confined to domestic operations, and second, no non-British or Indian-controlled banks could be given the privilege of handling the tribute remittances from India to Britain.

Thus during the period of colonial rule, until, say, 1920, the European banking system was itself segmented in many ways: it was regionally segmented with three Presidency banks with three distinct spheres of operation which overlapped only at a few points. It was segmented in terms of domestic versus foreign exchange operations, though some of the exchange banks mobilized deposits and lent money to mainly European firms on a large scale. It was segmented in terms of ownership and patronage, with the Presidency banks and later their amalgamated successor, enjoying state patronage within the borders of British India.

While in England or the Netherlands the establishment of state-backed banks put a system of public credit on a firm foundation, it led to no such development in colonial India. A colonially constrained set of state-backed banks in a society in which the authorities were least interested in creating a dangerously competitive class produced its own contradictions. First of all, none of the three Presidency banks acted as a lender of last resort, except to privileged European borrowers. In the case of the Bank of Bengal, this practice led to large losses in the 1830s, when the major British agency houses of Bengal collapsed like nine pins. Part of the losses resulting from their bankruptcy was made up by the bank by seizing the assets of the hapless Indian partners thus finishing off most of the bigger Bengali businessmen. In Bombay, since Indian businessmen were more powerful, the crisis resulting from the boom and collapse of cotton prices during and at the conclusion, respectively, of the US Civil War, had a slightly different outcome. The Bank of Bombay itself collapsed dragging down European speculators and their victims among the unwary Indians and Europeans. It ruined many Indian businessmen, no doubt, but some were at least partially protected by a pro-borrower insolvency law passed earlier by the Bombay legislature, and by the provisions of the Mitakshara law of property governing most Indian businessmen in that part of the country (Bagchi 1987a: chapters 25 and 26). The collapse of the old Bank of Bombay led to the cessation of any shareholding in the Presidency banks by the government. The New Bank of Bombay was established as a privately-owned institution, and from 1876, the government ceased to hold any shares in the other two Presidency banks as well. But it retained firm control over their basic constitution and rules of business.

In the period up to 1914, the British Indian government primarily raised loans both in India and London when they needed funds for military expeditions or public works such as the construction of railways, ports or irrigation networks. But sterling debt tended to grow faster than rupee debt. (All the figures of debt have been taken from Reserve Bank of India 1954: 880–81.) In 1821, for example, the rupee debt of the government was Rs 275 million, and the sterling debt was Rs 57.6 million; in 1860 the rupee debt grew to Rs 729.7 million and the sterling debt to Rs 243.6 million. By the year 1900, the rupee and sterling debts had grown to Rs 1272.0 million and Rs 1862.2 million, respectively. By 1914 the two figures had climbed to Rs 1797.9 million and Rs 2656.0 million, respectively. Much of the rupee debt was held by Europeans who had earlier worked in India. The public credit of the colonial government meant credit in the London money market. But the situation changed radically from the 1920s. Most of the new loans were raised in India. From the 1930s the government allowed most of the British-held debt to be repatriated and used loans in India to help the process. Against the general recession in the economy, this practice raised the cost of borrowing to Indian businessmen and was severely criticized by their representatives (Bagchi 1972: chapter 2; the point is also emphasized by Sunanda Sen and Aditya Mukherjee in the present volume).

Colonial Commercial Banking

In British India, the established Indian bankers continued to handle a considerable part of their usual business, that is, acting as *sarrafs* or money-changers, giving money that is acceptable for payment of taxes or for transactions over long distances for lower-order money which would be accepted only in local exchanges; advancing money to peasants, artisans or landlords for their consumption or production needs; engaging in the remittance of money from one location to another by using *hundis* or bills of exchange, Indian-style; acting as bankers to most of the Indian rulers whom the British kept on their thrones on strict condition of subservience to British rulers. Their capital and credit networks included communities all over India, but particular nodes of that network generally were controlled by family groups and clans. Joint-stock banking was practically unknown. The bankers and money-lenders often combined these activities with trade in a large variety of commodities. But with the establishment of British rule over most parts of India and those included generally the more densely populated and productive regions, they were deprived of their functions and the resulting profits as bankers to the government.

In the eighteenth century, private British merchants were setting up banks as part of their general business. They handled the funds of British officials and smaller European traders, invested them in profitable ventures and effected the remittance of the earnings to Europe. The last function often involved a circuitous route because much of the earnings of British officials were illicit gains and private European merchants required the permission of the East India Company, before it was deprived of the legal monopoly of trade in 1813. Private European banks were branches of European agency houses that were engaged in a wide variety of trades and mercantile activities. In that form some of them continued down to the beginning of the twentieth century. The last of the major banks of that type went out in 1906, when Arbuthnot and Company, mainly carrying on their banking and merchanting in South India, collapsed and in the process ruined many thousands of European and Indian investors (Bagchi 1989: 214–16; Bagchi 1997: 54–55, 445–47).

Before I enter the vast territory of Indian-controlled banking run on lines of family ownership and control, it is necessary to summarize briefly the series of 'infamous experiments' (phrase used by Karl

Marx to characterize the land revenue policy pursued by the British rulers in Bengal) the colonial rulers launched in the fields of coins and currency as their exigencies of rule, tribute extraction and remittance dictated. At the time the British were on their conquering spree in India, they found a tri-metallic system prevailing in the country for purposes of trade as well as payments of dues to public authorities (its lineage under Mughal rule is lucidly described by Habib 1987); below this system for local transactions, and even for payments of taxes to subordinate authorities, other media of exchange – of which the most prevalent were the *cowries*, a species of seashell mainly imported from the Maldives – were used. Of the three metals, gold coins were extensively used in South India, whereas in the north silver coins were the dominant media of exchange for large transactions and long-distance trade. Copper coins were used for smaller-value transactions. But coins issued by many different mints, usually under government licence, were used even in territories not under the rule of the authorities licensing the mints. Of course, money-changers and bankers facilitating remittances made considerable profit under this arrangement. But this free coinage system generally prevented the emergence of a shortage of media of exchange hampering trade.

The British could not remould the system to their liking before they had established control over most parts of the country. The British would not generally accept any medium except coins made of the two higher-value metals for payment of public dues. This was not only because they monopolized foreign trade in which such metals were used but also because the rulers had to pay a regular tribute to London and that had to be sent not only in monthly, but by the last half of the nineteenth century, fortnightly intervals, and only silver or gold coins would do the job. But the British also followed a policy of discouraging the use of gold coins in their dominion (Mitra 1974: chapter 6; Bagchi 1982; Bagchi 1987a: 41–48). For the period up to the 1860s, this was dictated by the fact that gold had a higher value in relation to silver in Europe than in India and China, and the British did not want to see gold coins misused by the Asians in this way. From the 1870s, when virtually all the major powers shifted to gold coinage, the British rulers were quite determined not to allow gold coinage in India. They wanted gold as the backing of the financial centre that London had become. John Maynard Keynes famously deprecated the Indians' irrational greed for gold: the shoe would much better fit the official view (including his own) of the use and monopolization of gold reserves as an instrument of capitalist competition (Balachandran 1996).

In 1835, the British Indian government passed a law making only silver coins issued by its mints the legal tender in its territories. This was a move to unify the currency system of the country. However, until 1861 the three Presidency banks continued to issue notes that were accepted for public payments within their designated territories. Moreover, a large number of the subordinate Indian rulers (styled 'native princes' officially) continued to issue their own coins. From 1862, the government took over note issues, and all note issues by banks were prohibited. However, the territory of British India was divided into a large number of currency circles, and notes issued for those circles would be accepted for payment of public dues only within those territories. One major reason for this was the fiscal motive: in many parts of India, the government treasuries were the only agents handling the remittance of money since no organized banks operated there, and the government did not want to lose the power and the revenues derived from that function. This division between currency circles was not given up until after World War II. Furthermore, at first notes of only high denominations were issued, the minimum with a value of Rs 10 or a pound sterling, equal to more than three months' earnings of an agricultural labourer and exceeding one month's pay of many an Indian clerk. Thus the governmental measures integrated the country in a single monetary system only at the highest levels but kept it segmented into many regions for most domestic transactions, and beyond the reach of most Indians when it came to the use of token currency.

Finally, the onset of British rule in most regions often led to the demonetization of those regions until their incomes had been depressed enough to come to an equilibrium with a smaller volume of the usual medium of exchange (Bagchi 1982). There were two principal reasons for this: first, many of the usual media of exchange were not acceptable to the British rulers and merchants and hence the older media had to be exchanged at lower and lower values, causing a drastic devaluation of the wealth held in the form of traditional kinds of money. Secondly, the coins of superior metals were exported in order to meet the tribute payments, and hence caused an acute shortage of those coins. A belief in the rigid quantity theory of money is not needed in order to understand this causal nexus. All that we need is to grasp the fact that a sudden alteration in the basic transaction arrangements would cause an enormous dislocation, especially in a society in which local exchanges predominated, and meeting the often escalating demands of the state in an appreciating medium would cause distress to poor peasants suddenly faced with such contingencies. A third reason for a fall in incomes would be a decline in demand for many of the domestically produced commodities and services because of the cessation of the custom of rulers who were overthrown by the British, plenty of evidence for which is available for Bengal after the acquisition of the Dewani by the British from the Mughal emperor in 1765, for Bombay Deccan after the fall of the Peshwa, and for Punjab after the fall of the kingdom constructed by Maharaja Ranjit Singh.

We can now turn to the way the Indian-controlled network of banking and credit worked and the way it interacted with the European-controlled network of what I have called 'apex banking' inside, and the imperial structure of governance and tribute remittance operations inside and outside the country. The papers by Rajat Kanta Ray and Dwijendra Tripathi bear on this issue, and the two papers by Aditya Mukherjee and Sunanda Sen are concerned respectively with how colonial compulsions led to losses of resources, incomes and dynamism in British India and how they were perceived by Indian businessmen. Finally, the paper by Indrajit Mallick deals with the activities of a dynamic banker in post-independence India.

Interpenetration of Indian and Anglo-Indian networks of banking in an open, colonial economy

Down to the 1950s, a watertight division was usually made in academic and policy-making circles between organized and unorganized banking, or synonymously between European-style and indigenous banking in India. The synonym itself was wrongly construed since firms such as Arbuthnot & Co. or Grindlays & Co. were also private partnerships, very much like family-controlled Indian *kothis*. One of the major aims of policy, supported by most academics, was to integrate the two sectors of banking. This objective was, however, largely based on a misconception, since European-style, limited-liability joint-stock banking utilized Indian bankers from its very inception, and the tradition continued down to the period of independence. The Indian money market was multiply segmented but the segments were linked from the joint-stock banks at the top to the village moneylender at the bottom. Some of the links were publicly displayed at least since 1909. From that date, the so-called *hundi* rates of the Presidency banks, that is, the rates at which *hundis* tendered by the *shroffs* recognized by those banks were discounted, became available through the reports and minutes of evidence before the various Currency Committees, the advertisements of the banks and the reports of the Controller of Currency of the Government of India (Reserve Bank of India 1954: 685–86, 694–95). The problem was not to create an integrated network but to change its pattern so that it could better achieve certain policy objectives such as channelling lower-cost credit to agriculture or small-scale industry, or to areas remote from major urban areas.

The Bank of Bengal, for example, from the beginning, employed Indian *khazanchees* whose main job was to keep in touch with the bazaar and guarantee that any credit granted to an Indian client did not turn into a bad debt. It employed *munshis* who would be able to read the Hindustani in which most *hundis* were written. For a long time, the *khazanchee* was expected to run his own department within the bank. Most of the Indian *poddars* and clerks were, of course, paid miserable wages, even while the British officers enjoyed sumptuous salaries and perquisites. The Indian *sahukars* or *mahajans* used loans from the bank to service Indian traders. The Presidency banks were barred from lending against real estate or other illiquid security. They got round this prohibition when the management really wanted to oblige a big *zamindar* by using the intermediary of an Indian *sahukar* who would take the loan on his own credit and then extend it to the ultimate customer. These banks used their *khazanchees, shroffs* or cash-keepers and the *mahajans* who worked closely with them as shock-absorbers as far as their Indian clientele were concerned, and were often financially ruined as a result.

With the exception of the Bank of Bombay, the other two Presidency banks discriminated severely against Indian, Sri Lankan, Myanmarese or other Asian borrowers (Armenians and Baghdadi Jews were a partial exception). While European borrowers could have their bills discounted on the basis of their presumed creditworthiness, or could be allowed to have cash credit accounts, Indians generally had to deposit government paper or, later on, other approved securities such as those issued by guaranteed railways or select municipal corporations, in order to obtain any credit. The *hundis* of Indian *sahukars* or traders were discounted but only on deposit of approved securities or on the guarantee of the Indian *khazanchee, shroff* or cash-keeper. Thus joint-stock banking also partook of the character of relationship banking: the degree of closeness or trust was decided on the basis of race or presumed qualification to be part of the ruling citizenry of Britain. The racial domination of the Europeans in these banks was consolidated by the ensconcement of European officers in all the major decision-making positions. Even when banks were set up under Indian initiative, as in the case of the Bank of Baroda analysed by Tripathi in this volume, or in the case of the Bank of India set up in 1906, or when Indians had a say in bank direction as in the cases of the Bank of Bombay or the Allahabad Bank, the secretary or general manager of the bank and most of the senior managers in the head office or branches were Europeans. The Indian Bank in Madras and the Central Bank of India in Bombay were probably the first Indian-controlled banks of any size that have survived until now to have appointed Indians as general managers. It was difficult for many Indian capitalists to shake off the ideology of racial superiority of Europeans.

When the so-called exchange banks began operating in India and Sri Lanka from the 1850s, the European companies had another source of credit to turn to. The exchange banks primarily financed exports and since the Presidency banks were forbidden to operate in the foreign-exchange market, there was a considerable degree of complementarity between the working of the two sets of institutions. But when the exchange banks, in search of liquidity, began to offer attractive rates on deposits with them and also took to financing the local working-capital needs of British-controlled plantations, mines and manufacturing concerns, the Presidency banks also regarded them as competitors. If the exchange banks resented the access the Presidency banks had to costless deposits from the government, the Presidency banks complained of access to the cheap source of credit in the London money market that the exchange banks enjoyed, from which the Presidency banks (and their successor, the Imperial Bank of India) were barred by legislative fiat. But the exchange banks, in fact, added but minuscule amounts to the Indian money markets from their operations in London. In the period of the depreciation of silver from the 1870s to 1893, they wanted to avoid any loss arising out of changes in the value of the rupee relative to sterling. Later too, as it became apparent from the evidence tendered by their representatives to official Currency Committees or Commissions, they would rather see the

India Office absorb any exchange risk through variations in changes in rates realized from Council Bills than obtain extra funds from London by telegraphic transfers on their own. If banks are often seen only as fair-weather friends, the exchange banks were doubly so, even as far as the apex banking system was concerned.

In his pioneering analysis of Indian currency and banking, Keynes (1913/1971) had claimed that linking the Indian rupee to sterling, in accordance with the recommendation of the Fowler Committee of 1898, would bring down interest rates in the Indian money market and moderate the extreme fluctuations in the rates of interest between the busy season – essentially the months in which the major agricultural crops were harvested and marketed, and when the government demands of the land tax had to be paid – and the rest of the year. During the period Keynes wrote about, the dominating bank rates in the apex market were those charged by the three Presidency banks. After examining the evidence of the movements of the rates charged by the Banks of Bengal and Bombay (the data on the rates of the Bank of Madras were incomplete) (Bagchi 1997: chapter 2 and its Annexure), I concluded (ibid., p. 64):

> in all the three phases [that is, the phase of the silver depreciation from 1876 to 1892, the phase of the 'limping standard' in the 1890s and the phase of the gold or sterling exchange standard since 1899], the prime rates charged by the two Presidency banks remained distinctly more variable than the rate declared by the Bank of England. There is no evidence *pace* Keynes that the gold exchange standard helped lessen credit stringency as measured by the variability of the rates of interest. The average *level* of the prime rates of the Presidency banks did come down, but that has more to do with the improving terms of trade of India's exports versus her imports and with the larger surplus generated by India in spite of the burgeoning Home Charges or tribute exacted by Britain than with the operation of the gold exchange standard as such.

The British officials knew that the rates of interest charged by moneylenders for loans to peasants and artisans were far higher than were paid either by the favoured customers of the joint-stock banks or by the well-heeled clients of the major Indian banking houses. The situation had worsened for most Indian peasants under British rule for a number of reasons. One of them was that the moneylenders could

now take over the peasants' land in case of default and could use the
threat of foreclosure for extracting higher rates of interest or harsher
terms of debt-service. After the Deccan riots of 1875, a group of
bankers from Poona, with the support of William Wedderburn (at the
time the district judge: he later took part in the founding of the Indian
National Congress in 1885 and presided over the all-India sessions of
the Congress in 1899 and 1910), floated a scheme for setting up an
agricultural bank for extending loans to peasants on less onerous
terms. But in an arid region with frequent crop failure and rigid land-
tax demands on the part of the government, they wanted an assurance
from the latter that the tax demands would not be raised for thirty
years and some explicit government support would be extended in
other forms. The scheme fell through since the government refused to
give any assurance of the kind demanded by the Poona capitalists
(Bagchi 1992: 41–43). The government remained contented by passing
an Act in 1879, curbing the power of moneylenders to take over the
property of agriculturists. Similar legislation was passed for Punjab,
where the government perceived a threat to security arising out of the
fact that most of the moneylenders were Hindus but the majority of
the peasants were Muslims. But in either case, beyond the partial
substitution of big farmers or landlords in the place of the professional
moneylenders and forcing all moneylenders to adopt the more circuitous route of subjecting the indebted peasants to debt bondage or
expropriation, such legislation by itself seems to have done little to
improve the condition of the ordinary peasant. In this anthology, the
paper by Manzur Ahsan examines the consequence of a series of legislative measures, starting with the Bengal Moneylenders Act of 1933,
taken by the provincial government in Bengal to relieve the peasantry
badly affected by the severe depression of the 1930s. These Acts
mandated Debt Settlement Boards which would make it easier for
debtors to pay back their dues and creditors to get back their loans by
scaling down the demands of the latter. The legislation was backed by
political clout when A.K. Fazlul Haque, leader of the Krishak Praja
Party, became the Prime Minister in the popularly elected government
of 1937. Ahsan shows that even then, the working of the Debt Settlement Boards fell far short of the expectations of the framers of the
legislation.

The relationship of the indigenous banking system with the
joint-stock banks long continued to fox the usual students of banking

in India. It was observed that the so-called bazaar rates were generally higher than the prime rates charged by the Presidency banks and their competitors. After all, the latter enjoyed many advantages including access to cheap deposits and implicit or explicit official backing. They also serviced a select clientele with deep pockets. The Indian bankers faced much higher risks in their lending operations. But it was also observed that in the lean season, the bazaar rates often went below the rates charged by the Presidency banks. Once data were systematically collected, the explanation could be proffered in terms of the greater stickiness of the rates charged by the joint-stock banks, and the latter could in turn be explained by the higher overhead expenses of the joint-stock banks and long-cultivated relationship of the Indian bankers with their favoured customers. (For extensive documentation of the phenomenon and its explanation on the lines indicated above, see Bagchi 1987, 1987a, 1989, and 1997.) But there were three other observations that still eluded systematic explanation. One was the claim made by several students of Indian banking (see, in particular, Jain 1929) that the rates of interest charged by Indian bankers to their long-term clients were remarkably stable and low. The second observation was that even in situations of extreme tightness of the money market as in the 1890s, during the period of the limping standard when the government was trying to stabilize the rupee exchange rate at 1s. 4d. by creating scarcity of Council Bills and metallic and paper currency, some Indian clients could still obtain loans from the indigenous bankers at lower rates of interest than were charged by the Presidency banks. The third observation was that in the period of monetary stringency some British firms could take recourse to indigenous bankers for obtaining loans when they could not procure them from the usual joint-stock banks, domestic or foreign.

The explanation for the long-term stability and the cheapness of loans extended by Indian bankers even in periods of tightness of the money market would run in terms of networks of trust (for a full discussion of these issues, see Bagchi 1997: 42–50). The indigenous bankers practised systematic discrimination in favour of members of their own community, who were generally their favoured clients (for further evidence of this, in the case of the Marwari bankers, see ibid. 1997: chapter 3). In periods of extreme monetary stringency, the indigenous bankers would ration their less-favoured clients, who would be the smaller traders or moneylenders lending to lesser fry, but they might then have funds available for lending to borrowers outside their usual networks of trust, if they perceived the risk of default to be low. Thus would, say, a few British firms obtain loans from the indigenous bankers in a period of extreme monetary stringency. If this analysis is correct, it would also prove that the view of some analysts such as Tomlinson (1993), that even in periods of long-drawn-out stringency in the apex money market, the access of Indian peasants or small traders to credit would remain unaffected, is found to be erroneous.

We are then left with another puzzle in the accepted discourse on the monetary and banking system of India. Why did so many policy-makers and analysts harp so long on the need to integrate the organized and the so-called unorganized money markets (the latter was anything but unorganized – only their principles of organization were different from those of joint-stock banks), and why did so many of them even argue that the integration would provide a solution to the lack of access of most peasants and artisans to cheap credit? I would hazard the guess that many of them did not fully grasp the fact that privately controlled credit markets are necessarily characterized by credit rationing and rate discrimination, and thought that injecting a greater degree of competition would eliminate such practices. On the part of policy-makers, there was an added reluctance to face the fact that only extensive state intervention and changes in production relations in rural society could bring down the debt burden or credit deprivation of the general run of small and medium farmers, and open up some avenues of credit to the landless workers or peasants. In the final section of this introduction, I will touch upon some of the structural constraints that kept credit either out of reach of the ordinary people or made it available only on usurious terms.

Structural constraints on the working of the banking and monetary system in British India and the perceptions of the policy-makers and publicists

During the colonial period, the imperative to transfer tribute to London on a regular basis without interruption played a major role in determining the policy stance of the Secretary of State for India, and ultimately of the British Parliament. On occasion, that stance was determined not by the views of the Government of India or the bureaucrats associated with the India Office but by the perceived needs of the capitalist–imperialist order, of which London was the principal seat of governance till World War I (Bagchi 1972: chapter 14; Bagchi 1989: chapter 2; and Bagchi 1997a).

The silver standard, for example, was maintained by the British Parliament during the years of silver depreciation in spite of repeated appeals by India Office bureaucrats, on occasion backed even by the Viceroy, for allowing India to move over to a gold standard or to work effectively to make a bimetallic standard internationally acceptable. With tribute payments fixed in sterling, the silver depreciation made life more difficult for the managers of the British Indian finances.

After World War I, in the 1920s, in a dogged attempt to keep the remittance mechanism smoothly working, the British Indian government, through the instrumentality of the Imperial Bank of India, pursued a tight monetary policy, and kept the rate of exchange pegged at the rate of 1s. 6d. to the rupee – a rate which virtually all Indian publicists (except for some conservative professors of economics) considered to be too high. In times of inflation, some of the Indian leaders of public opinion shared the conservatism of the British policy-makers and most, for example, supported the recommendations of the Indian Retrenchment Committee of 1922. But the experience of shortages of manufactures during the war and the perceived needs of Indian economic development had made some policy-makers sympathetic to demands for Indian industrialization, although as I argued (in Bagchi 1972), that sympathy was not translated into effective policies to induce or even support the faster induction of modern industry into India. During this period statesmen and economists such as M. Visvesvarayya and K.T. Shah were already talking about introducing planning as a means of stimulating economic development. Moreover, a section of British industrialists with their manufacturing enterprises mainly geared to the domestic market had often sided with Indian nationalists and industrialists in this respect. The views of the Bombay Chamber of Commerce and its European representatives during the agitation against the imposition of counter-vailing duties on mill-made yarn in India, and the views of the Upper India Commerce which primarily represented the British industrialists of Kanpur, may be cited in this regard. Sir George Schuster, the Finance Member of the Indian government in the early 1930s, had privately advocated many policy changes Indian nationalists had been agitating for and he went on to preach government planning for India after he had left his job (Bagchi 1972: 47). But as Finance Member he pursued orthodox budgetary policies which became instruments for aggravating the depression. So policy-making was often in conflict with the judgment of a policy-maker as an unbiased analyst, and imperial imperatives almost always prevailed.

As Aditya Mukherjee shows in his paper, Indian business opinion began to voice a trenchant and reasoned criticism of the policies of the Indian government from the 1920s and in the 1930s. Leaders of Indian business were advocating not only planning, government patronage and expansion of public expenditure even at the cost of violating the canons of sound finance, with the objective of stimulating industry and trade, but also for revitalizing agriculture by improving the conditions of living of the Indian peasantry.

Again, the condition of the heavily indebted Indian peasant had figured in hundreds of thousands of pages of Survey and Settlement Reports, reports of Collectors, Selections of Proceedings of the provincial and central governments, reports of Famine Commissions dating back to the 1880s and famine enquiries of earlier dates, and so on. In the 1920s, two Royal Commissions, one on agriculture and the other on labour and banking enquiries for all the major provinces and for all important 'native states', accompanied by a central banking enquiry, had produced thousands of pages of reports and minutes of evidence bearing on the condition of the Indian peasantry. But the only major positive initiative taken by the government was legislation for founding cooperative societies and providing some administrative framework for them, since the early 1900s. But the growth of the cooperative credit societies remained very slow, especially outside the Bombay and Madras Presidencies and Punjab. The total number of members of agricultural societies for the whole of India in 1935 was, for example, just above three million. The miserable condition of the peasantry, especially during the years of agricultural depression since 1927 (agricultural depression pre-dated the crash of 1929) and its effect in constricting the domestic market for manufactured goods was common knowledge and many sections of society, including Kanpur industrialists and representatives of Indian big business, were voicing their concern and demanding government action to remedy the situation. From the beginning of the 1930s, peasant movements had sprung up in various parts of the country including the United Provinces, Bengal and Bihar, and were voicing demands for rent reduction, better security for peasants on insecure tenure and vesting of property right on the actual cultivators of the land.

In 1934, in the final stages of the preparation of the Bill for establishing the Reserve Bank of India (RBI), the Government of India appointed Malcolm Darling, ICS, with long experience of rural administration in Punjab, to 'report on the most suitable organization' for the soon-to-be-founded Reserve Bank's Agricultural Credit Department, and to recommend the manner 'in which it might most effectively work with the cooperative banks and other agencies for providing credit to the agriculturists and landowners' (Simha 1970: 200–01). The Reserve Bank began working in April 1935 and Darling's report was submitted in June 1935. A major conclusion of Darling was that, under the prevailing circumstances, for purposes of refinancing of agricultural credit societies, the Reserve Bank could make advances to only three provincial cooperative banks, 'namely, those of Bombay, Madras and the Punjab, but since these banks had ample surplus funds, assistance was not likely to be required by them in the near future' (ibid.: 202).

From 1944 the Government of India was engaged in various exercises relating to post-war reconstruction and planning. As a component of those exercises, the RBI also appointed a number of sub-committees and committees under the chairmanship of eminent academics and bankers such as D.R. Gadgil and R.G. Saraiya. These committees recommended the further extension of the cooperative movement and providing infrastructural support such as the setting up of regulated agricultural markets and licensed warehouses. The recommendations also included the recognition of activities such as animal husbandry as a proper province of rural cooperatives and deserving of support of the RBI. Further recommendations in the same direction were made by the Nanavati Committee set up by the government of Bombay in 1947, and the Rural Banking Enquiry Committee of 1949 set up by the RBI under the chairmanship of Sir Purshotamdas Thakurdas, the elder statesman of Indian big business, and one of the authors of the industrialists' Bombay Plan of 1944 (Simha 1970: 761–70). All the committees recognized the fact that the cooperative movement had not spread its reach much further than when Darling submitted his report, nor had the RBI done much in the way of refinancing of rural credit. In 1945–46, for example, the RBI had lent a paltry sum of Rs 1 lakh to state cooperative banks. By 1950–51, the refinanced loans had increased to Rs 5.37 crore (Balachandran 1998: 231), which was still meagre in comparison with what was required for meeting even a fraction of the needs of rural credit. All the committee recommendations studiously avoided issues of land tenure and rural social structure in general and took the status quo for granted. Some of the committees strongly recommended the strengthening of land-mortgage banks as another instrument of spreading of cheap credit to rural areas. Basically, they were bankers' reports which only looked at the financial and physical infrastructure, and took little account of how that infrastructure was to be used.

My point is that while Indian capitalists wanted to introduce dynamism into an obviously stagnating rural economy, before independence, none of them had the foresight to grasp that only a basic change in rural social relations could impart dynamism to the rural areas by releasing them from the shackles of landlord and caste oppression, and enabling them to operate freely in the markets for output, labour and credit. Unfortunately, the situation did not change radically for the poor peasants even after independence, although in many parts of India, the formal abolition of revenue farming may have released the energies of middle farmers.

Ironically enough, while the demands of the rural areas as perceived at the highest levels may have given a thrust towards development banking, that is, banking operations aimed at long-term development with subsidization of operations by the state where necessary, the sectors which benefited first from the initiation of such banking after independence were primarily large or medium-scale industry and trade. The Indian Finance Corporation was established in 1948, and by the early 1950s, a clutch of state finance corporations had come up with a mandate to provide cheap, long-term credit to the industrial sector. The first major thrust towards providing developmental credit to the rural sector was made with the nationalization of the Imperial Bank of India and its conversion into the State Bank of India. The Imperial Bank authorities had obdurately ignored the direction of the Indian monetary authorities to cater to the small towns and large villages of India, and bringing it under direct government control was seen as the only remedy available (Balachandran 1998: chapter 9).

The activities of B.K. Dutt, which forms the subject of Mallick's paper, can be understood only against the emergence of development banking as an affordable activity after independence.

Mallick's paper also shows that much of development banking takes the character of relationship banking, for the banker has to assess the creditworthiness of potential clients in a situation in which many future-oriented projects are associated with considerable risk. Unfortunately, relationship banking has the potential of generating corruption and turning into crony capitalism, as we have witnessed in countries stretching from India and Indonesia to the USA and post-Soviet Russia. That the initiation of neo-liberal reforms and the retreat of the state from banking and industrial activities may aggravate rather than ameliorate the possibility of emergence of crony capitalism, is amply demonstrated by recent developments in all these countries.

References

Ali Muhammad Khan, 1761/1965, *Mirat-i Ahmadi*, translated from the Persian by M.F. Lokhandwala, Baroda.

Bagchi, A.K., 1972, *Private Investment in India 1900–1939*, Cambridge: Cambridge University Press.

———, 1981/2002, 'Merchants and Colonialism', Occasional Paper No. 38, Centre for Studies in Social Sciences, Calcutta; reprinted in Bagchi 2002, pp. 17–70.

———, 1982, 'Money and Credit as Areas of Conflict in Colonial India', Occasional Paper No. 51, Centre for Studies in Social Sciences, Calcutta, November.

———, 1987, *The Evolution of the State Bank of India, The Roots, 1806–1876, Part I, The Early Years 1806–1860*, Bombay: Oxford University Press.

———, 1987a, *The Evolution of the State Bank of India, The Roots, 1806–1876, Part II, Diversity and Regrouping 1860–1876*, Bombay: Oxford University Press.

———, 1989, *The Presidency Banks and the Indian Economy 1876–1914*, Calcutta: Oxford University Press.

———, 1992, 'Land tax, property rights and peasant insecurity in colonial India', *The Journal of Peasant Studies*, 20 (1), October, pp. 1–49.

———, 1997, *The Evolution of the State Bank of India, Vol. 2, The Era of the Presidency Banks 1876–1920*, New Delhi: Sage.

———, 1997a, 'Contested hegemonies and *laissez faire*: Controversies over the monetary standard at the high noon of the British empire', *Review*, XX(1), Winter, pp. 19–76.

———, 2002, *Capital and Labour Redefined: India and the Third World*, New Delhi: Tulika.

Balachandran, G., 1996, *John Bullion's Empire*, London: Curzon Press.

———, 1998, *The Reserve Bank of India 1951–1967*, Delhi: Oxford University Press.

Bernard, J., 1972, 'Trade and finance in the Middle Ages', in Cipolla 1972, pp. 274–338.

Besanko, David and Anjan V. Thakor, 1993, 'Relationship banking, deposit insurance and bank portfolio choice', in Colin Mayer and Xavier Vives (eds), *Capital*

Markets and Financial Intermediation, Cambridge: Cambridge University Press, pp. 292–319.

Braudel, F., 1972, *The Mediterranean and the Mediterranean World in the Age of Philip II,* Vol. 1, London: Collins.

———, 1982, *Civilization and Capitalism, 15ᵗʰ–18ᵗʰ Century,* Vol. II: *The Wheels of Commerce,* translated from the French by S. Reynolds, London: Collins.

Brewer, J., 1989, *The Sinews of Power: War, money and the English state, 1688–1783,* London: Unwin Hyman.

Chakravarti, R., 2001, 'Introduction', in Chakravarti 2001a, pp. 1–101.

———, (ed.), 2001a, *Trade in Early India,* New Delhi: Oxford University Press.

Chaudhuri, K.N., 1978, *The Trading World of Asia and the English East India Company 1660–1760,* Cambridge: Cambridge University Press.

Cipolla, C.M. (ed.), 1972, *The Fontana Economic History of Europe: The Middle Ages,* London: Collins/Fontana.

De Cecco, M., 1974, *Money and Empire,* Oxford: Blackwell.

Deyell, J., 1983/1994, 'The China connection: Problems of silver supply in medieval Bengal', in J.F. Richards (ed.), *Precious Metals in the Late Medieval and Early Modern Worlds;* reprinted in Subrahmanyam 1994, pp. 112–36.

Dickson, P.G.M., 1967, *The Financial Revolution in England: a study in the development of public credit 1688–1756,* London: Macmillan.

——— and J. Sperling, 1970, 'War finance 1689–1714', in J.S. Bromley (ed.), *The New Cambridge Modern History of Europe,* Vol. VI, *The rise of Great Britain and Russia 1688–1715,* Cambridge: Cambridge University Press, pp. 284–315.

Divekar, V.D., 1982, 'The emergence of an indigenous business class in Maharashtra', *Modern Asian Studies,* 16 (3), pp. 427–43.

Fossier, R., 1986, 'Europe's second wind', in R. Fossier (ed.), *The Cambridge Illustrated History of the Middle Ages, III, 1250–1350,* Cambridge: Cambridge University Press, pp. 399–453.

Frank, A.G., 1998, *ReOrient: Global economy in the Asian age,* Berkeley, CA: University of California Press.

Habib, I., 1982, 'Monetary system and prices', in Raychaudhuri and Habib 1982, pp. 360–81.

———, 1987, 'A system of trimetallism in the age of the "Price Revolution": Effects of the silver influx on the Mughal monetary system', in Richards 1987, pp. 137–70.

Haider, N., 1996, 'Precious metal flows and currency circulation in the Mughal empire', *Journal of the Economic and Social History of the Orient,* Vol. 39, pp. 298–364.

Jain, L.C., 1929, *Indigenous Banking in India,* London: Macmillan.

Keynes, J.M., 1913/1971, *Indian Currency and Finance,* London; reprinted as Vol. I of *The Collected Writings of John Maynard Keynes,* London: Macmillan.

Lamoreaux, Naomi R., 1994, *Insider Lending: Banks, Personal Connections, and Economic Development in Industrial New England 1784–1914,* Cambridge: Cambridge University Press.

Lane, F.C., 1965, *The Collected Papers of Frederick C. Lane*, Baltimore: The Johns Hopkins University Press.

——, 1965a, 'The Venetian bankers', in Lane 1965, pp. 69–86.

——, 1965b, 'The funded debt of the Venetian Republic, 1262–1482', in Lane 1965, pp. 87–98.

——, 1973, *Venice: a Maritime Republic*, Baltimore: The Johns Hopkins University Press.

Miller, E., 1972, 'Government economic policies and public finance 1000–1500', in Cipolla 1972, pp. 339–73.

Mitra, K.P., 1974, *Banaras in Transition (1738–1795)*, Delhi: Munshiram Manoharlal.

O'Brien, P.K., 1988, 'The political economy of British taxation, 1660–1815', *Economic History Review*, 41 (1), February, pp. 1–32.

——, 1994, 'Central government and the economy, 1688–1815', in R. Floud and D. McCloskey (eds), *The Economic History of Britain since 1700, Vol. 1, 1700–1860*, second edition, Cambridge: Cambridge University Press, pp. 205–47.

Pamuk, S., 1994, 'Money in the Ottoman Empire, 1326–1914', in Suraiya Faroqhi, Bruce McGowan, Donald Quataert and Sevket Pamuk, *An Economic and Social History of the Ottoman Empire*, Vol. II, *1600–1914*, Cambridge: Cambridge University Press.

——, 2000, *A Monetary History of the Ottoman Empire*, Cambridge: Cambridge University Press.

Nightingale, Pamela, 1970, *Trade and Empire in Western India, 1784–1806*, Cambridge: Cambridge University Press.

Parker, G., 1974, 'The emergence of modern finance in Europe 1500–1730', in C.M. Cipolla (ed.): *The Fontana Economic History of Europe: The sixteenth and seventeenth centuries*, London: Fontana/Collins, pp. 527–94.

Procacci, G., 1973, *History of the Italian People*, Harmondsworth, Middlesex: Penguin Books.

Raychaudhuri, T. and I. Habib, 1982, *The Cambridge Economic History of India, vol. I, c. 1200–c. 1750*, Cambridge: Cambridge University Press.

Reserve Bank of India (RBI), 1954, *Banking and Monetary Statistics of India*, Bombay: Reserve Bank of India.

Richards, J.F. (ed.), 1987, *The Imperial Monetary System of Mughal India*, Delhi: Oxford University Press.

Shirras, G. Findlay, 1919, *Indian Finance and Banking*, London: Macmillan.

Simha, S.L.N. (ed.), *History of the Reserve Bank of India (1935–1951)*, Bombay: Reserve Bank of India.

Subrahmanyam, S., 1991/1994, 'Precious metal flows and prices in western and southern Asia 1500–1750: Some comparative and conjunctural aspects', *Studies in History*, reprinted in Subrahmanyam 1994, pp. 186–218.

—— (ed.), 1994, *Money and the Market in India 1100–1700*, Delhi: Oxford University Press.

——, 1994a, 'Introduction', in Subrahmanyam 1994, pp. 1–56.

Subramanian, Lakshmi, 1996, *Indigenous Capital and Imperial Expansion: Bombay, Surat and the West Coast*, Delhi: Oxford University Press.

Tattara, G., 2002, *Institutional Changes and Its Reflection in the Capital Market Organization and Functions in 16ᵗʰ–17ᵗʰ Century Italy: Lyons's Tuscan Money Versus Bisenzone's Genoese Finance*, paper presented at the Summer School on Financial Market Reactions to Institutional Changes, Venice International University, 2–7 September.

Tomlinson, B.R., 1993, *The Economy of Modern India 1860–1970*, Cambridge: Cambridge University Press.

Torri, M., 1982, 'In the deep blue sea: Surat and its merchant class during the dyarchic era 1759–1800', *Indian Economic and Social History Review*, Vol. XIX, Nos 3 and 4, pp. 267–93.

———, 1991, 'Trapped inside the colonial order: The Hindu bankers of Surat and their business world during the second half of the eighteenth century', *Modern Asian Studies*, 25 (2), pp. 367–401.

Money, Market and Indian Feudalism
AD 600–1200

Krishna Mohan Shrimali

Writings on early medieval India in the last nearly four decades have focused on various features of the unfolding of the feudal social formation. Amongst these, considerable emphasis has been placed on the level of monetization in the dynamics of the overall economic scene. Beginning with the thrust on 'paucity' of metal money and its links with the relative decline in trade and urbanization between *c.* AD 600 and 1200, the construct of 'Indian feudalism' has negotiated some alternative paradigms that have questioned the afore-said early formulations.

There is now growing realization that the six centuries (*c.* AD 600–1200) need not be seen as an unchanging monolith. Rather, a case for 'revival' of metal money, trade and urbanization from about the mid-ninth century has been put on the agenda of historical enquiry. This paper is largely concerned with the latter phase, that is, from *c.* 850 to *c.* 1200.[1]

The seminar on 'Coins as a Source of the Economic History of Ancient India' held at Patna in 1969[2] represented the first recognition[3] of the relevance of coins from the point of view of the economic history of early India. It gave considerable fillip to the role of money and coinage in the early medieval Indian economy, specially the issues involved in the linkages between the paucity of coinage in the post-Gupta times[4] and trade and commerce, and the consequent emergence of feudal social formation. Some leading numismatists intervened in the debate that resulted in a four-fold response.[5]

Of these early interventions, B.N. Mukherjee's was the most significant in so far as he questioned both the paucity of coins and the decline in trade. Focusing his attention on mid-eastern India, comprising Bihar, West Bengal and Bangladesh during *c.* AD 750–1200, he

1

concedes that there was no coined money in the major portion of the territory and that the Palas and the Senas themselves did not strike coins. However, he adds that there was no dearth of media of exchange – there was not only a long series of Harikela silver coinage, (Mukherjee 1977: 135–38), *cowries* but, more importantly, *curnni* or *curni* (money in the form of gold/silver dust) also functioned as media of exchange.[6]

Notwithstanding such laboured reconstructions, the monetary history of centuries immediately preceding the establishment of the Turkish power in India is still very hazy.[7] One of our early reviews of these responses (Shrimali 1989: 237–51) had raised the following questions.

(a) What was the nature and extent of the sort of commercial activities that we find in certain regions of the early medieval period?

(b) Were they capable of generating a 'stable commercialized middle class', as Tarafdar puts it? (Tarafdar 1978: 274–86)

(c) Who took away the profits of this trade? Did it go to the foreign merchants or to the feudal lords?

(d) Did it give any incentive to the peasantry or to the artisans?[8]

The questions have largely remained unanswered.

II

In 1990 appeared the works of John S. Deyell (1990) and Andre Wink (1990), both seeking to demolish the paradigm of 'Indian feudalism'. The former recognizes that 'monetary history ideally is both an essential and interpretive source for the wider realm of economic history' (see Deyell 1990: 12). On the basis of his studies of forty-one hoards of early medieval coins, Deyell claims:

> it has been possible to order many of the series of early medieval coins, define the temporal period of their issue, fix the boundaries of their geographic distribution, attribute the control of their manufacture to known political authorities, establish their metrology and intrinsic value (and hence set their denominational parameters as money), trace their circulation history, and draw inferences as the pervasiveness of monetary usage and the relative volume of monetized exchange transactions. (ibid.: 18)

Broadly, as opposed to Sharma's contention of paucity of metal money, Deyell's conclusions are (ibid.: 233–48):

(a) Considered individually, the coins of early medieval North India present a sorry picture. Such coins are evocative of low culture, administrative disorder, local horizons of usage and quiescent trade.

(b) Economic history is concerned with money, and not coins *per se*. Considered collectively, the same medieval coins of *c.* 800–1200 constitute well-defined currency systems and currency spheres.

(c) Some extended currency spheres were probably congruent with major trade patterns, and the heartland/hinterland model of market hierarchy seems to be in operation.

(d) It was an age of mixed-metal coinage – every North Indian currency of the early medieval period contained significant proportions of copper. Precious metals were only used in alloy forms. Billon (silver/copper alloy) was used universally from AD 800 to 1200, except that it was displaced by trimetallic (gold/silver/copper) alloy in the Ganga basin from AD 1000 to 1200.

(e) Medieval moneyers provided coins of an intrinsic value suitable for the broadest range of exchange transactions, on several scales of magnitude.

(f) The weight of the coin was adjusted according to the dictates of handling convenience, while the mass of the precious metal contained therein was adjusted according to the dictates of the price structure.

(g) Pressure on the precious metal content of coins was not time-specific nor was it wholly place-specific. Rather, it was situation-specific, being a function of the political and economic circumstances of the place of issue and the economic horizons of the minting agency.

(h) Mintings and remintings were necessary to keep up the quantity and average weight of the coinage.

(i) The regional coinages of the Ganga basin underwent severe reductions in precious metal content – by 52 per cent in the silver *drammas* over two centuries, and between 63 and 100 per cent in gold of Lakshmi-type currency (*c.* 1000–1200). Such currencies had very little or no credibility in external trade transactions. The coinage of Gujarat and the northwest (Shahis), however, show some stability in their silver content and hence had a better reputation in trading transactions beyond their geographical confines. This explains why 'the hypothesis of a decline of trade is in conflict with the pattern of coin movements along the coastal axes centering on Gujarat, or the overland axis centering on Afghanistan and terminating in Delhi'.

(j) Foreign coins provided the majority of the circulating medium of Sind. (ibid.: 65)

(k) The precious metals available for coinage were obtained from royal and temple treasuries, from obsolete coinage, through trade, and as prizes of war. In spite of heavy debasement, the net silver or gold content of coins was still the determinant of value.

> Rather, dearth of precious metals caused a general deflation of prices, to the point where modest quantities of gold and silver had considerable purchasing power.... The Lakshmi-base gold coin at 4 g, the bull-and-horseman billon coins at 3.4 g, and the *gadhaiya* billon coins at 4.2 g, although all derived from different prototypes, fixed upon the same weight range as the minimum appropriate for general circulation purposes. By this means a vigorous exchange medium was maintained during a time of precious metal shortages. (ibid.: 190)

Andre Wink describes the early medieval world (seventh–eleventh centuries) as a period of 'Muslim economy' and 'the period of the economic supremacy of Islam' (Wink 1990: 225). Though familiar with Deyell's work, he seldom gives any evidence of marshalling his basic postulates. Thus, for Wink, the domains of the Rashtrakutas (ibid.: 308), the Palas (ibid.: 254–77), and the prosperous commercial regions of Gujarat and the western coast (ibid.: 308–09) show no evidence of an indigenous coinage tradition. Instead, the inadequacy of Sharma's hypothesis about the paucity of metal money is sought to be plugged by locating the pivot and driving force of early medieval economy and trade in the 'world-embracing exchange circuit with a unified monetary constituent and a fusion of formerly rival dominions in a new universalistic polity which bridged the divide between the Mediterranean and the Indian Ocean' (ibid.: 359). Thus, for example, it is underlined that the domain of the *dinar* and *dirham* (with special reference to the so-called 'millions of "*tatariya dirhams*" in Sind'; in the kingdom of al-Jurz or Gurjara-Pratiharas; in the Kabul valley, the Punjab and Gujarat) (ibid.: 175, 301), the universal gold and silver coinage of the early medieval world, integrated India and the Indian Ocean (ibid.: 309).[9]

4

Deyell's impressionistic quantification to make a case for manufacturing of coins in 'large quantities' in early medieval India and to show that these quantities were in no way inferior to those of the pre-Gupta coinage has recently been refuted by R.S. Sharma (Sharma 2001: 119–62, especially 141). The coin holdings in the British Museum (London), Indian Museum (Calcutta), The Asiatic Society of Bombay (Mumbai), Prince of Wales Museum (Mumbai), Indian Institute of Research in Numismatics (Anjaneri, Nashik), Andhra Pradesh State Museum (Hyderabad), Patna Museum (Patna), Directorate of Archaeology of Maharashtra (Mumbai), Bharat Kala Bhavan Museum (Varanasi), Central Museum (Indore) and National Museum (New Delhi), have been tabulated by him in eleven tables. These data show that the number of coins between *c.* 500 and *c.* 1000 should not exceed 20,000. The same tables show that the total number of coins for the 500 years preceding the rise of the Guptas (that is, *c.* 200 BC–*c.* AD 300) is around 97,000. Thus the coins of AD 500–1000 seem to be not more than a fourth of the coins from 200 BC–AD 300. There is also an indication that the per capita availability of coins in the post-500 period shrank substantially, for, agrarian expansion and multiplication of the states in both old and newly-settled areas suggest an increase in population. Some other aspects of Deyell's quantification of the numismatic data need special recalling, for these have important bearing on the reconstruction of monetary history.

(i) Of the forty-one hoards studied by him, there is none from Jammu and Kashmir, Himachal Pradesh, Gujarat and Bengal. The conspicuous absence of Bengal and the presence of only one hoard from Bihar (No. 34 from Rasulpur) are particularly inexplicable, for, Deyell stresses: 'Long-distance trade did not need to rely on a series of relay or entrepôt markets along an extended overland axis, since the Ganga was navigable its whole length from the Bay of Bengal to the Himalayas northeast of Delhi' (Deyell 1990: 239). Incidentally, all the 1,528 identifiable coins of the Rasulpur hoard of 1,565 coins have been assigned to the period between *c.* 1242 and 1266.

(ii) The Kasindra hoard (No. 5, Sirohi, Rajasthan) of over 94,000 coins has been arbitrarily assigned to the so-called 'Rajput period' and between *c.* 1000 and 1200. Since much has been said by Deyell about the role of billon coins of this hoard in the international and inter-regional trade of Gujarat (despite complete absence of any hoard of coins from Gujarat) with the Konkan coast and hinterland, certainty is needed about the period given to the Sirohi hoard. Deyell's allusion to the only published reference to this crucial data (Pokharna 1964: 51–52) contradicts his assumptions. Pokharna draws attention to the degraded character of these coins, the prototype of which is the 'bust-and-altar'-type coins belonging to the fifth century (cf. Pokharna, 'A New Variety of Indo-Sassanian Goins': 54–58; especially coin no. 04). Further, it is hinted that the Kasindra hoard might have been buried during the 'pressure of foreign attacks' between the fifth and eighth centuries. Michael Mitchiner has, in fact, attributed these coins to the Hepathalites (white Huns), and dates them in c. AD 550–650 (cf. Mitchiner, *Oriental Coins and Their Values*: 230; nos 1476–82).

(iii) The total number of coins in forty hoards (excluding Kasindra) is about 30,500. Of these, nearly 1,300 are unattributed. Coins datable up to c. AD 1000 number only about 200; whereas those of the period of Deyell's major concern, namely, AD 1000–1200, account for nearly 7,500, which is just about 25 per cent of the identifiable coins. Over 18,800 coins (more than 60 per cent of the identifiable coins) belong to the thirteenth century or thereafter.

(iv) Nine coin-types (nos 154 to 160 and 162–163) attributed to Gujarat and its dynasties between c. AD 750 and 1200 figure in eight different hoards, which have yielded, in all, 1,630 coins (excluding the Kasindra hoard). These hoards are located in Afghanistan (nos 6 and 7), Andhra Pradesh (no. 1), Madhya Pradesh (no. 4), Maharashtra (nos 3, 8 and 9) and Sind (no. 2). Of the aforesaid nine types, all except two (nos 162 and 163) are anonymous. Types 162 and 163 are attributed to Somala Devi and Jayasimha Siddharaja respectively, but their coins have not been found in any hoard reported by Deyell. The absence of coins of Jayasimha Siddharaja, who ruled for half a century, is particularly instructive. The details of Gujarat coins in hoards are as follows:

Chavdas: AD 760–940
    Type 154: nil; Type 155: 235 coins
Chaulkyas: AD 940–1210
    Type 156: 400 coins; Type 157: 104 coins; Type 158: 196 coins;
    Type 159: 674 coins
Vaghelas: AD 1210–1300
    Type 160: nil

'Associated Gujarat coinage'
> Type 162 (Somala Devi: *c.* AD 1200): nil;[10] Type 163
> (Jayasimha Siddharaja: AD 1094–1144): nil.[11]

Deyell's data on Gujarat pale into insignificance when compared with the data of hoards of the western Ksatrapa coins, ranging between the first and the fourth centuries. Of the forty-four known hoards of these coins, as many as twenty-six belong to Gujarat and more than 42,000 coins (about 10,000 in lead) of these kings are known. Incidentally, for nearly the first 250 years, the silver coins of this series show a very high silver content ranging between 90 per cent and 98 per cent – it is only in the late third century that the silver content goes below 90 per cent. The western Ksatrapa silver coins rarely show the fineness of less than 79 per cent silver (for data on these coins see Jha and Rajgor 1994: 57–77).

Deyell's *Living without Silver* is purely a numismatist's exercise which seeks to overawe the reader through questionable statistics and quantity. Its claim of being 'The Monetary History of Early Medieval North India' appears somewhat pretentious.[12] Nowhere does the work enter the realm of discussing the overall role of money in the life of peoples – specially its operation in the rural and urban areas.

Wink's much discussed work is neither a rigorous numismatic exercise nor a strict monetary history of India. His 'world-embracing exchange circuit with a unified monetary constituent' is marked by a conspicuous absence of empirical data. The *raison d'état* of his hypothesis, namely, the so-called 'internationalized *dirhams*', specially the '*tatariya dirham*', appears to be a usage not different from his equally famous imaginary *fitna*.[13] Further, how did the indigenous currency, wherever it was available, interact with this alleged international currency? What was the medium of exchange in the trade nexus of the Pandyas – specially in the context of their import of high-priced items such as horses? How did coins operate in the markets of peninsular India, specially under the Cholas who had raised their stakes in the trade of the Indian Ocean? One looks in vain for even probable answers to these questions. In addition, Wink seems to be completely oblivious of the following insights which have a bearing on the monetary transactions not only within the Islamic world but also on the alleged integration of the economy of the Indian Ocean in terms of 'internationalized *dirhams*'

(i) N.M. Lowick (Lowick 1974: 321; cited by Deyell 1990: 237) has argued that there was the virtual disappearance of coinage in the Persian Gulf from the ninth century.

(ii) A study of Islamic mint output between AD 685 and 743 based on dye variants shows that (a) in spite of the initial surge, the production of the reformed silver coinage ran into some impediments in the last years of Caliph 'Abd al-Malik's reign (AD 685–705), reaching its lowest level in the early years of al-Walid (AD 705–15); and (b) the reign of Hisham (AD 724–43) was characterized by the restriction of coin production to the mints operating in the areas remaining under the strict control of the Umayyad administration (Syria, Iraq) to the exclusion of mints in the eastern provinces. This centralizing policy is associated with a marked decline output of silver coins (University of Michigan 1966).

(iii) The Geniza documents of the Jewish merchant community in Egypt (Goitein 1980) are a testimony to the degree of economic autonomy of the trade networks in the western section of the Indian Ocean already in the eleventh and in particular in the twelfth century.[14]

(iv) Another study of the relevant Geniza material focuses on the relationship between *dinar* and *dirham*, that is, bimetallic currency of the Fatimid and Ayyubid times (AD 969–1250) (Goitein 1965) During most of the Fatimid period, the value of silver was indicated by its relation to the standard gold *dinar* and not *vice versa*. The situation was different in Ayyubid and Mamluk times. The most important fact emanating from the mass of evidence of these documents is the use of the word *dirham* in the general sense of a low-value silver coin. Thirty or more of these silver coins had to be paid for one *dinar*. It seems, however, that merchants and judges, the two arbiters on market values, were inclined to fix 1:40 as the normal rate of exchange. 'The frequent inquiries and statements about the market rate of the *dirham*, as well as the actual reports about their "sales" prove that the value of silver constantly was exposed to fluctuation' during the Fatimid times (ibid.: 43). By the Mamluk times, *dirham* became only a 'money of account' (Balog 1964: 45, cited in Goitein 1980: 42–43). Such volatility of value of the *dirham* must have concerned the 'lower middle class as much as the more affluent'. Goitein also hints that 'sudden and severe changes in the rate of exchanges would be felt as a calamity'. Wouldn't that affect the *Karimis*, a loose association of rich ship-owners trading under Ayyubid protection, who brought Indian spices to Egypt and the Yemen?[15]

(v) The Samanid *dirhams* too became very irregular in weight in the 930s when they varied between 2.7 and 4.5 gms,[16] leading to frequent cutting and breaking them into fragments. These fragments were used to bring the weight of a quantity of irregular silver *dirhams* down to, or up to, a regular weight. Spufford has argued that their existence in north Europe has misled some historians[17] into believing that fragments were deliberately made for small trading purposes, and has consequently conjured up an imaginary picture of vigorous, petty money-using exchanges.

(vi) The presence of 'foreign coins' in India, the outflow of Indian coins and their overall place in the network of foreign trade (Gupta 1976: 146–63) also does not support Wink's paradigm of overarching 'internationalized *dirhams*'. The biggest hoard of Indian coins found so far outside India was at Debra Dommo (Ethiopia), and comprises 103 gold coins of the Kushanas.[18] The number of coins in the several so-called hoards of Ohind coins of Spalapatideva and Samantadeva (ninth–eleventh centuries) found in Europe (recorded by Bykov 1965) never exceed three and have been treated as 'mere drifts' having no direct bearing on foreign trade. Even the existence of some eastern Chalukyan gold coins of Rajaraja (AD 1019–59) on the Arakan coast is not taken as evidence of its being an 'overseas province' of the Cholas. P.L. Gupta contends that the negligible outflow of the pre-Khalji Indian coins, as reflected in these finds, amply demonstrates that India had the potentiality to balance her imports with her own commodities without exporting much of her coinage (Gupta 1976: 154).

As far as the inflow of 'foreign coins' is concerned, Arab coins prior to the end of the twelveth century are considered to be rare. Some coins of the Egyptian rulers of the thirteenth and fourteenth centuries are not unknown. Amongst other known foreign coins were the Venetian *ducats* (fourteenth–seventeenth centuries) and Persian *larins* of the sixteenth century (Gupta, *Coin Hoards from Maharashtra*, nos 159, 162, 167; Husain, 'Dapoli Hoard': 160–61). Chinese coins (eleventh–thirteenth centuries) are known from the Coromandel coast. Absence of empirical evidence apart, as we shall see below (in Section IV), Wink seems to be totally oblivious of the nature of functioning of 'foreign' currencies outside the domain of their original jurisdiction.

9

III
Market Defined

To start with, it is necessary to define market transactions without reference to the presence of money. In a very limited sense, 'market' is a space where the buying and selling of goods[19] takes place as a regular activity. However, the market needs to be viewed not just in economic terms but also in its sociological, anthropological and cultural dimensions. For example, in the European Middle Ages, there was often an implied conflict between the workings of the market and the legal right of kings, landlords and borough communities. Since the state of the land market did not govern rents of tenures, certain disorders crept into the market. Evidently, there are issues here of concern to historians not primarily concerned with economic matters (Britnell 1993: 2). Some such critical aspects are discussed below.

(a) Negotiated exchange: In markets exchanges take place on the basis of supply and demand. Thus a free-market situation becomes restricted when the negotiated aspect has been eliminated (when exchange rates are determined by decree)[20] or minimized (when negotiations must take place within certain boundaries): both examples of administered markets (cf. Polanyi 1975: 63–66; Dalton 1975: 152–54).

(b) The second distinguishing feature of markets is voluntariness, meaning that the 'transactions can be accepted or rejected without wide-scale social repercussions' (Pryor 1977: 105).

(c) A third feature of market exchange, related to the first, is profit-making – market activity is engaged in because it is seen as an opportunity to accumulate surplus. Some of the best examples of profit-making appear in China. The Han text *Kuan-tsu* notes:

> It is human nature not to refrain from going after profit or warding off danger when either is in sight. Where profit is anticipated, traders will hurry around day–night, and make light of travelling over a thousand *li* to get it. So where there is profit, no mountain can remain unclimbed, and no water is immune from penetration even if it is unfathomable.[21] (Jichuang 1984: 39–40)

(d) A study of medieval England (AD 1000–1500) (Britnell 1993: 8–22) shows that the terms 'market' and 'fair' were foreign to the legal vocabulary of old English before the twelfth century. Ambiguities concerning the legal status of markets were resolved only gradually. In the twelfth century the king's clerks and justices employed *mercatum* and *feria* as standard technical terms for the franchises of market and fair, the essentials of which were (i) fixed time and place for trading; (ii) existence of seigniorial/community interest, whether this was the collection of tolls, charges for stalls, or charges for use of weights and measures. Markets and fairs were associated with castles or newly-founded monasteries. For example, some markets attached to Hundredals manors were those to which jurisdiction over a neigh-bouring hundred was granted. Landlords determined the economic viability of markets and their own interests induced them to limit the number of formal trading places. Most regulations controlling trade in pre-conquest England were of local concern. Briefly, then, evidence of early trading institutions is found only at the points where the inte-rests of landlords became actively involved. (iii) Markets were also at places to which institutions of law and religion regularly attracted large numbers of people.

(e) Commenting on the classic studies of Karl Polanyi on markets, redistribution and reciprocity (market exchange in spatial terms is redistribution), Colin Renfrew (Renfrew 1975: 10–11) not only draws attention to the difference between exchange centres and markets, but also stresses that all marketing implies some kind of order, security – ultimately, indeed, in the case of permanent markets, there is a strong case for the exercise of administrative jurisdiction.

IV
Early Medieval India: Localization of Markets and Monetary Transactions

In the early medieval context (*c.* AD 800–1250), studies have been able to focus on some regional pockets where the operations of . 'markets' have been identified. Some such important studies concern North India, Rajasthan, western India, Bengal and South India.[22] We have discussed elsewhere the role of money in the 'market' on the western (Konkan) coast.[23]

These regional studies, specially those of northern and western India, use such terms as *hattas, rajadhani, mandapika, patta-navara, mandavya-puriya-mandapika, mandavi, sulka-mandapika, nisraniksepa-hatta, sthanaka, pattana-mandapikas*, in the sense of exchange centres, warehouses, and port-markets. Ajay Mitra Shastri says: 'probably all or most of the flourishing towns had coin-exchange centres popularly known as *Nani vata* or *Sovani hata*' in the kingdom of the Yadavas who are known to have ruled over parts of Maharashtra, Andhra Pradesh and Karnataka in the twelfth and thirteenth centuries. The *Govindaprabhu-charitra* of Maimbhatta gives a vivid account of the functioning of these centres (Shastri, 'Yadava Coins', in Amiteshwar Jha (ed.), *Medieval Indian Coinages*).

In the case of the Cholas, Hall has focused on *nagarams*, which in some instances functioned as periodic markets, that is, which were convened on designated days of the week, identified in Tamil epigraphy as *tavalam* or 'fairs'. *Managaram*, literally 'great' or 'higher' *nagaram*, was a central market that functioned as a multi-purpose centre. *Erivirapattinam* ('place where the heroes of the road conduct trade') was also in the category of 'higher' marketing centres and probably constituted mercantile strongholds located in turbulent frontier areas. *Suradalam* has been called a 'fortified commercial centre'.

A case-study of early medieval Rajasthan has attempted to work out a trade network including the role of money therein (Chattopadhyaya 1985). Briefly, it argues for a proliferation of local centres of exchange situated within the domains of emergent Rajput lineages. These centres were points of intersection of traffic of varying origins giving rise to certain measures of hierarchy. The network was further elaborated with the growth of merchant lineages in the eleventh and twelfth centuries which operated both at the inter-regional and intra-regional levels. The range of merchandise started probably with agricultural produce (including dairy produce) but extended to such high-value items as horses, elephants, horned animals and jewels. All this activity took place with only 'partial monetization'.

The role of the 'market' in the Silahara economy also seems to have been somewhat limited. It is true that we read about *sthanaka* as a centre of sale, Friday market and paddy market at Sedambal, and about the superintendent of market (*krenikara*). But it is impossible to work out even a modicum of market networks. It is also true that a few goldsmiths are mentioned by name (Kakkala and Somaiya, Govyoja and Bammyoja and Nagoja), and that people and authorities to whom grants are addressed include artisans and trading guilds; there is a mention of thirty-five *settis* (traders and merchants) by name and there is even an allusion to 'additional taxes levied out of greed for wealth' (*dravyadilobhat nimitta siddhayadadhikam*). But it is still rather difficult to ascribe large-scale mercantile activity buttressed by an entrenched monetary economy. Amongst the economic products

12

figuring in the Silahara records, arecanut alone stands out as the principal commercial crop. Other items indicative of the nature of economic activity include agricultural products such as vegetables, spices (green ginger, turmeric, garlic, dry ginger, cumin, black pepper, mustard), eighteen kinds of grains (unspecified), betel leaves, fruits such as coconut, jackfruit, mango, dairy products such as clarified butter and oil, products of florists and potters, items of household furniture, and, finally salt and cloth. One looks in vain for such high-value goods. This can also be taken as an indicator of the limited long-distance overseas trade, notwithstanding some big vessel-owning merchants in control of ports such as Balipattana and Surparaka. Where are such big items of import as horses? Finally, the absence of security of transactions must have also impeded the growth of proper markets in the area. One may refer to Marco Polo's account of rampant piracy at Tana. Referring to this feature, Chakravarti has pointed out that the ports of southern and northern Konkan were apparently less prosperous than, and overshadowed by, ports on the Gujarat coast and in the Malabar littorals (Chakravarti 1991).

The monetary situation on the western coast under the Silaharas is marked by (a) localized usage of various types and denominations of coins, for example, coins of the north Konkan branch are not found under the Kolhapur branch and *vice versa;*[24] and (b) amongst major references to metallic money, barring *gadyanas* and *dharanas,* a great majority belong to land-based economic activities.[25]

Numerous studies in recent years have probed moving forces behind Chola forays in the Indian Ocean up to Southeast Asia. Kulke (1999), for example, builds on K.N. Chaudhuri's postulates of trans-oceanic or 'pre-emporia trade' giving way to 'the practice of organizing trade in shorter segments based on the intermediate urban emporia of the Malabar coast and the strait of Malacca'.[26] This fragmentation of the trans-continental maritime traffic in the Indian Ocean seriously dents Andre Wink's *Al-Hind.* Chaudhuri, following a Braudelian model (Braudel 1984: 48ff), seems to be arguing that the Indian Ocean trade was a monotonous repetition of pendulum movements where India, between the two wings (Islam in the west and China in the east), played only a minor role. Kulke controverts this paradigm and suggests that India too, from time to time, played an active role in the struggle for 'redistributing functions, power and political or economic advance' in the Indian Ocean trade. Further, with a focus on the eleventh-

century Bay of Bengal, India also played a significant role in the transformation of trade and emergence of the late medieval emporia in the
Indian Ocean as forerunners of the early 'European bridgeheads'.[27]

It was the emergence of the Cholas and their maritime
activities[28] accompanied by flourishing merchant guilds at the heart of
the Indian Ocean trade system which made South India an equal
partner along with China and Southeast Asia. Regrettably, however,
except for a brief mention of the well-known 1,838 Chinese coins
(second to the thirteenth century) found in the neighbourhood of
Nagapattinam, Kulke's piece is marked by absence of any hard numismatic evidence (cf. Kulke 1986).

Since the Cholas constitute an important case-study involving
linkages between the rural elite and participants of internal and
external trade networks, it becomes imperative to look at the dynamics
of the exchange mechanism. While Hall's study of 1980 on hierarchy
of 'markets' under the Cholas is well known, it needs to be supplemented by his exposition on the role of money in the trade and economy of the times (Hall 1991). The chief characteristics of the Chola
monetary system are as follows.

(a) Most epigraphic references to the use of gold coinage in
the Chola realm are associated with redistribution to temples and thus
the use of the relatively heavy *kalanju* coinage was appropriate to the
records of substantive long-term endowments.

(b) From the late tenth century, market networks extended
beyond the South Indian shores to Southeast Asia and China in the
east, and to the Red Sea region in the west. Appropriately, smaller units
of coinage (*kasus*) than the *kalanju* were necessary to facilitate the
enhanced marketing system.

(c) It is possible that each province retained its local currency
and thus there was a necessary calculated evaluation of coinage by a
realm-wide standard issued by the Chola monarchs.

(d) There were two systems of pricing, in gold and in paddy
rice. Market standards like pepper, ghee and arecanut were stated in
paddy equivalents, while staples of long-distance trade, such as carda-
mom seeds, *campaka* buds and camphor (all aromatics used in temple
ceremonies) were assigned a cash value. Livestock was bought and sold
either by cash or barter exchange.

(e) By the twelfth century, gold and silver were frequently
mixed with lesser metals (an alloy called *tara* is referred to in inscrip-

tions), as well as copper, in coinage. Thirteenth-century inscriptions also make reference to a new coin called *fanam*. The earliest concentration of low denominational coins was in or near coastal ports, where trade necessitated the exchange of non-perishable commodities.[29]

In his study of the currency system of South India, B.D. Chattopadhyaya (Chattopadhyaya 1977) divides South India (AD 950–1300) into a number of politically distinct currency areas based on the growing complexities of South Indian trade – particularly the import of expensive horses. He or his study points out that transactions at all levels of the society were not equally affected by coined money. No wonder, Hall raises the following questions: can we better examine the distribution of coinage finds relative to other historical evidence of internal development – especially in the Chola realm? Where, specifically, were large and small denominational coins used, and when? What is the relationship of coin-use to coastal, urban and rural population centres? When does small-unit currency penetrate the rural economy, and where? (Hall 1991). Questions somewhat similar to these lie at the root of our discussion of the level and degree of the penetration of money on the Konkan coast under the Silaharas (Shrimali 1996: 108–10).

Apropos the case of money and market in Mukherjee's mid-eastern India, including Bengal, some questions were raised above. In addition, it has been argued that the simplicity of predominantly rural life on the one hand, and the heavy expenditure of the Pala and the Sena rulers on the maintenance of their armies on the other, may account for the restricted use of money. Like the Konkan coast, the Bay of Bengal too was susceptible to the activities of pirates,[30] thus denting such essential components of the market as order, security and jurisdiction. Further, Dharmapala's grant of four villages (in the Pundravardhana *bhukti*) along with their market-places (*hattikas*) to a temple[31] also should be seen as examples of administered markets. Tome Pires, writing from early sixteenth-century Malacca, reveals that areas in contact with Java's east coast commercial centres – the Sunda Strait area of west Java and south Sumatra and the Spice Islands to the east – used Chinese cash, while the Bay of Bengal, notably Pegu and Ayuddhya, had become more regionally integrated and were using small tin coins and locally minted silver in their exchange.[32]

Since the exponents of a monetarist economy in early medieval India have often rationalized their positions in terms of long-distance external trade with Southeast Asia and East Asia (notably China), it is imperative that the dynamics of money in those areas are also configured. There has been some very substantive work in this area, such as that of Robert S. Wicks, Jan Wisseman Christie and J.N. Miksic (Wicks 1991, 1992; Christie 1996; Miksics 1979, 1996).

Wicks invokes a theory of monetization focusing on the importance of the measure of value as the basis for all monetary functions. He works out an overall valuation of concepts and chief substances used as money in early Southeast Asia[33] – gold, silver, cloth,[34] rice, salt and *cowries*[35] – and examines the ways in which control was maintained over external trade and an unexpected dichotomy between long-distance trade, typically conducted on a barter basis, and local exchange, which was often monetized.

Invoking Grierson's model of prioritizing the use of physical money in making administrative payments before its utilization in commercial (marketized) exchange,[36] Wicks shows that the geographical distribution of indigenous Southeast Asian coinage points overwhelmingly to local rather than regional usage, stressing its non-commercial function. It served, almost without exception, to fulfil fiscal or religious obligations and did not further the needs of merchants or traders. 'Metallic hierarchy' determined the choice of metal for coinage, not necessarily the availability of the metal. Bronze rarely served as a metal for creating coinage before the fifteenth century, but it was common for casting images throughout Southeast Asia. Though both gold and silver were evenly distributed throughout the region, silver was the most widespread measure of value on the mainland, while gold was preferred in island realms. The monetization of early Southeast Asia is an important manifestation of 'indigenization' process (Wicks 1992: 312–14).

The situation in the Javanese states (Christie 1996: 271–72) between the ninth and fifteenth centuries was no different. After the beginning of the tenth century, the need for large numbers of coins of smaller denominations grew more pressing, resulting in the import of Chinese copper cash that was imitated later on. As the newer copper currency became the preferred medium of exchange, first in market and then in official transactions,[37] the older gold currency, in turn, gradually acquired a ceremonial status. The distribution of coinage shows that the use of money in pre-thirteenth-century Java was not universal, but was restricted to the two core population centres in central Java and east Java. Chau Ju-kua reports that officials, except for the commanders of troops, were paid in local produce (perishables), while commanders, who had to take their belongings with them, were paid in gold.

Michael Mitchiner refers to the 'symbolic' coinage of Southeast Asia that was almost exclusively made of silver which was in use during a period before the end of the first millennium AD (Mitchiner 1991: 62–83). Gold coinage was restricted to a hoard found on the Malay peninsula (Krabi), plus a few related pieces found at Oc-eo in Vietnam. It is also argued that despite a strong Indian influence on this 'symbolic' coinage, which was also given a local interpretation, Indian coins of this period are not found in mainland Southeast Asia. Nor has any 'symbolic' coin of the Southeast Asia been found in India. The extensive commerce attested by cultural influences does not appear to have been served by coinage. Instead, bullion and barter seem to have serviced this early trade. With Arakan excepted, the primary links between India and mainland Southeast Asia appear to involve the Mon kingdoms of southern Burma and the Andhra kingdom and its successors in the Deccan.[38]

Wink's postulate of the 'internationalized *dirham*', specially the '*tatariya dirham*' circulating in India fails to take note of the nature of the operation of 'foreign' currencies outside the jurisdictions of the issuing authorities. Apart from the absence of empirical evidence and the known absence of silver in the late eleventh and twelfth-century Arab world (Mayhew 1987), some theoretical aspects also dent the money-market links suggested by Wink. Grierson had, of course, cautioned against assuming that the presence of coinage is indicative of market exchange. Collis, studying minted coinage from the anthropological rather than the numismatic standpoint, says: 'gold and silver coinage . . . had a prestige value, being employed in conditions of reciprocity, and bronze coinage was employed for market exchange'.[39] Wicks, however, cautions against Collis's assessment about base-metal coinage and its link with the market, and says that once it no longer becomes possible for the issuing authority to exercise jurisdiction (say, the Chinese cash in Java), there is no guarantee that the primary function within the recipient society will be to facilitate economic exchange. Indeed, in many societies imported goods become symbols of status and wealth.

Ibrahim ben Ya'qub, a Jew from Tortosa on the Ebro in

Muslim Spain, travelling through Mainz in AD 965, commented that he found there Indian goods such as spices, perfumes and *dirhams* struck at Samarkand in 913–14 at the beginning of the reign of the greatest of the Samanid emirs, Nasr bin Ahmad. Such non-European coins were not a part of its currency. Persons who did not possess their own state's coinage would treat the coinage of outsiders (Central Asian *dirhams*) as a commodity – commercial commodity – or as treasure, depending on whether the possessor was a 'merchant' or a chieftain of warriors. Coin, like other silver, was a commodity to be accepted by weight. Silver whether coined or uncoined was seen as a commodity, although a very precious and prestigious commodity, and was dealt in only by weight (Spufford 1988: 67–69).

In medieval England (AD 1000–1180), too, no foreign currency was allowed to circulate – foreign currency entering England had to be taken to a mint for remaking as English currency. The Crown supplied dyes to local mints – the number of coins per pound of silver was centrally determined. At least half the recorded population was largely independent of market for its subsistence.[40]

In the light of these limitations of 'foreign' coins, must we not look afresh at the alleged presence of Arab coins and '*tatariya dirhams*' in the territories of the Palas, Rashtrakutas, Silaharas and such other areas as are known for their 'monetary anaemia'?

V
Credit, Rate of Interest and Money Supply

The availability of credit is an integral element of a real monetary economy. The early medieval *Smrtikaras* laid down norms for regulating pledges, sureties and rates of interest. The post-tenth-century evidence throws additional light, in so far as we are informed about the strong presence of land, cattle, grains, cloth and houses for raising loans. The documentary evidence of the *Lekhapaddhati* showing the practice of mortgage (twelfth/thirteenth centuries) as a means of credit has been too well known to be repeated here. Similarly, varieties of *hundikas* (bills of exchange) mentioned in post-tenth-century sources also take cognizance of agricultural products, animals, etc. – for example, *dhanya-hundika, yava-godhuma-hundika, ghoti-kanama-hundika.*[41]

The role of money in a society can also be understood in terms of the rate of interest on investments and loans. An analysis of the cumulative evidence of literature and epigraphs of early medieval texts (both literary and epigraphic) shows that the rate of interest varied between 10 and 33.3 per cent per annum. Generally, historians have tried to explain such a phenomenon in terms of the money supply. Thus, the high rate at Bhinmal (30 to 33.33 per cent) was the result of the need to encourage donations, while the low rate (12 per cent) mentioned in the Jalor inscription (VS 1323 = AD 1266) was possible because of the capital being easily available. A deposit in the Mahavira tem-ple at Arasana fetched only 10 per cent interest, which is sought to be explained thus: 'its credit was high and with the rich Jain community to patronize it, it had no need of bringing in fresh deposits by promising high rates of interest' (D. Sharma 1959: 300–01).[42] Traders undertaking high-risk ventures on the high seas or in forests infested with robbers had to be prepared for very high rates of interest that ranged between 120 per cent and 240 per cent per annum. It has also been argued that the increase in the rate of interest 'does not seem to be so much the result of a stronger tendency of exploitation or of the growing importance of the rentier class as of the comparative absence of coins and decline of trade' (Sharma 1983: 193–217). Occasionally, disturbed political conditions also accounted for fluctuating rates of interest. The possibilities of these factors notwithstanding, we have in our case-study of the Silaharas (Shrimali 1996: 111) raised several questions to underline that the explanation of the rate of interest in terms of money supply is an oversimplification, and that it calls for a more intensive analysis of the actual functioning of the cash-nexus.

A dialectic relationship exists between the rate of interest on the one hand and investment-savings on the other. Also, if the supply of money is regarded as a factor, we cannot be oblivious to the speculative demand of money as well, which is no less integrally linked with the rate of interest. Finally, what about the 'transaction demand' of money? After all, in a society based on monetary economy, cash liquidity should be an important consideration. The Bhinmal stone inscription of Udayasimhadeva of (Vikrama) *Samvat* 1306 (AD 1249), and the dole (*vyavastha* settlement) given by the *mahajanas* to the *sthanikas* of Kalikatti in south Karnataka in the early thirteenth century enable us to see the linkage between cash and non-cash resources and the transfer of cash resources.[43] Another important example of the cycle of cash and non-cash resources is seen in the Kolhapur stone inscription of Bhoja II (of the Kolhapur branch of the Silaharas) (*CII* VI: 266, lines

13–19) recording three donations between *Saka* years 1112 and 1115. The second of these made in SE 1114 (AD 1192) refers to a donation of some land and some houses. The donor (Kaliyana Nayaka) purchased it from the *mahajanas*, who had in turn purchased it for a gift from the previous owner, Lakhumana Ghaisasa.

The early medieval evidence also throws important light on many other aspects of the network of interest bearing a close relationship with the changing socio-economic formation. The consideration of *varna* in determining the rate of interest; detailed laws on the growing practice of loans in kind, including foodgrains and milk products; the emergence of *kayika* or bodily interest as a form of interest paid through services; and the introduction of land in the mechanism of the early medieval mode of interest – all these fit in the economic scenario marked by limited monetary transactions and reflect the lesser capacity of members of the lower order to repay their debts (for details, see Sharma 1983: 193–217).

VI
Bullion Flow

'Coins will not carry much meaning for economic history unless we identify the ancient sources of gold, silver and other metals' (Sharma 1976: 7). The flow of metals, specially the precious ones, across the globe are known to have affected the production and dissemination of coins and money. To illustrate, the American treasure imports initiated, by the sixteenth century, a lively, broad-ranging pan-European debate and inquiry into monetary theory, or in Michel Foucault's terms, 'the analysis of wealth' (Foucault 1971: 168–74, cited by Richards 1983: 4–5). Reflecting a general shift from 'Renaissance' to 'classical' thought, Foucault postulates an important alteration in the conception of precious metals as money:

> For the Renaissance 'economists' . . . the ability of money to measure commodities, as well as its exchangeability, rested upon its intrinsic value . . . [gold and silver] possessed, both in the natural scale of things and in themselves, an absolute and fundamental price, higher than any other, to which the value of any and every commodity could be referred. . . . Fine metal . . . had a price; for this reason too . . . it was a measure of all prices; and for this reason, finally, one could exchange it for anything else that had a price.

In the 17th century, these three properties [price, measure, exchange] are still attributed to money, but they are all three made to rest, not on the first (possession of price), but on the last (substitution for that which possesses price). Whereas the Renaissance based the functions of coinage (measure and substitution) on the double nature of its intrinsic character (the fact that it was precious), the 17th century turns the analysis upside down; it is the exchanging function that serves as foundation for the other two characters (its ability to measure and its capacity to receive a price) thus appearing as qualities deriving from that function.

The dynamics of pre-Turkish money in India has seldom been explained in terms of bullion flows.[44] Deyell's map showing distribution sources of precious metals in medieval India (Deyell 1990: 249–52[45]) and his hypothesis of North Indian people living without silver raise more questions than they actually answer. For example, is Deyell's cartographic delineation exhaustive? Was India 'Living without Silver' for the first time during *c.* AD 800–1200? A geological survey of the nineteenth century records ancient silver mines in the Kadapah and Karnul districts in the south (now Cuddapah and Kurnool districts of Andhra Pradesh) which were identified with the extensively worked mines of Narae reported by Pliny (Ball 1881: 232). The same survey also lays emphasis on numerous place names with *chand* (silver) in the Bhagalpur region of present-day Bihar (ibid.[47]). Deyell's mapping ignores these areas of eastern and southern India.

Further, how did the western Ksatrapas strike silver coins of very high purity for as many as four centuries? And even before that, the silver punchmarked coins had a truly pan-Indian character, which no other pre-British Indian currency ever achieved. From where did silver come for these hundreds of thousands of coins known through hundreds of hoards? How is it that, notwithstanding the aforesaid Narae silver mines, the Satavahanas preferred to issue coins with substantial lead content? Why do coins of the Indo-Greeks, Scythians, Parthians, Kusanas, etc., show a decline in the use of silver and a corresponding preference for the so-called non-precious metals/alloys such as copper, bronze, nickel, etc.? (Prasad 1969) Why are the post-punchmarked coins of the Panchala and Magha kings of such high-tin (ranging between 17 per cent and 23 per cent – the tin content in normal bronze is usually put between 10 per cent and 15 per cent) bronze?

(Shrimali 1983: 110, 182–85) Even in the case of the Ksatrapa silver coins, one notices the presence of as much as 14 per cent to 18 per cent copper as opposed to about 8 per cent required to strengthen silver alloys. Is this also related to a limited supply of silver? (Sharma: 123[47]) In short, the choice of any particular metal for minting coins was not determined solely by the availability or paucity of one or the other metal. The determining considerations seem to be many and somewhat complex. The shift to the so-called less valuable metals, for example, in the case of the Satavahanas and other post-Mauryan powers of northern and northwestern India, may have something to do with conscious changes in monetary policy, particularly when we find that both lead and tin were scarce in India and had to be imported. Such policy changes have indeed been carefully worked out in the cases of (a) the Kusana gold and copper coins and (b) the Bactrian Nickel theory in respect of the Indo-Greek coins. Apparently, India did live without silver long before the early medieval centuries delineated by Deyell. Even in the early medieval context, we are told that the debasement in the coins of the Turk Shahis (seventh–nineteenth centuries) was not due to the alleged loss of the Panjhir silver mines, for, the areas around Panjhir were lost only after the battle of Ghuzak in AD 986–87. Instead, unscrupulous and cunning private *sahukars* were behind the move in order to make illicit profits (Rahman 1979: 168–72). Incidentally, Deyell too is aware that the silver mines at Panjhir, Anderaba, Zebak and Wakhan were active until the Mongol conquest in the early thirteenth century and recognizes: 'these must have been the dominant "local" sources of coinage silver [*sic*]' (Deyell 1990: 251).

In another connection Deyell has argued that between AD 1200 and 1500 the Sultans of Bengal probably obtained their supplies of silver from southwest China and eastern Burma through an overland route using pack animals. This has been suggested as an alternative to the well-known sea route to India from Southeast Asia (Deyell 1983: 207–27[48]).

VII
The Feudal Order Stayeth

Skinner had, in his classic study of markets in rural China, defined a 'standard' market as

that type of rural market which met all the normal trade needs of the peasant household: what the household produced but did not consume was normally sold there, and what it consumed but did not produce was normally bought there. The standard market provided for the exchange of goods produced within the market's dependent area, but more importantly it was the starting point for the upward flow of agricultural products and craft items into higher reaches of the marketing system, and also the termination of the downward flow of imported items destined for peasant consumption. (Skinner 1964: 6)

As already mentioned, the study of marketing structures goes beyond the immediate concerns of the economy and, therefore, interests sociologists and anthropologists. Sharing this outlook, Skinner contends that marketing structures defined by him 'appear to be characteristic of the whole class of civilizations known as "peasant" or "traditional agrarian" societies' (ibid.: 3)

Assuming that markets in early medieval India met manifold criteria as laid down above,[49] the overall role of money therein will have to be assessed in a broad spectrum. In our case-study of the Konkan coast under the Silaharas (Shrimali 1996: 95–123), we had been able to stress that there had neither been a 'rocket-like rise in the volume of money'[50] nor any operation of sophisticated 'fiduciary currency' (postulated by Aymard 1980: 11–20). It is well known that once the cash system comes into use, even when it falls into comparative disuse, the old practice of computing prices and payments in cash continues. It is, therefore, not improbable that some of the allusions to cash donations may have been spelt out only in a notional sense rather than in specific monetary terms.[51] Even in the heyday of the Mughal empire under Akbar, the limitations of monetary transactions were apparent when we find that coins were not regarded as fixed standards of value but rather as a form of merchandise – a merchant who offered payment in money was, in fact, entering into a particular kind of barter. Similarly, the land revenue demands on peasants and the salaries of *mansabdars* in the seventeenth century were expressed in terms of *dams* (copper coins) which were used only as 'money of account' (cf. Habib 1999: 280–81, 432–44 Appendix C;[52] see Moreland 1983: 59–60). Such calculations differed from real transactions in rupees and argue for an extremely limited monetization of economy which was not able to make any significant dent in the predominant feudal socio-economic formation despite revival of trade – both inland and long-distance overseas trade.

That land continued to occupy a more conspicuous place in the overall economic structure under the Silaharas is possible to infer from: (a) references to 66 fields, very often identified in terms of crops sown; (b) eighteen instances of donations of plots of land mentioned in six inscriptions; (c) fifteen epigraphs recording the donation of twenty-six villages; (d) seventeen allusions to donations of orchards in sixteen inscriptions; (e) eighteen fields as objects of donations in fourteen inscriptions; and (f) numerous donations of crop produce in 64 inscriptions. The rigorous control of the ruling elite over the rural populace, a typical feature of the feudal order, may be seen in the influential members of the village Turubhamra issuing a tough warning to prospective miscreants that if they damaged the water channels of moneylenders, they would be severely punished.[53] The cash-nexus on the western coast, even in its extremely limited form, was being actually manipulated by the ruling elite in such a way as to curb the free activity of not only the peasants but of small craftsmen and artisans as well.[54]

It is argued that 'full monetization' implies 'full marketization', or at least that all goods and services are available for purchase with money. According to Grierson, Polanyi and Dalton (Grierson 1977: 162–20; Dalton 1975: 88 where Polanyi has been cited; see also Neale 1976), the use of a single money as a medium of exchange, means of payment and general standard of value only occurs with the rise of a marketized economy. Could the reverse also be true, namely, 'partial monetization' implying only 'partial marketization'? How did partial monetization and 'commercialization' of revenue affect social differentiation or the functioning of various grades of *samantas* and *mandalesvaras*? Is it possible to comprehend the dynamics of money in early medieval India without looking at the control of numerous grades of lords and chiefs who seem to be the real arbiters of exchange patterns and whose interests shaped many of the institutions of commercial activities?[55] Didn't *samantatatva* imply moral and legal claim to call upon all kinds of resources of the dependent peasants and non-peasants alike?

As one of the examples of elite control, one may invoke Hall's analysis of *nagarams* under the Cholas. In return for their support to the king, the merchants operating in the *nagarams* derived such benefits as (i) systematization of weights and measures that made it easier to determine a fair price in trade negotiations between local and itinerant merchants; (ii) honour of double conches and drums; (iii) state intervention in collecting commercial dues; (iv) right of administrative autonomy and to raise private armies (*velaikkarar*). Amongst these, militarization among merchants would have allowed commercial centres to assume coercive power, prompting Hall to talk about a 'tendency towards independent warlord control'. With the support of the *nattar*, the landholding elite of the *nadu*, the dominance of the *nagaram* over its community was considerably facilitated.

The predator-like mentality of merchants, which was particularly marked amongst itinerant petty merchants, is commented upon in the *Smrtis* and their commentaries. To illustrate, the *Mitaksara*[56] eloquently informs us about modes of cheating and tampering with commodities. Thus, the odour of the *mallika* flower could be added to give the appearance of *amalaka*, the odour of sandal to a piece of *bilva* wood, and silver obtained by polishing black metal.

The Watkura inscription (a sima charter) from east Java, first issued in AD 902 and then reissued in 1348, is an interesting example of shifting the burden of agricultural taxes on to each hamlet within the village corporation (Christie 1996: 279–80). The growing control of the ruling elite in early medieval India is reflected in varied levies, both in cash and kind. The Kolhapur stone inscription of Gandaraditya (SE 1058 = AD 1136) (*CII*, VI, pp. 229–35), the Miraj stone inscription of Vijayaditya (SE 1065–66 = AD 1143–44) (ibid., pp. 241–46), refer to such cash and kind levies as (a) arecanuts, (b) betel leaves, (c) one sollage on each pitcher of clarified butter and oil, (d) *palas* on cloth, (e) items of furniture on carpenters' houses, (f) spices, (g) eighteen kinds of grains, (h) dry and fresh fruits, etc. Levies in kind are often mentioned in terms of differing units of cartloads and headloads. To this may also be added the rising and perhaps also oppressive commercial taxation which has been extensively documented (Srivastava 1999; Jain 1990).[57]

Epigraphic evidence, specially from North India, frequently refers to *turuskadanda*, that is, a levy possibly to meet the threat of the Turks. One is tempted to compare it with war taxes in medieval Europe. The mode of payment of this *danda* is not clear. Is it possible that the number of coin hoards that we encounter for the medieval centuries were the result of such hard times? Economists usually assume that velocity of coin circulation[58] moves in unison with the trade cycle. This conforms to the commonsense observation that in good times people are more inclined to spend and that they tend to save for hard times. Mention was made above that the Kasindra hoard was probably buried under 'pressure of foreign attacks'. Indications of hard times are also noticeable in western India where a rise in cost of living during the twelfth/thirteenth centuries has been postulated (Jain 1990: 208).

It is well known that early medieval land grants were very often made in the months of *Vaisakha* and *Karttika*, that is, the end of one agricultural season and the beginning of another.[59] Since these were also the occasions when the inhabitants of the donated lands were informed about the levies they were expected to pay to the donees, it would not be unreasonable to suggest that the forces of money and market may also have been linked with this seasonal cycle. If at all any money reached the hands of small peasants and rural artisans and craftsmen, it may have been recycled in favour of landed magnates, both in the rural and urban areas. After all, the ruling elite comprising influential *mahabrahmanas*,[60] *mahajanas*, *settis* and their assemblies, functioned in league with the king and his feudalized bureaucracy. The growing interest of the mercantile community as well as bureaucracy in landed investments is easily recognizable in land grants from different parts of India. At one level this meant locking up of cash liquidity, and on the other, generating sources of social tensions. Conflict between a Vaisnava establishment and a *matha* of Devi over landed property has been recorded in a tenth-century inscription from Chinchani near Sanjan (north Konkan coast). It also seems to have acquired the ugly form of a tussle between the local inhabitants and 'outsiders' who were merchants. The hold of religious beneficiaries and mercantile community on these religious establishments was quite pronounced (Chakravarti 1990: 199–201).

In late medieval England (*circa* fourteenth–fifteenth centuries) there had developed a remarkable convergence of the interests of the mercantile class and those of the gentry comprising knights. The fourteenth-century knight and merchant among Chaucer's Canterbury pilgrims may have been men with opposing interests in life and a different scale of values, where trade and gentility did not mix. The ground reality, however, was different. The common interests of the landed and commercial classes contributed to the fluidity of English society which allowed the son of a wool merchant, William de la Pole, to become the Earl of Suffolk. At the other end, Sir Guy Brian and Hugh, Lord Stafford, the Knights of the Garter, did not hesitate to call themselves merchants. Military commanders such as Sir John Fastolf were as keen to invest their booty in trade as in rural manors.[61] This transformation of the English society is easily comparable with the triumvirate of the rural, commercial and bureaucratic elite – all with distinctive landed interests, as sketched above in the context of early medieval India.

The dynamics of money, markets and trade in India during the four centuries between *c.* AD 800 and 1200 could not make any significant dent in the land-based and exploitative social order which was the hallmark of feudalism.

I am grateful to my colleague Dr Najaf Haider and Dr Himanshu Prabha Ray of Jawaharlal Nehru University. They not only discussed various problems connected with this presentation but also made available to me some inaccessible reading material.

Notes

[1] Peter Spufford divides the Middle Ages into two periods, namely: (i) seventh to twelfth centuries, and (ii) thirteenth to fifteenth centuries. See Spufford (1988: 378–80).

[2] A seminar held on the occasion of the 58th Annual Conference of the Numismatic Society of India. Its proceedings were published only in 1976. See Shastri (1976).

[3] This is being suggested on the basis of our understanding that no organized effort in the direction was made before this. This is, however, not to deny the extremely significant and seminal contributions made by D.D. Kosambi. His numerous writings on punchmarked coins raised very important and fundamental questions about the utility of coins. For example, his emphasis on the need to determine the relationship between the loss of coin weight and circulation of coins, the relevance of the volume of coins, his painstaking suggestions about the chronology of punchmarked coins on the basis of the sequence of symbols thereon, and his rational tenacity in showing the link between the number of obverse and reverse symbols and the period of circulation of these coins. Some of Kosambi's representative writings have been compiled in the volume entitled *Indian Numismatics* (1981) with an introduction by B.D. Chattopadhyaya and published by Orient Longman, New Delhi. Kosambi, indeed, was the founder of scientific numismatics in India.

[4] Though first suggested by Kosambi, it was the publication of R.S. Sharma's *Indian Feudalism* in 1965 that brought it into focus.

[5] First, we have those contributions which have upheld Professor Sharma's basic contentions. Professor Lallanji Gopal's findings on early medieval coin-types are already well known in this respect. Amongst some more contributions on the subject can be added Bela Lahiri's observations (1980: 87–89), made in her Presidential Address delivered at the 66th Session of the Numismatic Society of India held at Bangalore in March 1980. R. Vanaja's compendium (1983: 18–19) also concedes the paucity of coins in the period between *c.* AD 600 and 800. Similarly, Amal Kumar Jha and Sanjay Garg (1991) underline the 'gap between ancient and medieval coin-age traditions' in Kangra (*c,* seventh–ninth centuries).

Second, we have D.K. Ganguly's case-study (1982: 114–29). Here he is absolutely explicit in saying that Orissa has not yielded any coin of the period between AD 600 and 1200. However, he does not accept R.S. Sharma's contention about the decline of trade, pleads for trade with Southeast Asia, argues rather unconvincingly about the usefulness of gold coins in terms of only bullion, and, like P.L. Gupta (1976: 146–47), goes to the extent of over-emphasizing the role of barter in foreign trade. See also A.P. Sah (1970: 178–82).

Third, the case of Kashmir represents yet another aspect of the problem. Y.B. Singh talks about the emergence of the copper coinage of Kashmir from about the eighth century, but prefers to explain its poor quality in terms of the 'decline of trade-based economy and rise of agricultural pursuits in the valley'. See Y.B. Singh (1982: 180–81).

Finally, one has to mention B.N. Mukherjee's contention, wherein he not only questions the idea of paucity of coins but also the decline in trade. See B.N. Mukherjee, 'Money, Trade and Rulers in Mid-Eastern India (*c.* AD 750–1200)', paper presented on 'Trade and Patterns of Commerce in Early Medieval India (*c.* AD 700–1200)' organized by the American Institute of Indian Studies in Delhi from 29 to 31 July 1983 (later published as Mukherjee 1983: 159–65). Further amplified versions of the ideas of this author are Mukherjee (1982: 65–83; 1986: 91–105).

[6] D.C. Sircar observes, 'the word *curni* usually means a hundred *cowrie* shells': *EI*, XXIX, 1951–52, p. 48 (on the Algaum inscription of the Ganga King Anantavarman, twelfth century). This is in consonance with early medieval lexicographers such as Amarasimha, Halayudha and Hemachandra, who take *churni /ni* to mean 'the shell Cypraeamoneta (one *kaparda*)', and scholasts such as Unadi, who in fact treats *churni* as equivalent to 100 *kapardas* (IV. 52).

[7] There may have been some regional exceptions but the pan-India perspective perhaps fits in well with Sharma's hypothesis. Though it was recognized long ago that not all links in the chain of arguments originally advanced in favour of Indian feudalism were equally strong and that the concept needed to be strengthened both theoretically as well as in details (cf. Jaiswal 1979–80: 19–20), yet, the feudal model has made a significant contribution towards the study of the agrarian class structure by focusing on the changes in the nature of the class exploiters and the peasantry and

the methods of expropriating the surplus. However, more documentation on the problem would always be welcome.

8 Even Mukherjee (1982: 75–76 and fns 154–55) ends his detailed exposition by pointing out: (a) 'the sources relevant to our zone and period are silent about the participation of indigenous people in the maritime trade of the area in question'; (b) trading activities were confined to the ruling elite; and (c) the miserable conditions of the common man – the word *Vangali* (literally meaning 'a resident of Vangala') now denoting somebody 'very poor and miserable'.

9 For our initial critique of Wink's postulates and their neo-colonialist strains, see Shrimali (1993: 25–39); for other critiques, see also Jha (1991; 1992: 93–103), and Sunil Kumar (1994: 147–52).

10 Two specimens have been mentioned on p. 353, but 'Index to coin-types in the coin hoards' (p. 319) does not give any details.

11 Sixteen specimens have been mentioned on p. 353, but again, 'Index to coin-types in the coin hoards' (p. 319) does not give any details.

12 It has been pointed out that even the title of the work, namely, *Living without Silver*, is 'intriguing' because 'two of the chief currency systems identified by the author, viz., the Bull and Horseman and gadhaiya types, are of silver (or billon in the later ages)', which served as the medium par excellence in North India between AD 850 and 1200; cf. Biswajeet Rath's review of the work in *Numismatic Digest*, 15, 1991, p.160. Rath, however, relies on Deyell's coin hoards' data to argue that these coins represent a transition from 'early medieval' to 'medieval', where the defining parameter was the introduction of an 'Islamic' legend on both faces of the coin in the thirteenth century (cf. Rath 2001: 73–83). We regret the usage of such a parameter which, in essence, is a reiteration of the periodization of Indian history in terms of religious category that formed the basis of the James Mill-type colonialist communal overtones.

13 For a critique of Wink's use of *fitna*, see the review of Wink (1986) by Irfan Habib in Habib (1988).

14 Wink (1990: 97–99) is quite dismissive about Goitein's reconstruction of the presence of the Jews between the Mediterranean and the Indian Ocean, and in his typical judgemental manner, brands it as 'extremely biased and anachronistic'. Wink himself is looking at the problem solely from the point of view of slave trade. He does not realize that his own documentation on the subject is quite arbitrary. See also, Jha (1991–92: 96–97).

15 The state of *dirhams* elswhere in the Islamic world was no better. In Spain it declined both in weight and fineness between the eighth and early eleventh centuries. Cf. Spufford (1988: Appendix 1, 400).

16 It weighed only two grams under the Almoravids (*c.* 1085–*c.* 1170) and 1.5 gms under the Almohads (*c.* 1130–1269); cf. Spufford (1988: Appendix 1, 400).

17 Ibid.: 69, n. 3, where Peter H. Sawyer, *The Age of the Vikings* (2nd edn), London, 1971, p. 193, has been cited as evidence for this formulation.

18 Gupta is intrigued why a trader, whether Abyssinian or Indian, took Indian

gold coins to a country which was itself rich in gold and even exported it to India along with pearls and slaves!

[19] *Kraya-vikraya* mentioned in the Bijapur inscription of Dhavala of Hastikundi, VS 1053 = AD 996, *EI*, X, 1909–10, No. 3, p. 24, line 27.

[20] One wonders if in this sense the famed 'market regulations' of Alau-ud-Din Khalji were really helping the cause of 'markets' in the real sense.

[21] A similar passage, dating to 1088, can be found in Yoshinobu (1970: 48).

[22] Malik (1998); Chattopadhyaya (1985, 1994); Jain (1990; numerous contributions of B.N. Mukherjee on what he calls mid-eastern India – that includes Bengal – mentioned earlier; Nandi (1986, esp. chapters 1, 2, 13); Chakravarti (1996); Hall (1980); Champakalakshmi (1996, 1996a); Spencer (1983).

[23] Shrimali (1996). Other relevant studies on the Konkan coast are Ranabir Chakravarti's contributions, including Chakravarti (1986, 1990, 1998, 1991).

[24] An interesting comparable case is the trifurcation of the *mahmudi* which signified the localization of fiscal and commercial networks within the Sultanate of Gujarat on the eve of the Mughal conquest. A case has been made to disaggregate the collective designation *mahmudi*, for, at least three varieties of the *mahmudi* (of different weights, fineness and exchange rates), all modelled on Mahmud's principal silver coin, circulated in various parts of Gujarat, namely, western (peninsular) Gujarat, southern Gujarat (chiefdom of Baglana), and the region of Baroda and Broach in between. See Najaf Haider, 'Mughals and Mahmudis : The Incorporation of Gujarat into the Imperial Monetary System' (unpublished, courtesy the author). On localization and regionalization of currency, Spufford (1988: 380–86) has pointed out that the extraordinarily long time-lag in the adoption of innovations between different parts of Europe meant that at any one time there were very distinct regional differences in the type and amount of money available and in the way it was used. Difference in scale of the monetary base also meant qualitative differences in credit; for example, much Hanseatic trade involved no credit at all, but at the other extreme, Genoese merchants did 160,000 *lire* of business in four years with under 12,000 *lire* of coins.

[25] For further details, see Shrimali (1996), which anticipates most of the contentions of Ranabir Chakravarti (1998: 120–21).

[26] Chaudhuri (1985: 49). For local and regional trade networks and the presence of numerous powers in the Indian Ocean in an earlier period (*c.* 400 BC–AD 400), see Ray (1994). It has been reviewed by Shrimali (1994–1995).

[27] Indrapala (1971) has also argued that South Indian merchant guilds which established a number of bases in Southeast Asia in the eleventh century may well have operated in a manner similar to that adopted by the European East India Companies, mixing diplomatic, military and commercial roles.

[28] These include spectacular attacks on Srivijaya in order to control the Straits of Malacca and the Sunda Straits; occupation of Ceylon and the Maldives;

elimination of all possible opponents on the eastern coast up to Bengal. On these developments, see also Kenneth Hall and John K. Whitmore, in Hall and Whitmore (1976).

[29] In Java, for example, trade was conducted using copper coinage, but also gold, which was said to be very pure, soft, easily worked, cut, and sold in whole or in part. The cost of a purchase would be weighed and cut. Filipino merchants were known to carry small scales around with them. Tagalogs surprised the earliest Spanish by taking touch-stones and checking the quality of gold offered even for small food purchases. For a general overview of the use of gold and silver at the time of the initial European incursions, see Reid (1988: 96–100).

[30] Dandin's *Dasakumaracarita* refers to a piratical expedition undertaken by a prince of Tamralipti. Cf. also Devi (1976), for references to piracy in the Bay of Bengal.

[31] *EI*, IV, 1896–97, No. 34, p. 250, Khalimpur copper plates, lines 48–56.

[32] Cortesao (1944: 93–100, 104–05, 114–15, 140, 170, 181, 203, 106–07). On the evolution of the Bay of Bengal regional trade network, see hall and Whitmore (1976: 303–40). See also note 35 below for attitude to the use of *cowries* in Yunan.

[33] Wicks (1992: chapters 1 and 9, specially his observation on 'moneyness' on p. 6). Miksic (1996: 291) makes a point that the study of monetization in early Southeast Asia should focus not on the objects used, but on the transactions which took place. The symbolism of exchange in many cases may have been more important than the objects exchanged. The early Southeast Asian sources which might have given us clearer understanding of the social and psychological connotations of giving and receiving require much more exploration before we will feel confident that such concepts as 'trade', 'markets', and 'money' can be satisfactorily glossed.

[34] The most detailed description of cloth as a standard of value is provided by Fan Chuo in his account of Nanchao in the ninth century: 'Whenever they trade in silken stuffs/or felt or hair-rugs or gold, silver, turquoise or cattle, sheep, etc., they reckon the price as so many *mi* (lengths) of silken stuffs, "Such and such a thing", they say, "is worth so many *mi* (of silk)"' (cited by Wicks 1991: 307).

[35] In Yunan, however, dire penalties had to be threatened to force the people to abjure the use of *cowries*; in 1650 those who used *cowries* could have their noses and feet amputated. Cf. Vogel (1993).

[36] Grierson (1977). Polanyi, on the other hand, argued that monetization occurs first in marketized exchanges and only then comes to be adopted for administrative payments.

[37] This is Polanyi's position and is opposed to Grierson's model adopted by Wicks.

[38] A study undertaken by Sahai (1971) dealing with two centuries of the post-Gupta times (AD 600–800) mentions very emphatically that Southeast Asia failed to evolve a system of coinage and barter, based largely on paddy and only marginally on cloth, provided the essentials of the Khmer economy.

[39] Collis (1971), cited by Colin Renfrew in Jeremy A. Sabloff and C.C. Lamberg-Karlovsky (eds), 1975, *Ancient Civilization and Trade*, Albuquerque: University of New Mexico Press, p. 53.

[40] When in 1124 Henry I's knights in Normandy protested about the quality of coins in which their wages had been paid, his moneyers lost their right hands and their testicles. Cf. Britnell (1993: 30–31).

[41] It has been emphasized in the context of medieval Europe's bills of exchange that many international payments were only a superstructure, and that a great body of commercial transactions, and in consequence of monetary payments, was intensely local in character. The majority of men were fed and clothed by the products from their own vicinities. Even the town-dwelling minority were largely dependent on the surrounding countryside for their basic necessities from a great distance. The interplay between town and country was far more important than the interplay between one town and another. Cf. Spufford (1988: 395).

[42] Strictly speaking, this is not an index of 'money supply' in sheer economic terms, for that is the activity of the government. This, in fact, is a case of release of accumulated money.

[43] *EI*, XI, 1911–12, pp. 55–57; *Epigraphia Carnatica*, V, Ak., no. 51. For a useful discussion of the problem, see Chattopadhyaya (1990: 112–13).

[44] Amongst the rare examples would be D.W. MacDowall's analysis of Kushana gold and copper coins (*JNSI*, XXII, 1960, pp. 63–74) and contributions on Bactrian Nickel theory in respect of the Indo-Greek coins (for details, see Shrimali 1989: 249).

[45] Deyell's proposition that precious metals for coins were obtained from royal and temple treasuries, from obsolete coinage and as prizes of war (p. 190) is not sufficient explanation.

[46] That an analysis of place-names can throw up interesting insights about the material resources of their surrounding can be illustrated by invoking examples of such place-names as Vellore and Velurpalayam. It can be suggested in these cases that they possibly owe their origin to *vailurya*, a derivative of *vaidurya*, which stands for beryl. The area continues to be an important zone of beryl mining in India. Needless to emphasize that Suvarnagiri of the Asokan inscriptions is known to have been so named because it lies close to the renowned Kolar gold mining area of Karnataka.

[47] Citing K.T.M. Hegde's opinion on the copper content in the Ksatrapa silver coins.

[48] Richards comments (1983: 14, n. 16) that this exploratory essay contradicts his own assumption of Indian metals flowing northeast to pay for imports of horses over the same routes, and thinks that this contradiction needs further probing.

[49] For example, Kenneth Hall's study of *nagarams* (1980) shows that it came very close to Skinner's model of 'standard' market. These were integrated both horizontally and vertically in a network that was governed by rhythmic movement of villages through periodic market schedule.

[50] This happened in England between 1180 and 1280; cf. Britnell (1981: 209–21); see also Britnell (1993: 79–127).

[51] Moreland (1968: 11) notes that during the first century of the Turkish rule (thirteenth/fourteenth centuries), when the payments of landed intermediaries were ordinarily assessed in terms of cash, there were a few cases of the revenue of a province being stated in commodities, for example, elephants from Bengal. It may also be recalled that as late as the sixteenth century, Sher Shah framed assessment rates on the basis of the state claiming one-third of the average produce stated in grains, with rates fixed in cash for a few crops only (ibid.: 82–83).

[52] The 'notional' character of numerous epigraphic allusions to numismatic terms in early medieval inscriptions could be seen in this context.

[53] British Museum stone inscription of Haripaladeva, North Konkan branch of Silaharas, SE 1076 = AD 1154, CII, VI, pp. 148–50, lines 4–6.

[54] A study of craft guilds of a somewhat later period in England (c. 1350–1530s) shows how these guilds were deliberate and artificial constructs of the medieval urban authorities, bore little relation to economic structure and largely performed policing role as agents of civic authorities. Cf. Swanson (1988: 29–48).

[55] Britnell (1993) has underlined that commercialization was compatible with survival of serfdom; serfdom declined in fifteenth-century England because of failure of commercialization rather than its success in the thirteenth century.

[56] On *Yajnavalkya Smrti* II. 246.

[57] In the context of medieval Europe, too, it has been pointed out that the burden of direct taxation in the countryside was frequently much greater than that of indirect taxation in towns – in the 1280s the countryside of Pistoia supported a tax burden six times as high as that paid by the city; cf. Spufford (1988: 246–47).

[58] Apropos the Fisher Equation, also known as the equation of exchange, this is an important component having a bearing on overall money supply, levels of transaction and vicissitudes in price structures. A useful contribution on the problem is Day (1987: 108–16).

[59] The practice is followed in modern times as well for purposes of leasing land to sharecroppers and the British also adopted end of March (*Vaisakha*) as an end of financial year. The government of India has also not made any change in the practice.

[60] Cf. *CII*, VI, p. 57, line 38; p. 62, line 27; and p. 79, line 60. The references to *Mahabrahmanas* in these inscriptions are not in the derogatory and inauspicious ritualistic sense. Rather, these allusions clearly hint at brahmins acquiring the status of being big and powerful by virtue of their proprietory land rights.

[61] We have derived this data from Nightingale (2000: 36–62).

Abbreviations

CII: *Corpus Inscriptionum Indicarum*
EI: *Epigraphia Indica*
IESHR: The *Indian Economic and Social History Review*
IHR: The *Indian Historical Review*
IMB: *Indian Museum Bulletin*
JESHO: *Journal of the Economic and Social History of the Orient*
JNSI: The *Journal of the Numismatic Society of India*
PIHC: *Proceedings of the Indian History Congress*

References

Aymard, Maurice, 1980, 'Money and Peasant Economy', *Studies in History*, Vol. II, No. 2.

Ball, Valentine, 1881, *Economic Geology*, Part III of *A Manual of the Geology of India*, Geological Survey of India.

Balog, Paul, 1964, *The Coinage of the Mamluk Sultans of Egypt and Syria*, New York.

Braudel, Fernand, 1984, *Civilization and Capitalism: 15th–18th Century Vol. III: The Perspective of the World*, tr. S. Reynolds, London.

Britnell, R.H., 1981, 'The Proliferation of Markets in England, 1200–1349', *The Economic History Review*, 2nd Series, XXXIV, No. 2.

———, 1993, *The Commercialization of English Society, 1000–1500*, Cambridge: Cambridge University Press.

Bykov, A.A., 1965, 'Finds of Indian Medieval Coins in Eastern Europe', *JNSI*, XXVII, Pt II.

Chakravarti, Ranabir, 1986, 'Merchants of Konkan', *IESHR*, XXIII, No. 2, April–June, pp. 207–15.

———, 1990, 'Monarchs, Merchants and a *matha* in Northern Konkan (*c.* AD 900–1053)', *IESHR*, XXVII, No. 2, April–June, pp. 189–208.

———, 1991, 'Horse Trade and Piracy at Tana (Thana, Maharashtra, India): Gleanings from Marco Polo', *JESHO*, XXXIV, pp. 159–82.

———, 1996, 'Trade at Mandapikas in Early Medieval North India', in D.N. Jha (1996).

———, 1998, 'Coastal Trade and Voyages in Konkan: The Early Medieval Scenario', *IESHR*, XXXV, No. 2, April–June, pp. 97–123.

Champakalakshmi, R., 1996, 'The Medieval South Indian Guilds: Their Role in Trade and Urbanization', in D.N. Jha (1996).

———, 1996a, *Trade, Ideology and Urbanization: South India 300 BC to AD 1300*, Delhi: Oxford University Press.

Chattopadhyaya, B.D., 1977, *Coins and Currency Systems in South India, c.* AD 225–1300, New Delhi: Munshiram Manoharlal Pvt. Ltd.

———, 1985, 'Markets and Merchants in Early Medieval Rajasthan', *Social Probings*, II, No. 4, December, pp. 413–40.

———, 1990 'Aspects of Rural Settlements and Rural Society in Early Medieval India', *S.G. Deuskar lectures on Indian History and Culture (1985)*, Centre for Studies in Social Sciences, Calcutta: K.P. Bagchi and Company.

34

————, *The Making of Early Medieval India*, Delhi: Oxford University Press.

Chaudhuri, K.N., 1985, *Trade and Civilization in the Indian Ocean: An Economic History from the Rise of Islam to 1750*, Cambridge: Cambridge University Press.

Christie, Jan Wisseman, 1996, 'Money and its Uses in the Javanese States of the Ninth to Fifteenth Centuries AD', *JESHO*, Vol. 39, Part 3 (special theme issue on 'Money in the Orient'), August.

Collis, J.R., 1971, 'Market and Money', in D. Hill and M. Jesson (eds), *The Iron Age and its Hill Forts*, Southampton.

Cortesao, A. (ed.), 1944, *The Suma Oriental of Tome Pires*, London.

Dalton, George, 1975, 'Karl Polanyi's Analysis of Long-Distance Trade and His Wider Paradigm', in Jeremy A. Sabloff and C.C. Lamberg-Karlovsky (eds), *Ancient Civilization and Trade*, Albuquerque: University of New Mexico Press.

Day, John, 1987, 'The Fisher Equations and Medieval Monetary History', *The Medieval Market Economy*, Oxford: Basil Blackwell.

Devi, Sushil Malti, 1976, 'Paucity of Coinage in North-Eastern India after the Fall of the Imperial Guptas', in Shastri (1976).

Deyell, John, 1983, 'The China Connection: Problems of Silver Supply in Medieval Bengal', in J.F. Richards (1983).

————, 1990, *Living without Silver: The monetary History of Early Medieval North India*, Delhi: Oxford University Press.

Foucault, Michel, 1971, *The Order of Things*, New York.

Ganguly, D.K., 1982, 'Medieval Orissan Coins as Source of History', *JNSI*, XLIV, Pts I–II.

Goitein, S.D., 1965, 'The Exchange Rate of Gold and Silver Money in Fatimid and Ayyubid Times', *JESHO*, VIII, pp. 1–46.

————, 1980, 'From Aden to India: Specimens of Correspondence of Indian Traders of the Twelfth Century', *JESHO*, XXIII, pp. 43–66.

Grierson, Philip, 1977, *The Origins of Money*, London: The Athlone Press, University of London.

Gupta, P.L., 1976, 'India's Foreign Trade and the Coins', in Shastri (1976).

Gupta, P.L., *Coin Hoards from Maharashtra*, Numismatic Society of India Monograph Series, No. 16.

Habib, Irfan, 1988, 'Review of Andre Wink's *Land and Sovereignty in India–Agrarian Society and Politics under the Eighteenth Century Maratha Swarayja*', *IESHR*, XXV, No. 4, October–December, pp. 527–31.

————, 1999, *The Agrarian System of Mughal India, 1556–1707*, New Delhi: Oxford University Press.

Haider, Najaf, 'Mughals and Mahmudis: The Incorporation of Gujarat into the Imperial Monetary System', unpublished.

Hall, Kenneth R., 1980, *Trade and Statecraft in the Age of the Cholas*, New Delhi: Abhinav Publications.

————, 1991, 'Carriage, Trade and Economy in Early South India and Southeast Asia', in Amal Kumar Jha (1991).

Hall, Kenneth and John K. Whitmore, 1976, 'South East Asian Trade and the Isthmian

Struggle, 1000–1200', in Hall and Whitmore (eds), *Explanations in Early Southeast Asian History*, Ann Arbor.

Husain, M.K., 'Dapoli Hoard of Silver Larins', *JNSI*, XXX.

Indrapala, K., 1971, 'South Indian Merchant Communities in Ceylon, 950–1200', *Ceylon Journal of Historical and Social Studies*, New Series, Vol. 2.

Jain, V.K., 1990, *Trade and Traders in Western India (AD 1000–1300)*, New Delhi: Munshiram Manoharlal.

Jaiswal, Suvira, 1979–80, 'Studies in Early Indian Social History: Trends and Possibilities', *IHR*, VI, pp. 19–20.

Jha, Amal Kumar (ed.), 1991, *Coinage, Trade and Economy*, Nasik: Indian Institute of Research in Indian Numismatics.

Jha, Amal Kumar and Sanjay Garg, 1991, *A Catalogue of the Coins of Katoch Rulers of Kangra*, Nasik: Indian Institute of Research in Numismatic Studies.

Jha, Amiteshwar and Dilip Rajgor, 1994, *Studies in the Coinage of the Western Ksatrapas*, Anjaneri, Nasik: Indian Institute of Research in Numismatic Studies.

Jha, D.N., 1996, *Society and Indeology in India: Essays in Honour of Professor R.S. Sharma*, New Delhi: Munshiram Manoharlal.

Jha, Vishwa Mohan, 1991 and 1992, 'The Artless Pirennian', *IHR*, XVIII, Nos 1–2, July and January, pp. 93–103.

Jichuang, Hu, 1984, *Chinese Economic Thought before the Seventeenth Century*, Beijing: Foreign Language Press.

Kosambi, D.D., 1981, *Indian Numismatics*, New Delhi: Orient Longman.

Kulke, Hermann, 1986, 'The Early and the Imperial Kingdom in Southeast Asian History', in David G. Marr and A.C. Milner (eds), *Southeast Asia in the 9th to 14th Centuries*, Singapore.

———, 1999, 'Rivalry and Competition in Bay of Bengal in the Eleventh Century and its Bearing on Indian Ocen Studies', in Om Prakash and Denys Lombard (eds), *Commerce and Culture in the Bay of Bengal, 1500–1800*, New Delhi: Manohar and ICHR.

Kumar, Sunil, 1994, in *Studies in History*, X, No. 1, January–June.

Lahiri, Bela, 1980, 'Complexities in the Study of Early Medieval Coins of Northern India', *JNSI*, XLII, Pts I–II.

Lowick, N.M., 1974, 'Trade Patterns on the Persian Gulf in the Light of Recent Coin Evidence', *Near Eastern Numismatics: Studies in Honour of George C. Miles*, Beriut.

Malik, Anjali, 1998, *Merchants and Merchandise in Northern India, AD 600–1000*, New Delhi: Manohar.

Mayhew, Nicholas J., 1987, 'How far can Coins Provide Evidence of Bullion Flows? A Review of the European Evidence from c. 1000 with Methodology and Historical Implications for India', in Parmeshwari Lal Gupta and Amal Kumar Jha (eds), *Numismatics and Archaeology*, Nasik: Indian Institute of Research in Numismatic Studies.

Miksic, J.N, 1979, 'Archaeology, Trade and Society in Northeast Sumatra', Ph.D. Dissertation, Cornell University, Ithaca.

———, 1996, 'Archaeology, Ceramics and Coins' 'Review' of A. Reid, *Southeast Asia* in the Age of Commerce, Vol. II: Expansion and Crisis, JESHO, Vol. 39, Part 3, August.

Mitchiner, Michael, 1991, 'Early Trade between India and Mainland Southeast Asia as Reflected by Coinage', in Amal Kumar Jha (1991).

Mitchiner, Michael, *Oriental Coins and their Values: The Ancient and Classical World, 600 BC–AD 650.*

Moreland, W.H., reprint 1968, *The Agrarian System of Moslem India*, Delhi.

————, 1983, *India at the Death of Akbar*, Delhi.

Mukherjee, B.N., 1977, 'A Note on a Few Series of Silver Coins', *JNSI*, XXXIX, Pts I–II, pp. 135–38.

————, 1982, 'Commerce and Money in the Western and Central Sectors of Eastern India (c. AD 750–1200)', *IMB*, XVII, pp. 65–83.

————, 1983, 'Media of Exchange in Trade of Mid-Eastern India (c. AD 750–1200)', *JNSI*, XLV, Pts I–II, pp. 159–65.

————, 1986, 'Media of Exchange in Early Medieval North India', *Numismatic Digest*, X, December, pp. 91–105.

Nandi, Ramendra Nath, 1986, *Social Roots of Religion in Ancient India*, Calcutta: K.P. Bagchi.

Neale, Waltor C., 1976, *Monies in Societies*, San Francisco: Chandler and Sharp.

Nightingale, Pamela, 2000, 'Knights and Merchants: Trade, Politics and the Gentry in Late Medieval England', *Past and Present*, No. 169.

Pokharna, Prem Lata, 1964, 'A Huge Hoard of Gadhaiya Coins from Kasindra', *JNSI*, XLVI, Pts I–II.

————, 'A New Variety of Indo-Sassanian Coins', *Numismatic Digest*, VI, Pts I–II.

Polanyi, Karl, 1975, 'Traders and Trade', in Jeremy A. Sabloff and C.C. Lamberg-Karlovsky (eds), *Ancient Civilization and Trade*, Albuquerque: University of New Mexico Press.

Prasad, H.K., 1969, 'The Economic Aspects of Coins of Northern India between 185 BC to AD 320', *The Indian Numismatic Chronicle*, VII, Pts I–II.

Pryor, Frederick L., 1977, *The Origins of the Economy: A Comparative Study of Distribution in Primitive and Peasant Economies*, New York: Academic Press.

Rahman, Abdur, 1979, *The Last Two Dynasties of the Shahis*, Islamabad.

Rath, Biswajeet, 2001, 'Transition from Early Medieval to Medieval: Evidence from Coin Hoards and the Dravyapariksha', in Amiteshwar Jha (ed.), *Medieval Indian Coinages: A Historical and Economic Perspective*, Anjaneri, Nasik: Indian Institute of Research in Numismatic Studies.

Ray, Himanshu P., 1994, *The Winds of Change: Buddhism and the Maritime Links of Early South Asia*, Delhi: Oxford University Press.

Reid, Anthony, 1988, *Southeast Asia in the Age of Commerce, 1450–1680*, New Haven.

Renfrew, Colin, 1975, 'Trade as Action at a Distance: Questions of Integration and Communication', in Jeremy A. Sabloff and C.C. Lamberg-Karlovsky (eds), *Ancient Civilization and Trade*, Albuquerque: University of New Mexico Press.

Richards, J.F. (ed.), 1983, *Precious Metals in the Later Medieval and Early Modern Worlds*, North Carolina: Carolina Academic Press.

Sah, A.P., 1970, 'Currency in Medieval Orrisa (*circa* AD 600–1200)', in *Proceedings of Indian History Congress*, Vol. I, Jabalpur session.

Sahai, Sachchidanand, 1971, 'Medium of Exchange in Ancient Cambodia: A Study in the Contemporary Economic Life (AD 600–800)', *JNSI*, XXXVIII, Pt 1.

Sharma, Dasharatha, 1959, *Early Chauhan Dynasties*, Delhi.

Sharma, R.S., 1976, 'Coins and Problems of Early Indian Economic History', in Shastri (1976).

————, 1983, 'Usury in Early Medieval Times', in *Perspectives in Social and Economic History of Early India*, New Delhi: Munshiram Manoharlal.

————, 2001, 'Paucity of Metallic Coinage (*c.* 500–1000)', in R.S. Sharma, *Early Medieval Indian Society: A Study in Feudalization*, Hyderabad: Orient Longman.

Shastri, Ajay Mitra (ed.), 1976, *Coins and Early Indian Economy*, Memoirs Series, No. 6, Varanasi: Numismatic Society of India.

Shastri, Ajay Mitra, 'Yadava Coins: Some Aspects', in Amiteshwar Jha (ed.), *Medieval Indian Coinages*.

Shrimali, K.M., 1983, *History of Pancala*, Vol. I, Delhi: Munshiram Manoharlal.

————, 1989, 'Early Indian Coins and Economic History: Trends and Prospects', in Devendra Handa, *Ajaya-Sri: Recent Studies in Indology*, Vol. I, Professor Ajay Mitra Shastri Felicitation Volume, Delhi: Sundeep Prakashan.

————, 1993, 'Reflections on Recent Perceptions of Early Medieval India', *Social Scientist*, Vol. 21, No. 12 (247), December.

————, 1994–1995, 'Early Maritime History: A Fresh Look', *Social Science Probings*, Nos 11 and 12, pp. 137–44.

————, 1996, 'How Monetized was the Silahara Economy?', in D.N. Jha (1996).

Singh, Y.B., 1982, 'Copper Coins and their Minting in Early Medieval Kashmir: A Problem', *JNSI*, XLIV, Pts I–II.

Skinner, G. William, 1964, 'Marketing and Social Structure in Rural China Part I', *Journal of Asian Studies*, Vol. XXIV, Nos 1–4.

Spencer, G.W., 1983, *The Politics of Expansions: The Chola Conquest of Sri Lanka and Sri Vijaya*, Madras: New Era.

Spufford, Peter, 1988, *Money and its Use in Medieval Europe*, Cambridge: Cambridge University Press.

Srivastava, O.P., 1999, *Commercial Taxation in India, c. AD 600–1200*, Allahabad: Kitab Mahal.

Swanson, Heather, 1933, 'The Illusion of Economic Structure: Craft Guilds in Late Medieval English Towns', *Past and Present*, No. 121.

Tarafdar, M.R., 1978, 'Trade and Society in Early Medieval Bengal', *IHR*, Vol. IV, No. 2, January, pp. 274–86.

University of Michigan, 1966, 'Early Islamic Mint Output: A Preliminary Inquiry into the Methodology and Application of the "Coin-die count" Method', *JESHO*, IX, pp. 212–41.

Vanaja, R., 1983, *Indian Coinage*, New Delhi: National Museum.

Vogel, H.U., 1993, '*Cowry* Trade and its Role in the Economy of Yunan: From the Ninth to the Mid-Seventeenth Century', Part II, *JESHO*, Vol. 30.

Wicks, Robert S., 'Money Use and the Controls of Trade in Early Southeast Asia' in Amal Kumar Jha (1991).

————, 1992, *Money, Markets and Trade in Early Southeast Asia: The Development of Indigenous Monetary Systems to* AD *1400*, Ithaca: Cornell University.

Wink, Andre, 1986, *Land and Sovereignty in India: Agrarian Society and Politics under the Eighteenth Century Maratha Svarajya*, Cambridge: Cambridge University Press.

————, 1990, *Al-Hind: The Making of the Indo-Islamic World, Vol. I: Early Medieval India and the Expansion of Islam, 7th–11th Centuries*, Delhi: Oxford University Press

Yoshinobu, Shiba, 1970, *Commerce and Society in Sung China*, Ann Arbor, Michigan.

The System of Credit in Mughal India

Om Prakash

An outstanding feature of the Mughal Indian economy was the existence of a highly sophisticated and efficiently run monetary and credit system. The system had evolved over a period of time and was conditioned by a variety of developments in the economy. In turn, it held important implications for all sectors of the economy. Between the sixteenth and the eighteenth century, the economy undoubtedly continued to be overwhelmingly agrarian in character both in terms of the proportion of national output generated in the sector and of the share of total gainful employment provided by it. But within the agricultural sector, important institutional and other developments with far-reaching implications were taking place, affecting not only the sector itself but indeed the entire economy. One such major development, for example, was a restructuring of the land revenue system during the reign of Emperor Akbar. Land revenue had traditionally accounted for an overwhelming proportion of state finance in India and the government's concern with a steady flow of revenue on this account was perfectly legitimate. Adjustments in the procedures for assessing and collecting this revenue were, therefore, a routine feature in all administrations. But under Akbar, these adjustments were rather extensive and, among other things, involved a continuing shift away from the collection of land revenue in kind to that in cash. The process would evidently have been gradual, and long after the introduction of the measure, a part of the land revenue continued to be collected in kind. But the point to emphasize is that both at a qualitative as well as at a quantitative level, this innovation served to promote in an important way the growth of a money economy. Considering that land revenue amounted to anywhere between 40 and 50 per cent and perhaps even more of gross agricultural output, which, in turn, accounted for an overwhelming proportion of gross national output, the implications of a shift of land-revenue demand from kind to cash would have been quite significant. Quite clearly, the land-revenue assessees would have been marketing a certain proportion of their gross output in any case. But under the new situation of compulsorily having to generate a rather large flow of cash to meet the revenue demand, the volume of monetized transactions entered into by this group would have gone up significantly. At the macro level too, the overall volume of monetized transactions in the system would have gone up substantially in relation to an earlier situation where the conversion of land revenue received in kind into cash would have been effected at the level of the state.

The growth in the volume of monetized transactions would have been possible only under a situation of continuously rising supply of money and perhaps in its velocity of circulation. It was a fortunate coincidence that at a time when the need for money was rising in the Mughal Indian economy, so was its supply. As is well known, the Mughal Indian coinage consisted of the gold *muhr*, the silver rupee and the copper *dam*. The Mughals followed a system of 'free' minting under which anyone was free to bring metal to an imperial mint and get it converted into coins. The cumulative supply of money at any point in time was, therefore, largely determined by the public, itself subject to a ceiling prescribed by the availability of metals in the system and the coining capacity of the imperial mints (for details, see Om Prakash 1988). Since India herself produced virtually no gold and silver, the increment to the supply of these metals was determined entirely by the volume of the import of these metals. The Middle East had traditionally provided large quantities of solvent: from the sixteenth and particularly from the early seventeenth century on, the European trading enterprises – the Portuguese followed by the English and the Dutch – added considerably to the total volume of silver and gold that entered the Indian subcontinent. Most of the silver brought in was of American origin, though the Dutch also brought in considerable quantities of Japanese silver in addition to Japanese gold and copper. As a result, there evidently was a considerable increase in the supply of money in the system, though it is as yet not possible to quantify this increase in any satisfactory manner.

The crafting of refined metal into coins at the Mughal imperial mints was done under at least two distinct entrepreneurial and technical arrangements. Under the dominant model, the work of coin production was organized by state officials. A significant proportion of the total clientele at the mints working under this arrangement was provided by professional dealers in money known as *sarrafs*. The role played by this group in the less dominant model, represented by the imperial mint at Surat, was even more important. The running of the Surat mint was farmed out to a number of *sarrafs* of the city on an individual rather than a group basis, with the role of the *daroga* being limited to a supervisory one of ensuring that the quality of the coins manufactured conformed to the Mughal standard in respect of the weight, the purity level of the metal used and the alloy content in the coin (Om Prakash 1988). This arrangement would almost certainly have involved a recurring revenue loss to the imperial exchequer, but would seem to have nevertheless been followed in view of the greater flexibility in output of coins that it ensured. Given the very special place of Surat as the premier port and trading centre of Mughal India, it is not surprising that this arrangement was followed at the imperial mint in the city. (ibid.)

In the Mughal coinage, the problem of wear-and-tear of a coin through use was tackled ingeniously by a complex system of equivalence based on a varying degree of premium being enjoyed by a new coin over older issues. The *sikka* rupee, defined as a coin minted during the current or the previous year, enjoyed such a premium over all older issues which routinely carried the year of issue on them. The rate of this premium was controlled for all practical purposes by the *sarrafs*. Once the premium enjoyed by a new over an earlier issue exceeded a threshold level, defined by the wear-and-tear and the cost of reminting, the old coin would simply be brought to the mint for recoinage.

Coined money constituted an important, perhaps an overwhelming, segment of the total money supply in the economy, but it by no means accounted for the whole of it. Small-value transactions were often carried out through an extensive use of uncoined non-standardized money. Important varieties of this kind of money were the small seashells known as *cowris*, bitter almonds known as *badams*, pieces of lead and tin, and so on. In addition, there were the credit instruments constituting near-money which were used to settle mutual claims.

The *sarrafs* constituted the core group around which the money-and-credit markets were organized. It might be noted that in addition to dealing in money and credit, many of the *sarrafs* simultaneously engaged in other economic activities such as trading, brokerage and so on. This obviously resulted in a certain amount of interlocking of resources across different activities, but it was not necessarily a negative feature in all situations. It might also be pointed out that while the level of development and sophistication achieved by money-and-credit markets in different parts of Mughal India was on the whole quite high, the existence of significant regional differences in this regard must be recognized. These differences were reflected in a chronic and, at times, large variation in the structure of interest rates in vogue in different markets. These variations often created a situation where large amounts of funds were borrowed in a particular region for use in another on an almost regular basis.

It would seem that perhaps the most highly developed money-and-credit market in Mughal India was the one at Surat. This was partly because this port was the principal point of entry of foreign treasure into the Mughal empire. This treasure was minted locally before it found its way to other parts of the empire. Available evidence suggests that very large sums of money could be raised in this market on loan for varying periods of time with relative ease. Thus the records of the Dutch East India Company's factory at Surat reveal that the Company almost regularly raised large sums of money locally on interest. As early as 1622, when the Company had been operating in the city for less than five years, it managed to borrow 406,000 *florins* (approximately 290,000 rupees). In 1639, this figure had gone up to 1.2 million *florins* (approximately 864,000 rupees). This high level was not attained again for many years, but we find that in the closing years of the seventeenth century, the Company's borrowing in the local market in the course of a year often exceeded 1.5 million *florins*.[1] The duration of the loans raised by the Company was ordinarily between one and three months and it almost never exceeded a maximum of six months at a time.[2] Also, the Company ordinarily dealt with a relatively small number of rather substantial *sarrafs*. Thus, of the total loan of 304,500 rupees raised in 1670, as much as 227,500 rupees had been borrowed from one Vanmali Das, 49,000 rupees from Virji Balkam Das, and the remaining 28,000 rupees from one Sundar Das.[3] In 1694–95, the total amount raised by the Company was as much as 914,000 rupees. Though this amount had been borrowed from a total of twenty-two *sarrafs*, six of them between themselves accounted for 55 per cent of the total amount.[4] The single largest creditor was Vanmali Das Hari Das who had provided 147,000 rupees, accounting for 16 per cent of the total. The bulk of the *sarrafs* at Surat were Gujarati Hindus with only a smattering of Muslims. Thus, of the total of 80 *sarrafs* the Company did business with between 1693 and 1696, only five were Muslims.[5]

Whenever a loan was negotiated, the borrower was obliged to sign an IOU in favour of the creditor indicating the amount of the loan, the mutually agreed rate of interest and the duration of the loan, though the last was not obligatory. It was customary to pay the interest on the loan at the end of one year or to add it at that point to the principal sum. The addition of the interest to the principal sum before the end of a year was rare and was done only in situations of acute shortage of funds when the interest rate would perhaps be going up (van Santen 1982). In every money-and-credit market, there would be a structure of interest rates and the actual rate applicable to a particular category of borrowers would depend upon its creditworthiness and other circumstances. An institutional borrower such as a European trading company would ordinarily be able to negotiate a loan at a rate almost at the bottom of this structure. But in situations of rather large borrowings by such bodies, the interest rate would be under pressure and the companies would have no option but to agree to a hike in the rate. Thus, in 1688, when the Dutch Company's demand for money at Surat went on increasing in a situation of great shortage of cash till a sum of 1.88 million *florins* had been raised, the factors reported that they would have to agree to a rather large increase in the interest rate, from 7.5 to 9 per cent per annum.[6] Also, different loans negotiated in the same market by the same agency at points in time quite close to each other, might bear considerably varying rates of interest. Thus, of the total of 864,000 rupees owed by the Dutch factory at Surat in June 1696, the interest rate at which different sums had been borrowed ranged between a low of 3.75 per cent to a high of 6 per cent per annum.[7]

These peculiarities and problems notwithstanding, one could broadly argue that in the seventeenth century, the average rate of interest in a highly developed money market such as Surat would be lower – at times substantially lower – than in a somewhat less-developed market such as Hugli in Bengal. For reasons that are not quite clear, these differences not only persisted but in fact became even more marked over time. The average annual rate of interest applicable to the European trading companies in Hugli and other places in Bengal in the second half of the seventeenth century generally fluctuated between 12 and 15 per cent: the figure given by Streynsham Master, writing in the 1670s, is 15 to 18 per cent per annum Temple 1911: 137). As for the rate at Surat, van Santen has argued that it registered a sharp decline in the course of the seventeenth century. According to him, the average rate the Dutch Company was obliged to pay at Surat was 12 per cent per annum until about 1640. In the second half of the century, this figure came down to 6 per cent and in 1683 to as little as 4.5 per cent. In 1700, this figure was reported to have been around 5 per cent, though in the first decade of the eighteenth century it tended to go up somewhat in the context of the growing shortage of cash at Surat (van Santen 1982: 118). The explanation of this decline in interest rates given by the official historian of the Dutch East India Company, Pieter van Dam, is that it simply represented a tighter control of the Company over its factors in Surat, which prevented them from entering in the books a rate higher than what they had actually paid and pocketing the difference (van Dam 1939: 39). In so far as the decline in interest rates at Surat is also suggested by the documentation of the English East India Company, van Dam's explanation does not appear to be particularly useful. Van Santen's own explanation runs in terms partly of the further growth of Surat in the second half of the seventeenth century as a financial centre, and partly of the increase in the creditworthiness of the European companies (van Santen 1982: 119). A closer look at the evidence suggests that van Santen's position on the behaviour of interest rates at Surat needs to be modified somewhat. For the fifty years between 1635 and 1685, van Santen has a total of thirteen observations. The first five of these relate to the period between 1639 and 1644, and the next five to that between 1652 and 1658. The last three observations relate to the years 1682, 1683 and 1685. If one looks at the information for the period from the 1660s on more closely, the picture that emerges is broadly of the following kind. The rate of interest was between 9 and 12 per cent in 1665, and 9 per cent in 1666 and 1667. In the two years in the 1670s for which information is available, namely 1677 and 1678, the rate had come down further to 7.5 to 9 per cent. The 1680s witnessed a wide fluctuation of the rate between 4.5 to 9 per cent, except for an occasional year such as 1685 when it ranged between 9 and 12 per cent. A substantive and sustained decline took place only in the 1690s, with a low of 2.25 per cent in 1691 and a high of 6 per cent in several other years. The exceptional year in the 1690s was 1698, when the rate fluctuated between 6 and 7.5 per cent. The overall picture suggested is one of fairly marked fluctuations in the rate of interest at Surat all through, with an overall decline characterizing the second half of the seventeenth century. This process got considerably accelerated in the last decade of the century.[8] Whatever the reasons behind this development, it substantially increased the gap in the interest rates between Surat and other markets where no such distinct downward trend was discernible. This, in turn, created an incentive for an entrepreneur to borrow money in Surat and use it elsewhere in the empire. It is not clear whether this was done on any scale by private individuals, but there is evidence to show that the Dutch Company engaged in this practice on a fairly substantive scale. The Company's exports from Surat to Batavia almost always contained a treasure-chest containing silver rupees of local mintage. For example, in 1678–1679, of the total cargo sent from Surat to Batavia valued at approximately 1.4 million *florins*, as much as 0.6 million *florins* consisted of silver rupees (van Dam 1939: 39). The bulk of the Surat rupees received at Batavia were sent on to Bengal, where the investment of the Company at this time was registering a rapid increase (for details, see Om Prakash 1985: ch. 3). At times, the export of Surat rupees to Bengal was arranged directly without the intervention of Batavia.[9] If one analysed the import of non-Japanese Asian silver bullion and coins into Bengal by the Dutch East India Company in the seventeenth century as a whole, Surat would perhaps turn out to be the single largest source of such silver. In addition to Bengal, Surat rupees were also sent to the Dutch factories in Coromandel and Malabar. It might be noted that the Mughal authorities were generally opposed to the transfer of Surat rupees outside the area. In 1693, for example, acting on a complaint by the local *sarrafs* regarding the export of Surat rupees by the Dutch East India Company, the *mutasaddi* at Surat, ostensibly acting on instructions from the emperor, summoned the Company's brokers and instructed them to ensure that no such transfer of Surat rupees took place.[10] However, there evidently was no mechanism whereby this could be enforced.

How did the *sarrafs* finance themselves? In the absence of any detailed definitive evidence, this query cannot be answered satisfactorily. Probably the principal source the *sarrafs* fell back upon was accumulated family wealth. It would also appear that they were able to raise a certain amount of money by accepting deposits from the public. In the present state of our knowledge, however, it would be impossible to indicate how significant this phenomenon was quantitatively. It would seem that the profit of the *sarrafs* consisted basically in paying a lower rate of interest on these deposits than what they themselves charged on loans they made available.

We noted earlier that the growing monetization of land revenue demand in Mughal India involved a possibly substantial expansion in the volume of monetized transactions, and, therefore, in the demand for money in the system. Considering that under the Mughal land revenue system, the revenue in respect of the *khalisa* lands belonged to the imperial exchequer, enormous sums of money needed to be transferred regularly from the provinces to the heartland of the empire in Delhi/Agra. The reverse flow consisted of funds needed to run the provincial administrations, for organizing military campaigns of various kinds, and for purposes of acquiring goods in the provinces either for trade or for consumption in the heartland. The large-scale business of remitting funds from one part of the empire to the other and indeed to areas outside the empire but within the sub-continent, was also carried on by the *sarrafs*. There was an extensive network of branches, agents and correspondents that these *sarrafs* had, and the basic document used to effect the transfer of funds was the bill of exchange or the *hundi*. This document, which is essentially a binding written promise to pay a named person or its presentor a certain sum of money at some future but proximate date, usually in another town, came in general use in Europe in the fourteenth century. It is not quite clear when it first began to be used in India, but there is no question at all that by the seventeenth century, the *hundi* was used extensively to effect money transfers on a large scale. The standing of the *sarrafs* engaged in the *hundi* business ranged from relatively small dealers to very large houses with agents or correspondents all over. In the seventeenth century, one such major house was that of Virji Vohra with its headquarters in Surat. During the first half of the eighteenth century, by far the most important *sarraf* establishment in the empire was that of the Jagat Seth family operating from its headquarters in Murshidabad in Bengal. Among its other extensive activities, this house handled the remittance of central revenues from Bengal to Delhi amounting to over 10 million rupees per annum.

The *hundi* was used both as an instrument for remitting funds from one place to another as well as for raising short-term credit which would be repaid on maturity at another place. An example of the former kind of *hundi* found in the records of the Dutch East India Company reads as follows:

> Zeogdeuw [Sukhdev] and Sieuwdeth [Shivdatt] Shahs are greeted by Kasinaeth [Kashinath] and Mitterseen [Mitrasen]. This is to inform you that we are issuing on you a letter of exchange of the sum of rupees sixty thousand whose half is thirty thousand and which amount has been received from the Director of the Dutch Company to be paid to the Dutchman Van Hoorn in Patna after a lapse of forty days in the *siccas* of the second year.[11]

Under this arrangement, the amount to be transferred was handed over to the *sarraf* together with the cost of the transaction, which would depend upon the current rate of discount on *hundis* between the two cities. The *sarraf* would then issue the *hundi* to the party, who would arrange to send it on to its representative in the city to which the funds were to be transferred. This representative would present the document to the local agent or correspondent of the *sarraf* who had issued the *hundi*, and collect payment at the expiry of the stipulated period. As for the number of days after which a *hundi* matured for collection, there was a great deal of variation depending upon specific needs and circumstances. Under one of the arrangements, the number of days mentioned in the document was counted from the day it was presented for collection to the agent/correspondent. In the case of *hundis* obtained by the Dutch East India Company's factors at Surat on Ahmedabad this number was stated to be nine,[12] while in the case of those obtained in Agra the number most often mentioned was seventeen or eighteen (van Santen 1982: 119). Another arrangement involved the counting of the days not from the day of presentation for collection but from the day of issue of the document.[13] In the case of such *hundis* obtained in Surat on Agra, the number of days most often quoted was forty-one.[14] The other oft-quoted number was 61 days.[15] There is at least one case available where the number of days to maturity was counted neither from the date of issue of the document nor from that of its presentation for collection. In 1661, the Dutch Company factors at Surat bought a *hundi* from a local *sarraf* Mohandas Naan in Masulipatnam for 50,000 rupees. The terms of the *hundi*

included the stipulation that it would be encashed twenty days after
the arrival at Masulipatnam from Bengal of one of the ships of Mohandas called '*Surat Furza*'.[16]

On the whole, the system, as outlined above, worked remarkably efficiently and large sums of money got transferred. But as far as
the party remitting the funds was concerned, the arrangement did
involve a certain amount of risk arising from the possibility of the
sarraf going bankrupt before the *hundi* had been encashed. The extensive interlinking of financial enterprises across houses of *sarrafs* made
even a chain of bankruptcies a distinct possibility. It is true that such
bankruptcies did not happen frequently or on any scale, but the possibility was always there. Indeed, there is evidence available that such
chain bankruptcies happened twice in Patna within a period of sixteen
years. Six leading houses of *sarrafs* are known to have collapsed in the
city in 1673. Another group bankruptcy of five houses was reported in
1689 (Om Prakash 1967: 19). Unfortunately, the causation behind and
the precise mechanism of these collapses is not recorded in the documents.

From the point of view of a businessman or a trading company who wanted to remit funds to another city to enable its representative there to invest them in the procurement of local goods, one way
the loss arising out of a possible bankruptcy of a *sarraf* could be avoided
was to use the alternative method of raising the resources locally. This
was done by the local representative going to a *sarraf* and drawing a
hundi on his principal. In the example of the Dutch East India Company given above, this would mean that the Company's factor at Agra,
rather than being provided with a *hundi* bought by the Company at
Surat, would instead be asked to go to the local agent/correspondent
of the *sarraf* in Surat and ask for accommodation for a specific sum of
money. The agent/correspondent would then provide the accommodation asked for, less the commission/discount to be charged. The
document exchanged between the agent and the factor would be sent
by the latter to the chief factor at Surat, who would arrange for the
money to be paid to the local *sarraf* after the lapse of the stipulated
period. This period normally was again seventeen to eighteen days after
the arrival of the document in Surat and the formal acceptance of the
liability by the Company. Under this arrangement, the *hundi* really
became an instrument for raising short-term credit. In addition to ob-
viating the risk arising out of bankruptcies, this method of drawing a

hundi also implied that the Company had the use of the funds for the duration of the journey between Agra and Surat and for the maturity period of seventeen to eighteen days thereafter (van Santen 1982: 119–20). The discount or commission charged at the time of drawing a *hundi*, therefore, was always greater than if a *hundi* had been bought for remitting the same sum of money. Since both the options were available to the Company, the discount-rate differential in the two options was carefully regulated by the *sarrafs*. We have a case available to us relating to 1689 where the Company's factors at Agra made a detailed calculation of the net cost of getting 60,000 rupees at Agra through remittance from Surat as against that of raising it locally by drawing a *hundi* on Surat. It turned out that if the additional cost on account of the higher discount rate in respect of the second alternative was offset against the saving on interest on the amount for the additional period that the funds were available to the Company under this alternative, the net additional cost of the second alternative was a mere forty rupees.[17] It is a moot question whether this amount would correctly measure the probability of loss under the first alternative due to bankruptcy.

The discount or commission charged at the time of issuing or drawing a *hundi*, say, at Agra, depended a good deal on the city on which the *hundi* had been asked for. It was partly a function of the distance and partly of the volume of bill traffic between the two cities. Thus, in the 1640s, while the discount rate for issuing *hundis* in Surat on Ahmedabad was between 0.62 and 1.25 per cent, that between Surat and Agra over the same period was between 2.69 and 3.5 per cent (van Santen 1982: 223). The small amount of evidence available for the latter part of the century would seem to suggest that the Surat–Agra rate had gone up slightly. Thus in 1689, *hundis* were obtained in Surat on Agra at 3.56 per cent, 3.75 per cent and 3.68 per cent.[18] Only in one case relating to 1688 was this rate reported to be 4.25 per cent.[19] An interesting, though seemingly unrepresentative, case available pertains to 1667, where not only was a commission of 2.5 per cent charged at the time of issuing a *hundi* in Surat on a city on the Coromandel coast, but it was also stipulated that at the time of encashment a further commission of 1.25 per cent would be charged by the agent/correspondent of the *sarraf*.[20]

Sudden abundance or shortage of funds in a given city at any given point of time could bring about a violent fluctuation in the discount rate on *hundis* between that city and any other. H.W van Santen has cited a very interesting case illustrating this. The year 1636 witnessed an acute shortage of funds in Ahmedabad because of several reasons. A bad trading season in general had been compounded by the plundering of a *kafila* to Surat and the obligatory encashment of a bill of 150,000 rupees drawn at Surat on the city on behalf of Subahdar Azam Khan. The acute shortage of money got reflected in a rise in interest rates in the city as well as in the discount rate on bills drawn on Ahmedabad. At the same time, the interest-cum-commission charged on bills drawn in Ahmedabad on other cities registered a sharp decline. Indeed, on bills drawn on Agra, not only were the Ahmedabad *sarrafs* willing to waive the charges altogether but were even ready to pay a premium. This, of course, reflected not only the shortage of money in Ahmedabad but also the large demand to transfer funds to Agra. The situation was taken full advantage of by both the English and the Dutch East India Companies, who remitted fairly large sums of money from Surat to Agra via Ahmedabad. This, of course, helped the liquidity position in Ahmedabad to get back to normal with the necessary effect on interest and discount rates (van Santen 1982: 121–22).

On the question of the negotiability of the *hundis*, the evidence is disappointingly meagre and very little can be said in this regard which would be definitive. In Italy, bills of exchange had generally become negotiable by the late sixteenth century. In the Netherlands, endorsed bills (with an assignation of the bill to a third party written on the back) had become common in Antwerp from the 1570s onwards. In England, however, it was only from about the middle years of the seventeenth century that the bill of exchange had become negotiable (Parker 1974: 543). For Mughal India, there is some evidence available which suggests that the provision of endorsement of the *hundi* to a third party did in fact exist. Thus, during a phase of shortage of liquidity at Agra in the 1630s, anybody presenting a *hundi* to a *sarraf* for encashment was being asked to bear a half per cent additional charge. But this person was given the option to have the document endorsed in favour of someone to whom he owed money, thus clearing himself of that obligation (van Santen 1982: 121–22). But the critical question really is whether such endorsements were possible only under special situations, such as the one described above, or had assumed the character of a general practice. No definitive answer seems possible at this stage.

The credit network in the Mughal Indian economy also had a very close relationship with the structure of manufacturing and other production for the market. By far the most important manufacturing industry in the economy was that producing textiles. The production of a certain amount of relatively standardized varieties of textiles for conventional markets was usually undertaken by the weavers on the basis of their own resources and at their own risk. These goods were then transported to urban centres and sold to merchants. Some of these merchants might themselves be engaged in trade in these goods, while others bought them on inventory for sale to other merchants. There is evidence, for example, that several varieties of comparatively coarse cloth were produced on this basis in the district of Malda in Bengal, for eventual sale to merchants engaged in trade with Pegu, North India (Hindustan) and Persia, which had traditionally been important markets for these varieties.[21]

But only a small proportion of the total marketed output of cloth seems to have been manufactured on this basis. For the rest, the production was on the basis of agreements between merchants – many of whom were intermediary merchants known as *paikars* – and weavers specifying details such as the quantity to be supplied, the price to be paid and the date of delivery. A part – often a substantial part – of the final value of the contract was given in advance to enable the weaver to buy the necessary raw materials as well as sustain himself and his family during the period of production. This sum of money was essentially an interest-free loan to be adjusted against the final value of the contract. Clearly, the three key elements in the system were the weavers' need of finance, their relatively limited access to the market, and a desire on their part to avoid risks arising out of their inability to forecast correctly the behaviour of the demand for a given variety of textile. This system, which could be described as the contract system, was somewhat different from the standard European putting-out system. Most often, the European producer was provided with the necessary raw materials and the money payment made to him was only an advance on his wages. At all stages of production, the output belonged to the merchant. The Indian artisan, on the other hand, retained his status as an independent worker buying his own raw material and exercising formal control over his output until it changed hands. Of course, the merchant who had given the advance had the first claim on the output and debt obligations often rendered the artisans subject to coercive control by the merchants.

The intermediary merchants themselves operated on the strength of orders obtained from other merchants engaged in coastal or overseas trade. The orders had to be accompanied by a cash advance which provided the bulk of the working capital of the intermediary merchants. The precise proportion of the cash advance to the value of the contract was obviously a matter for negotiation, but in Bengal, the norm appears to have been between 50 and 65 per cent. The trading and the intermediary merchants were ordinarily brought together by a class of brokers who worked either on salary or on a commission basis.

In addition to the manufactured goods, there was a substantial amount of trade carried on in foodstuffs as well as commercial crops such as opium and indigo. The structure of production and of procurement for trade in respect of the commercial crops was in many ways similar to that for the manufactured goods. The producers pledged specified quantities of their crops to the intermediary merchants at predetermined prices against a part of the total value of the contract received in advance free of interest cost. The intermediary merchants entered into similar agreements with the trading merchants. This picture would hold for most major commercial crops, such as opium. But in respect of at least one such crop, namely indigo, grown in and around Bayana near Agra, there were sufficient interesting deviations from the norm to merit a somewhat closer look. Perhaps the most distinguishing characteristic feature of the production organization of this crop was the distinct role played in it by credit. The principal groups of merchants engaged in the procurement of and trade in indigo were the Dutch and English East India Companies, and the Persian and Armenian merchants. The commodity was a highly volatile one in so far as the fluctuations in both output and price could be fairly marked. It was perhaps because of this peculiarity that the normal procedure of procurement adopted in relation to other commodities, including commercial crops such as opium, was not followed in the procurement of Bayana indigo. Neither party wanted to commit itself to honouring a predetermined price. As a result, the norm developed in relation to this commodity was that contracts between the buyer and the producer were made only after the harvest was in and deals concluded at the ruling market price.

This, however, did not prevent certain buyers from entering into prior contracts with the producers and giving them fairly large sums of money in advance. Ordinarily, the producers of indigo, including the fairly substantial ones, were in constant need of finance, and welcomed any advances coming their way. But the conditions that accompanied such a contract were very different from those in the case of, say, opium or textiles. In the first place, the funds advanced to the producers of indigo were not interest-free and ordinarily carried an interest rate of 1.5 per cent per month. Secondly, no mutually binding price was worked out at the time of the contract. Once the harvest was in, price negotiations would be held between the producer and the person who had given the advance. If a mutually acceptable price emerged, the deal would go through and the advance together with the interest on it would be adjusted in the final payment. Should the price negotiations, however, fail, the producer would be free to sell to anyone else, and his obligation to the person giving the advance would be limited to returning the advance together with the interest on it. The only firm right that the person giving the advance had was the right to be offered the output first. In other words, he had the first right of refusal but nothing else. Note that this was a radically different situation from that obtaining in respect of other commodities where the contract obliged the producer to supply under all situations at the mutually agreed predetermined price.

Why did anybody then give out advances? It would seem that different categories of persons giving out advances had a different set of objective functions. In the first place, there were the speculative dealers in the commodity. This group emerged essentially in the 1630s when the international demand for the product was rapidly on the rise. The basic idea was that by using the right of first purchase at the current market price soon after the harvest was in, they would be able to cash in on the continuously rising market price. The other important category engaged in the business of giving advances to indigo producers was that of the employees of the Dutch East India Company, who did it clandestinely and without the approval of their employers. The considerations that led these employees to do this were quite different from those of the speculative buyers. Often, the funds given out as advances belonged to the Company but were not officially entered in the books as advances. The implication was that whether or not the deal with the producer went through, the proceeds of interest at 1.5 per cent per month between the time of giving of the advance and the coming in of the harvest into the market would be available to the employees for being pocketed. In situations where Company funds were not available for such advances, these employees borrowed the money in the money market at Agra in the name of the Company at 1 per cent per month. In that case, the difference of half per cent per month would still be available to them (van Santen 1982: 153).

From the point of view of both the speculative buyers as well as the servants of the Dutch East India Company, the giving of advances to producers of indigo carried with it certain inherent risks. In the event of a poor crop, it might not always be possible to recover the full extent of the money advanced together with the interest earned on it in the form of either indigo or cash. This is precisely what happened in 1637 to both the speculators as well as the servants of the Dutch Company. Several of the speculators went bankrupt as a result (ibid.: 153–58). After 1645 or so, when the international demand for Bayana indigo registered a steep decline, the remaining speculative buyers too had no option but to go out of business. The failure of the crop in 1637 also hit the Company servants hard and when the matter accidentally came to the attention of the Company, a major scandal was created. Eventually, in 1642, the Company was obliged to write off the bad debts still outstanding against the names of the indigo producers (ibid.). There is no evidence that the servants of the Company engaged in this activity from this point on. The special role of credit in indigo cultivation was thus a rather short-lived affair.

To conclude, the system of credit in Mughal India had attained a level of development and maturity that one would probably find hard to match in many other Asian economies of the period. Credit had become an inseparable part of the structure of production and procurement in the economy: the advanced structure of credit organization was amply reflected in the sophistication achieved by the structure of production.

Notes

1 The information for 1622 and 1639 is from van Santen(1982: 41). The information for the years from 1662 on has been taken from the correspondence between the Surat factors on the one hand, and the Governor-General and Council at Batavia and the Heeren XVIII, on the other. See in particular, Algemeen Rijksarchief (ARA), Batavia to Surat (B.S.) 3 November 1666, VOC 890, f. 863; B.S. 26 September 1669, VOC 893, f. 758; Surat to Directors (S. XVII), 27 April 1690, VOC 1476, f. 45v; S. XVII, 19 May 1691, VOC 1496, f. 156; B.S. 16 May 1694, VOC 923, f. 1301; S. XVII, 11 December 1694, VOC 1548, f. 643; S.B. 15 August 1695, VOC 1571, f. 312; S.B. 25 September 1696, VOC 1582, f. 289; S.B. 10 March 1698, VOC 1611, f. 152.

2 S.B., VOC 1598, f. 11; Pieter Ketting at Surat, 28 April 1698, VOC 1611, f. 288.

3 See VOC 1279, f. 834.

4 Letter from Dirck de Buson at Surat, 6 July 1695, VOC 1571, ff. 486–87.

5 S.B. 13 September 1698, VOC 1620, f. 368.

6 Directors to Batavia (XVII. B), 30 September 1689, VOC 322, f. 546v.

7 Batavia to Directors (B. XVII), G.M., 19 January 1697, VOC 1573, f. 225v.

8 For van Santen's figures, see van Santen (1982: 120, Table 13). The information for the period from the 1660s on, except for 1682 and 1685, is from the following: Algemeen Rijksarchief, B.S. 13 September 1665, VOC 889, f. 493; B.S. 13 September 1666, VOC 890, f. 592; S.B. 11 May 1667, VOC 1264, f. 615v; S.B. 9 June 1677, VOC 1329, ff. 1496 and 1502; B.S. 27 October 1678, VOC 902, ff. 1310–1311; Ahmedabad to Surat, 29 January 1679, VOC 1341, f. 916; B.S. 15 September 1681, VOC 906, f. 811; B.XVII (G.M.), 19 September 1683, VOC 1371, f. 558; S.B. 31 March 1683, VOC 1388, f. 2019; S.B. 26 April 1685, VOC 1398, f. 536; VOC 322, f. 546v; S.H. 27 April 1690, VOC 1476, f. 45v; S.H. 15 May 1691, VOC 1495, f. 156; B.S. 3 August 1693, VOC 922, f. 1401; S.B. 28 May 1693, VOC 1539, f. 47; S.H. 11 December 1694, VOC 1548, f. 643; S.B. 15 August 1695, VOC 1571, f. 312; B. XVII (G.M.), 19 January 1697, VOC 1573, f. 225v; S.B. 22 November 1698, VOC 1620, f. 32.

9 For example, a sum of 100,000 Surat rupees was received in Bengal directly from Surat in September 1661 (H.B. 20 December 1661, VOC 1236).

10 Diary kept at the Surat factory, 22 May 1693, VOC 1548, f. 469.

11 Enclosure to H.B. 16 February 1709, VOC 1777, ff. 192–93.

12 Surat–Ahmedabad, 23 January 1679, VOC 1341, f. 915.

13 The exact words used in the letter from the Dutch factory at Surat to the factory at Agra are: 'na 't verloop van 41 dagen heden ingaande ginder door de houders na behooren voldaan te werden'. (Surat–Agra, 3 June 1689, VOC 1475, ff. 236–37).

14 See, for example, S.H. 12 April 1667, VOC 1265, f. 619; VOC 1273, f. 1804v; Agra–Surat, 9 March 1689, VOC 1475, ff. 262–63; Surat–Agra 5 June 1689, VOC 1475, ff. 236–37.

15 Agra–Surat, 9 March 1689, VOC 1475, ff. 262–63.

[16] Coolhaas (1968: 436). The name of the ship given in the document is 'de Suratse Alphandigo'.

17 Agra–Surat, 19 August 1689, VOC 1475, f. 285.

18 Surat–Agra, 5 June 1689, VOC 1475, ff. 236–237.

19 Surat-Agra, 11 January 1689, VOC 1475, f. 216.

20 Batavia's instructions to Andries Bogaert, 19 September 1667, VOC 891, f. 641.

21 Report by Hendrick Cansius on Malda dated 7 September 1670, VOC 1278, ff. 2173v–2174; English factor Peachy at Malda to Job Charnock and the English Company Council at Calcutta, 23 October 1690, Factory Records, Calcutta, Vol. 9, f. 100; the English Company Council at Calcutta to factors at Malda, 30 October 1690, Factory Records, Calcutta, Vol. 5, f. 81.

References

Coolhaas, W.P. (ed.), 1968, *Generale Missiven van Gouverneurs Generale en Raden aan Heren XVII der Verenigde Oost Indische Compagnie*, Vol. 3, The Hague.

Om Prakash, 1967, 'The Dutch East India Company and the Economy of Bengal, 1650–1717', unpublished Ph.D. Dissertation, University of Delhi.

————, 1985, *The Dutch East India Company and the Economy of Bengal, 1630–1720*, Princeton.

————, 1988, 'On Coinage in Mughal India', *The Indian Economic and Social History Review*, 25, pp. 475–91.

Parker, G., 1974, 'The Emergence of Modern Finance in Europe: 1500–1730', in C.M. Cipolla (ed.), *The Fontana Economic History of Europe, The Sixteenth and Seventeenth Centuries*.

Temple, R.C. (ed.), 1911, *The Diaries of Streynsham Master, 1675–1680*, Vol. I, London.

van Dam, p., 1939, *Beschryvinge van de Oost-Indische Compagnie*, edited by F.W. Stapel, Rijks Geschiedkundige Publicatien 83, Vol. 2, Part 3, The Hague.

van Santen, H.W., 1982, *De Verenigde Oost-Indische Compagnie en Gujarat en Hindustan, 1620–1660*, Leiden.

The Monetary Basis of Credit and Banking Instruments in the Mughal Empire

Najaf Haider

Introduction

In medieval monetary economies, coins were the lifeblood of exchange and commerce. While the use of metallic money served to overcome the restrictions of barter transactions, its absence threatened to disrupt the continuity of economic activities. To ensure continuity in economic exchange, a system of credit was devised in developed market economies by allowing claims to money to be used for making payments and settling obligations. Such a system of credit, where payments could be deferred or money could be transferred from one sector to another, brought about an expansion in the existing volume of currency money and, at the same time, an increase in its velocity of circulation. The volume of money increased automatically when banking instruments, such as bills of exchange and letters of credit, were used in place of currency, while deposits and money-loans facilitated the circulation of currency among individuals.

The close coexistence of metallic money, credit and banking instruments is widely discussed by historians and economists and there is a lively debate over the exact nature of this relationship in the event of a change in money supply. In an argument against the role of money in triggering the economic depression of the Renaissance, credit was presented as a substitute for actual money capable of performing specific acts of exchange on its own (Postom 1959; Hatcher 1977: 53). Monetarists, on the other hand, argued that credit is only a supplementary means of payment for the reason that medieval transactions were structurally tied to settlement in specie (Spooner 1972: 54–57; Day: 145, Nightinga 1990: 560–75).

In the present paper, we probe the relationship between money, credit and banking instruments in the Mughal empire by examining the evolution of a monetized network of exchange that created the necessary conditions for the emergence of an organized system of credit and banking. In order to understand the dynamic nature of this relationship, we also examine the ways in which monetary movements regulated the functioning of banking instruments in particular, and the expansion and contraction of credit in general.

The term banking is used here for any form of a regular, usually recorded, business of accepting deposits and advancing loans (out of funds made available by those deposits), carried on by individuals or firms. Implicit in these functions is the ultimate ability of the deposit banker to create credit or 'bank money'. Though modern banks perform a variety of functions besides these two, they still remain the essential elements of all banking (Usher 1932–34: 399–400). The term banker is used in our study precisely in the sense in which it was employed for the Genoese money-changers who combined, in the fairs of Champagne and in the money market of Bruges, currency exchange with credit operations and book transfers.[1]

Money in the Exchange Economy of the Mughal Empire

Within the monetized sector of the Mughal empire one can identify two broad streams of exchange: one largely local in nature, and the other linked to long-distance trade and foreign markets. The demand for money in the local network of exchange stemmed from the consumption of goods and services and the tax obligations of the rural population. At the lowest level, the village community obtained its weekly supplies of goods from the nearest *qasba*, made cash payments to its functionaries, who included money-changers (*sarrafs*), and to the state in the form of revenue.[2] The money supply of the village came from the sale of its agrarian products in the *qasbas* and nearby towns with the help of rural merchants (*baniyas, mahajans*) and itinerant traders (*banjaras*) who brought the cash back to the countryside (*Waqai Sarkar Ranthambhor wa Ajmer*, nos 78–79; *Mirat-i-Ahmadi*: 260–61; *English Factories*: 224–25). Villages situated near trade routes developed their own markets for specific commodities and held big seasonal fairs which attracted buyers from near and afar (*Ain i Akbari*: 433–34; *Khulasat ut Tawarikh*: 43–44).

The other stream of exchange extended from the countryside to the urban entrepôts for the seasonal supplies of export goods. All major commodities which generated trade surplus (textiles, indigo, saltpetre and sugar) were produced and processed in villages before being fed into the market chain which led to export. This network of exchange involved peasants and manufacturers at the local level and merchants, brokers, bankers, transporters and a host of other people at multiple intermediate stages.

It appears that in the sixteenth and the seventeenth centuries the size of the product sold beyond the village for money increased not only under fiscal pressure but also out of the need of the rural community to transact in the markets of the *qasbas* and towns to sell its surplus product for profit as well as obtain commodities for consumption. The specialization which grew in the rural hinterland in response to export demand and the internal demand for food-and-craft products indicated greater orientation of the village and intermediate economies towards monetized exchange than has been acknowledged so far.

The urban centres and entrepôts of the Mughal empire were immersed far more deeply in the circuit of monetary exchange. Here, the concentration of the military–bureaucracy, mercantile classes and artisans created a permanent demand for food supplies, craft goods and services. Urban taxes, such as customs and transit dues, and mint seigniorage were always paid in cash and were spent towards meeting the administrative costs and consumption expenses of the resident ruling elites.

Both networks of exchange were based on a cash-nexus and required the use of money at each point. Since there was no domestic extraction of gold or silver and very little of copper, in each season the internal circulating medium had to be reinforced with fresh supplies from foreign markets. This was accomplished by defining the terms of the foreign trade in a manner in which Indian imports consisted predominantly of monetary metals (Haider 1996: 298–325). This peculiar and permanent feature of India's pre-colonial trade attracted the attention of a large number of contemporary observers from Pliny to James Grant, and was attributed more often than not to the cultural greed of an ostentatious orient.

The transformation of foreign gold and silver into Mughal money was done at the mint but it was largely mediated through an organized bullion market dominated by the *sarrafs* or professional money-changers, who acted also as bullion merchants, bankers and insurers. Although the Mughals had an open coinage system, the practice of assigning fixed days to the merchant–suppliers often clashed with the timetable set by them to make investments in hinterland markets and to keep commodities ready for shipment in the right seasons. This was a positive factor in the growth of the money market and the business of the *sarrafs*, who turned to offering facilities to the merchants for cash investments at the coasts as well as at distant markets in the hinterland. The *sarrafs* used their skills as assayers and money-changers to evaluate foreign specie and bullion and fix their price in the legal tender. Apart from dealing in currency, the *sarrafs* also organized commercial credit and their position as deposit bankers (on which, see below) and discounters of bills of exchange (*hundi*) enabled them not only to provide merchants with the cash they immediately required, but also the facility to transfer funds from one place to another on payment of a small commission (Haider 1996: 326–35).

Evolution of the Mughal Monetary System

This was the structure of exchange within which the Mughal monetary system functioned. In the first stage of its development, the monetary system symbolized a continuation of the billon-copper regime of the late Delhi Sultans. Although the Mughal state took over the trimetallic currency of Sher Shah (silver *rupiya*, gold *muhr* and copper *paisa*), it lacked the apparatus and resources to bring about a permanent change in the pattern of economic exchange and money usage. The conjuncture which placed it in a position to articulate a new monetary system came with two major developments in the second half of the sixteenth century: an enormous increase in the eastward migration of international silver, and the westward expansion of the Mughal empire with the conquests of Gujarat and Sind (Haider 1996: 342–47).

A massive surge in the imports of Spanish-American silver and its distribution by the Portuguese, together with the political unification of trade routes stretching from the Levant to the Indian Ocean, signalled a new era of international commercial exchange. The configuration of these forces created a chain of entrepôts across the territorial nexus of Europe, Africa and Asia and a class of mercantile communities feeding the arteries of commerce. The coastal-and-caravan cities of the Mughal empire became the principal beneficiaries of these changes at a time when political and commercial links between entrepôts and the hinterland were deepening and a new fiscal and monetary structure was evolving. The significance of the unification of the two distinct political and monetary zones of coastal and insular India was enormous. It established a direct link between the production of the rupee in coastal towns and its circulation in the hinterland, and allowed the Mughal state, merchants and money-changers to incorporate silver, a readily available and more efficient medium, into the circuit of exchange.

The incorporation of silver into the Mughal economy was both gradual and complex, and it was accomplished by a series of administrative, fiscal and monetary measures taken between 1575 and 1600. It was facilitated, as mentioned earlier, by the functioning of the mints and money markets situated in all important commercial centres, notably at the entry points of foreign imports. The monetary structure which emerged after three decades of intense administrative and market changes set a benchmark in the monetary history of the Mughal empire. This meant a uniform and standardized currency system in place of the old regime of billon-copper and of variegated regional issues, geared to a constant flow of silver through foreign trade on the one hand, and its constant absorption into the circuit of exchange on the other (Haider 1996: 348–50; Haider 1999: 328–33). The domain of petty transactions was dominated by the use of fractional pieces of the silver rupee (*ana*) and copper currencies. At those levels of exchange where prices needed to be expressed in units lower than the copper coin, metallic currency was supplemented by *cowrie* shells (Hindi *kauri*; Persian *khar muhra*) in Bengal, Bihar and Orissa, and bitter almonds (*badam*) in Gujarat. Imported respectively from the Maldives and Iran, *cowries* and almonds were more abundantly available at the coast but were in greater demand in the hinterland (*Kitab-i-Sikkaha*: 15bf; *Ain* I: 391–92; Tavernier: 23–24; Habib: 12–13).

The Network of Mercantile Credit

Within the Mughal monetary economy, the continuous movement of goods across various levels of the market and the reciprocal flow of money in the reverse direction was supported by an organized system of credit. The most important point in the complex cycle of credit was the one at which money loans were advanced to commodity merchants. These loans were the most popular form of financing commerce and trading on borrowed capital was a norm among small and big merchants (Banarasidas 1981: 261, verse 494). Indeed, a standard way for merchants of the Mughal empire to calculate profit and loss was to deduct interest paid on loans from the proceeds of commodity sales (ibid.: 247, verse 314).[3] One reason for the popularity of money-loans was the accessibility of a market free from theological restrictions, where the obligation for payment of debts and bills was governed by customary laws enforceable in local courts (*Farmans and Sanads*: 19–106; *Mirat-i-Ahmadi*: 250–51; Manucci: 77–78; Habib 1964: 416–17).

The demand for money and freedom to charge interest on loans provided a firm foundation to the business of moneylending and banking. In commercial centres, the *sarrafs* took a leading position in financing commodity trade by advancing short and long-term loans depending on the seasons and circumstances of the borrowing. The network of loan transactions which brought together merchants, moneylenders and intermediaries is described by the French factor, Roques, in the following terms:

> If a merchant, for example, is going to make a purchase at some place, he will not undertake his journey empty-handed. He will either carry or send some money (*argent*) or bill of exchange (*lettre de change*) to give the broker an advance for his purchases. The first [the merchant], whose money is spent on purchases, is his security for the broker to obtain more loans [from the *sarraf's*], who [the broker] would be happy at the lack of money in order to deal with the seraf and conceal his dishonest dealings under his [the *sarrafs'*] wings. The seraf, seeing that the merchandise has already been bought will happily lend him about as much money as can be raised, the only condition being that the buyer can do nothing to it [the merchandise] unless he [the *sarraf*] is satisfied. . . . Moreover as the broker receives this money in small amounts at a time and uses it in the same way, he accounts to the seraf for the interest on a day by day basis and includes this interest in the principal which he counts as running from the date of the first loan he took out. (Roques: 223–24 ff)

Roques' account is a good illustration of the link between commerce and credit and also of the role of the *sarrafs* in financing commodity trade. In big cities like Surat and Agra, the dominance of the *sarrafs* can be explained by the presence of the mint-and-bullion market, the main centre of their business activities. In townships (*qasbas*) and villages, or even in big towns where the line separating commerce and moneylending was thin, it was the *mahajans* and *sahukars* who financed commercial and consumption loans and offered banking facilities to a diverse clientele.

The *mahajan* was basically a grain merchant who also engaged in lending money at interest on a regular basis to peasants and members of the upper rural strata. It was for this reason that he was often classified differently from an ordinary merchant (*beopari*) in contemporary documents (*Waqai*: 345–46ff; *Mirat*: 240–41). It seems that in eighteenth-century Bengal the *mahajans* primarily carried on the business of moneylending, for there the term *mahajani* became synonymous with usury in popular parlance (*Risala*, 10b, 11a; Habib 1964: 395). Petty *mahajans* are also portrayed in our sources as modest pawnbrokers trafficking in the goods of insolvent debtors (*Waqai* no. 78: 219ff., 420ff.).

In so far as the demands of the Mughal ruling class created a permanent market for grains and manufactured goods, the consumption loans advanced by the *mahajans* and *sarrafs* also assumed importance for the commercial sector. In big cities, those who advanced loans to the nobles (*umara*), small *mansabdars* and resident soldiers were described as 'big serafs [who] set the exchange rates [of money]' and who assessed the collateral held by their clients including *jagir* assignments and promotions (Roques: 248–49ff; Manucci: 354). In quite a similar fashion, the *mahajans* combined financial assistance to the agrarian communities to raise crops or pay tax with loans advanced to *mansabdars* against tax-yields (Habib 1964: 394–98).

In these cases, money-loans were offered to merchants and consumers to make purchases in the commodity market. The facility was further extended to the level of production where merchant-borrowers themselves supplied credit to the manufacturers (known by the technical name of *dadani*) to ensure commodity supply at bargain prices (*English Factories*: 137, *Diaries* I: 26, II: 14–15; Moreland: 134–35; Habib 1964: 399–400; Raychaudhuri: 281–82). Although artisans producing commodities for mid-distant markets themselves visited the local marts, they often relied heavily on brokers and merchants for the sale of their products.[4] This dependence came about on two counts: the latter's greater experience of the market and its mechanism and the inadequacy of artisan capital to buy raw material and undertake the manufacturing process.[5] In areas where merchants had to face competition for supplies, credit was extensively used to establish precedence over other buyers (*Factory Records:* 45–46ff; *English Factories:* 245; Moreland: 140, 141, 145). Where the manufacturers happened to be peasants and were required to pay land revenue, the dependence on merchant capital was often dictated by the need to keep production going if taxes had to be paid before the harvest. In the indigo tract of Bayana, the Dutch went a step ahead in the system of advances when they began to underwrite the payment of land revenue to the state on behalf of indebted peasants (van Santen: 211). While the need for cash created a burden of dependence on peasants and artisans making it difficult for them to obtain the true value of their product, cash loans also enabled them to meet their obligations, obtain raw materials and maintain the desired level of production which could find a regular market.

Deposit Banking and Bills of Exchange

The expansion in commodity exchange and a concomitant rise in the demand for money exerted pressure on the resources available for credit. Given the complex nature of the credit cycle and the diverse portfolios of the Mughal moneylender, it is difficult to determine the volume and composition of the various types of capital flowing into his coffer. An unknown and self-generating portion of this capital was indeed made up of profits earned from interest and ploughed back into the reserve funds. But the capital which originated outside the money market also constituted a regular source of running moneylending and banking operations.

The device which performed an outstanding function of attracting idle balances towards the *sarrafs, mahajans* and *sahukars* was deposit banking. Mughal bankers accepted cash deposits essentially in two ways: short-term time deposits accepted against bills of exchange (*hundi*), and demand deposits accepted from individuals, merchant-groups and state officials who had cash to put out on interest. Roques indeed took a critical look at this business when he tendered the following advice to his compatriots in the second half of the seventeenth century:

> Take great precautions when transacting business with the serafs, especially when giving them money for a bill of exchange, or to get interest on it, because they risk your money with great ease in order

to gain on these exchanges and remittances which they make you pay for without having any capital. (Roques: 236f)

Roques' statement alludes to both elements of the *sarrafs'* banking activities: the acceptance of deposits directly from investors or by discounting bills of exchange, and the employment of these sums as interest-bearing loans. The classic description of direct deposits payable on demand comes from Agra where the entire amount deposited by diverse creditors was suddenly withdrawn probably as a result of some immediate demand for cash (to be called back at different intervals in the case of time deposits). The difference between rates paid on deposits and loans, mentioned separately, constituted the profit of the bankers.

> Those that are great monied men in the towne, and live only upon interest receive from the sheroffs noe more than 5/8 per cent per month. The sheroffs they dispose of it to others from 1 to 2 ½ per cent, running some hazard for the same, and that is their gaines. Now when the sheroff (for lucre) hath disposed of great sommes to persons of qualities at great rates, not suddenly to be called in to serve his occasions, then beginn his creditours (as in other parts of the world) like sheepe one to runn over the neck of another, and quite stifle his reputacion. Thus . . . hath two famous sheroffs bynn served within a month, one of which failing for above three lack of rupees, diverse men have lost great somes and others totally undone thereby; which hath caused men of late to bee very timerous of putting their monies into sheroffs hands. (*English Factories*: 303; Habib: 392)

The *sarrafs* are here clearly identified as deposit bankers, although the 'great monied men' who appear as depositors remain difficult to detect. Pelsaert indeed speaks of a class of people at Agra who lived mainly on interest (Pelsaert: 28–29). Perhaps these were Mughal nobles who were not unfamiliar either with usury or other means of making profit from commerce. Alternatively, they could also be big merchants who employed reserve capital for earning interest in lean seasons (Mundy: 290; Chandra: 321–22; Athar Ali: 154–60; Sloane 1910: 45bf; *English Factories*: 186, 199).

In addition to individual capital, the cash reserves of the state were also put on deposit with the *sarrafs*. In 1623, when Prince

Khurram (later Jahangir) ordered his 'treasure' to be transported to Mandu, the *sarrafs* of Ahmadabad were asked to make the remittance which caused a 'great scarcity of money' in the city (*English Factories* 1622–23: 181). Had the 'treasure' already been in cash-hoard and now put with the *sarrafs* for transmission through bills of exchange to Mandu, it should have caused a superfluity, not scarcity, of money at Ahmadabad.[6] It appears that the 'treasure' had been previously deposited with the *sarrafs* to be lent out by them at interest and now that it had to be transferred to Mandu, the *sarrafs* at Ahmadabad were compelled to recall their loans, thereby causing a scarcity of money available for credit.

The *mahajans* too accepted deposits from both merchants and state officials and we have numerous references to such transactions in the news-reports sent from Rajasthan. Mughal revenue collectors, instead of depositing cash with the treasury, often lent it out to the *mahajans* for personal gain, a practice deemed fraudulent by the state. In one such instance, three revenue officials (*amin*, *karori* and *fotadar*) were found falsifying revenue records in order to earn interest from money held with a *mahajan* (*Waqai*: 27, 29–30, 32, 319–20ff). These deposits combined with the *mahajan's* own capital, obtained through commodity trade, to finance their banking operations.

The second important source of banking capital was short-term time deposits which the *sarrafs* and *mahajans* received by issuing bills of exchange (*hundi*) – the species of commercial paper in Mughal India which functioned simultaneously as a mode of money transfer from one place to another. In order to avoid the risks of transportation, merchants deposited the cash with a banker in exchange for a *hundi*. It almost paralleled the traveller's cheque of modern times if the deliverer himself happened to be the payee and carried the *hundi* to the destined place. Otherwise, the *hundi* was delivered to the shop (*dukan*) of his agent or correspondent by a messenger (Hindi *pathmar*, Persian *bazar qasid*), where it was honoured. The English and the Dutch were two of the several merchant-groups trading in India who remitted money through *hundis* in order to supply capital to their areas of investments. Individual merchants, such as John of Julfa and Tavernier, too travelled with little cash and kept their main capital in circulation by transferring it from one place to another through the *hundi* (Khachikian 1966: 153–56, 173–74).[7]

The remittance of the state's resources to the central

exchequer and from the latter to the treasuries throughout the empire was also affected through *hundis* drawn by the *sarrafs*.[8] The *hundi* facilitated the remittance of sums as small as Rs 50, in the case of John of Julfa, and as big as Rs 3 lakh sent by the Governor of Patna to Agra or, in another instance, sent by Akbar to the Deccan (Khachikian 1966: 174; *English Factories 1618–21*: 236, Abul Fazl: 762). However, though the *sarrafs* were able to combine resources to handle the remittance of large sums of money, such efforts were limited and the state often had to arrange the transportation of its treasures to distant provinces under armed escort (*badarqa*) (Lahori: 379; Bhimsen: 47–48, 177; *Surat Documents*: 99af; *Mirat*: 382; Tavernier: 93).

From our description of the two stages of credit transactions, it can be seen that the incoming streams of cash into the bankers' books, one from the investors in direct deposits and the other from merchants and travellers through *hundis*, were matched by an outflow of loans advanced against debt contracts. In the same way as merchants advanced credit by buying bankers' bills to make cash remittances, the bankers too accepted *hundis* drawn by creditworthy clients. This was done out of two considerations. First, to offer short-term loans and transfer their own funds. Second, and this is more important, to make payments on behalf of an individual who already had an account with them.[9] In this case the flow of credit was reversed from the one witnessed in the first type of *hundi*. Instances of merchants drawing such *hundis* to obtain loans are too numerous to be cited and even though the preference for credit bills, which required no prior capital holding and were redeemed usually after the sale of commodities, must have been greater among merchants, the two types of *hundis* effectively performed the same function: the exchange of cash for credit (claim to cash) from one person and place to another.

When the *hundi* carried a statement, in an Indian language (*Hindwi*) or in Persian, promising payment of a specified sum on demand to a person within or after a stipulated time, the conversion of credit into cash was regulated by the details mentioned therein. But if the *hundi* was made payable to the bearer, the conversion of credit into cash was freed from the constraints of time and place.[10] The *hundi* then became saleable in the market at a small discount which accounted for the gain of the buyer whose cash was locked up till the date of the bill's maturity.[11] The buyer could use the bill to make a payment, satisfy his debts or receive cash (*anth*) from the drawee.[12]

This form of credit, emerging out of the negotiability of the bill, endowed it with a purely monetary function and contributed directly towards increasing the volume of money in circulation. While the money deposited for the bill was lent out by the banker, claims against it were used simultaneously to settle other transactions.

The terms of negotiability of such *hundis*, protecting the rights of the buyer in the event of non-payment, were brought up in a case in which a renegade Mughal prince left some of his debts floating in the market:

> When Mr Blake went home in 1659 he had in his hands bills of debt owing by Shah Shusah [Shuja], the Prince of Bengalla, to the amount of 6000 rupees and odd, which he sold at his departure to some merchants of this country at something under rate. Now the law of these nations is in such a case that, if a merchant can not recover ... what is due on such bills, that he shall returne them to the person of whom he bought them and receive his money without interest. (*English Factories* 1668–69: 177)

The saleability of *hundis* was facilitated by another device which freed them further from the restriction of being sold at a specific place in a specific currency. Currency exchange was indeed the original function of a bill of exchange, and in respect of bills drawn at Surat on the rupee areas of the Mughal empire, the transaction automatically involved the exchange of the local Gujarat currency, as well as Spanish and Mexican dollars, into rupees (*Supplementary Calendar:* 55; *English Factories:* 104–05). However, within the rupee areas, different regions showed their preference for a particular type of coin and gave currency to its circulation. Added to this, of course, was the fact that merchants preferred to receive payment in silver coins of a superior quality, while the *sarrafs* tried to pass on inferior specie. The terms *pakka* and *kachcha anth* were used by the market respectively for superior and inferior coins received for the bill (OIOC, *Original Correspondence:* 217a–bff).

This practice interfered with the negotiability of the bill and became a cause for conflict between the payee and the drawee (Roques: 227f). To avert this, it seems, the word *hundi* was prefixed as a technical term to the amount specified in the bill referring to the coins current at the place of receipt on such transactions, whatever the place or coin-type may be. At Agra, for instance, payments specified in *hundi* rupees were always made in the current (*chalani*) rupees.[13] The case was different with bills paid at Ahmadabad and Burhanpur, where the coins used were respectively new (*sikka*) and old rupees (*khazana*).

Each *hundi* was bought and sold at a price known as the exchange rate. The exchange rate was determined by a variety of factors, such as usance of the bill and the demand for credit. But the most important factor was the cash-balance position of the places involved in the bill traffic (Habib 1972: 294–95). A comparison of the rates current at Surat, Ahmadabad and Agra demonstrates the monetary basis of the bills of exchange. Figures available for bills drawn at Surat on Agra suggest that the normal discount rate was 2 to 2.75 per cent even though the *sarrafs* conceded interest on deposits. The reason for this was that Surat was an entry-point for foreign bullion and merchants required remittances to be made for their inland investments. Agra, on the other hand, was a primary market for commodities requiring ready money for investment. Delivering money at Surat and collecting it in Agra therefore meant that merchants had to pay in the form of discount on bills they bought.

Bills drawn at Agra on Surat enjoyed much higher exchange rates ranging between 4 and 5 per cent. Although the bills performed the same function – transferring merchants' funds from Surat to Agra – these were in fact bought by the merchants from the *sarrafs* to raise credit. Since the discount rates included interest payable to the *sarrafs* and probably the cost of reverse remittance as well, the charges were higher compared to those at Surat.

Bankers' *hundis* drawn at Ahmadabad, on the other hand, always carried a premium for the reasons which had to do, once again, with the cash position of the city. Ahmadabad had lost its coveted position to Surat as a market for bullion and a mint town and its supply of fresh currency had gone down substantially in the seventeenth century. The bankers of Ahmadabad were thus using the bill traffic to transport money from Surat and remit it to Agra and other towns on favourable terms.

With the demand for each type of bill guided principally by the nature of commercial links, this meant the accumulation of money at one end (Surat) and its growing demand at another (Agra). In order to ensure a smooth functioning of this network, the bankers had to strike a balance between the credit they received and the credit they gave at any one place while issuing and discounting bills. Since the network was widespread, they also had to keep a constant cash-flow in order to maintain an overall balance. This was achieved partly by altering exchange rates to induce merchants to buy or sell bills and partly by transporting money physically to their agencies through couriers, if it was in gold, or by carts, if large quantities of silver were required to be delivered (Roques: 227, 229–31ff).

Expansion in Money Supply and Volume of Credit

Interest rate represents the cost of credit and we have at our disposal a sufficiently large number of interest-rate quotations for commercial loans extended to the European and Armenian merchants which can be analysed to indicate changes in the demand and supply of money and credit (Moosvi 2000: 337–38). These are '*bezar*' or 'customary' rates determined by the leading bankers of a region on the basis of an assessment of the money and credit market, and followed by 'all the rest'.[14]

The inter-regional structure of interest rates broadly divides the highly commercialized regions of the Mughal empire into two groups. Surat, Ahmadabad and Agra formed a uniform region and Bengal and Golconda constituted another, rates in the latter appearing to be much higher than the former. If we look at the movement of the rates over time, two things immediately strike our attention: the long-term stability in the rates, and a fall some time towards the middle of the seventeenth century.

It is difficult to explain all the variables in the structure of the interest rates by referring to a single factor whether monetary or real. Monetary historians have indeed considered the link between money and interest rates to be a critical one, the former determining the behaviour of the latter. The bullion famine of the late fourteenth and early fifteenth centuries saw the collapse of banking houses in the most creditworthy city of Venice, and a rise in the level of interest rates throughout Europe (Spufford: 347–48). Conversely, credit grew in direct proportion to specie money with the influx of American bullion into Europe, and resulted in the revival of banking and a fall in the rates of interest (Spooner: 56–71; Cipolla 1993: 216–17, Table 9.3).

In the commercial correspondence of the European merchants trading in India we get several examples of money driving the course of interest rates in the short run. When the supply of foreign bullion was once threatened by dangers on the sea, the English factors sent the following report from Surat:

> Tis tho[ugh]t [that] those 5 ships gone into the Gulph wil not
> returne for fear of the pyrates. So that no treasure wil be bro[ugh]t
> from thence this year; if so interest of money wil be rise and scarce
> any to be had and wee shal find it a hard task to take up any on use
> ... [at] 3/4 p.ct. (*Factor Records, Surat,* Vol. 94: 69A–bff)

Here, the evidence points to a positive link between the fall in money
supply and rise in interest rates. We also get the impression that the
money and credit market of the port city was fully saturated and tied
to the seasonal imports of precious metals. Conversely, a sudden
increase in money supply exercised a downward pressure on interest
rates, as illustrated by another instance quoted in a letter of the English
Company from London:

> Mr Penning ['who lately arrived from Surat'] ... informs us that our
> sending lately such large stocks, hath made such a fall of interest
> there that persons of good credit could take up money at 4 per cent,
> and that our old broker Bhimgee Parrack was arrived at so vast an
> estate as to be computed worth one million of pound sterling, which
> give us cause to suspect that he hath made too great advantage of us.
> (*Letter Book:* 1af)

Apart from reiterating the relationship between money supply and
interest rates, the second passage also alludes to an increase in the
profits of the broker, Bhimji Parakh, apparently over the period of time
he was associated with the English Company. This was perhaps an
indication of the rise in the fortunes of the commercial classes, notably
those associated with big merchant groups in major market centres.

In these instances, money supply was the prime determinant
of interest rate in the face of a fixed demand for credit. The other
important variable was the absolute demand for credit linked to the
rate of profit.[15] In pre-industrial economies this meant buying cheap
and selling dear, and the greater the rate of commercial profit the
higher the demand for credit and the rate of interest.[16] Instances of
merchants taking advantage of opportunities created by short-term
fluctuations in prices are numerous and it will suffice to cite here only
two such cases reported in the letters exchanged between Masulipatam
and London: '[The English] can not raise meanes by sale of their goods
to make an investment this year [1638], especially now that the cloth is
so cheap, "being at least a sixt penny fallen in its former price." The

Dutch are taking up money at extra-ordinary rates in order to benefit by it' (*English Factories 1637–41*: 55).

The close correspondence between commodity prices, mercantile investments and the demand for credit was brought out in another letter sent to the Company a year later:

> Fresh demands are made upon them daily; while money is extra-ordinary scarce (as shown by the low prices of the goods). The Dutch owe here [Masulipatam] upwards of 70,000 pagodas, and the Danes 28,000 or 30,000. The former (possibly 'to break the Danes altogether') are selling their cloves at 4½ and 4 pagodas per maund; and at that rate the 'moneyed men' choose rather to invest in this commodity than to lend at interest to the English. (ibid.: 186)

There are two important points which emerge from this description. First, the merchants viewed the widening difference between the buying-and-selling price as a favourable opportunity to make additional investments. The second, and equally important, point is that such an opportunity also induced professional moneylenders to divert investments from commercial usury into commodity trade. These tendencies would have had the effect of pushing interest rates up by creating additional demand for loanable capital and a simultaneous fall in its supply.

Thus, we can visualize that both monetary and real factors were operative in the market economy of the Mughal period, at one time or another, exercising a dialectical influence over the cost of borrowing.[17] In the long term, it was the sustained dominance of one over the other which would have determined the course of movement of interest rates in the seventeenth century. If we take the position that the reason for a fall in interest rates was an increase in money supply, for which we have substantial qualitative and quantitative evidence, this could have only come through an increased accumulation of banking capital in the form of deposits as well as profits generated from other portfolios. We observed that the bankers exclusively handled the business of money-changing (both local and foreign) and also held a near-monopoly of buying and minting foreign bullion. This monopoly was strengthened in the second half of the seventeenth century by the creation of a class of *sarrafs* holding exclusive rights for supplying bullion to the mint. In the meantime, an expansion in the volume of bill traffic ensured a substantial increase in the absolute level of bankers' profits. They also sold marine and inland insurance and collected premiums and high interest rates from respondentia loans for offering protection to goods and capital in transit as well as to credit transactions (Haider 1995).

With the possibility of an increase in bankers' income from these sources, there was to be a proportionate increase in the size of the commercial capital available with them to be loaned out. By looking at the size of the capital borrowed by the European merchants, we find that towards the last decades of the seventeenth century, it assumed considerable proportions (Om Prakash 1991: 476–77). One explanation, therefore, for the decline in interest rates could be a faster growth in the capital accumulated by the bankers relative to commercial expansion, which simultaneously created the paradox of placing new demands on credit.

At the regional level, interest rates in Bengal remained higher than those in Gujarat and at Agra. If we accept that monetary factors lay behind the movement of interest rates, one possible explanation could be the lower level of money supply in Bengal *vis-à-vis* its demand relative to Gujarat and Agra. The amount of bullion which made its way to Bengal by direct foreign exports was comparatively smaller, and much of what it received came from Delhi, Agra and Patna. But the specie which Bengal received from these regions was partly held by the bankers who issued bills of exchange to transfer merchants' funds (Habib 1972: 294). At the same time, there was a reverse remittance of Bengal's money to Agra, Delhi and Gujarat in the form of the surplus revenue of the province and up-country remittances of Mughal nobles and non-resident merchants. Some of this money was remitted through *hundis* and some of it was transported physically (Foster 1798: 7; Mehta 1967: 22–23; Tavernier: 93; Moreland: 178–82; Bayly 1983: 64). Although it is difficult to assess the precise extent of the net transfer of bullion from one region to another from the limited evidence we have on Bengal's economic and administrative relationship with the rest of the empire, it would seem on balance that the pressure on Bengal's monetary stock was greater than either Agra or Gujarat, and the situation described in an early eighteenth-century source may be considered as typical of the provincial monetary economy:

> As the king's revenues and other money are annually sent to the Mughal courts at Delhi . . . not only the bullion, but also the rupee of

other provinces imported into Bengal, in the course of trade, [is swept away]. It goes to Delhi, from whence it never returns to Bengal; so that after such treasure is gone . . . there is hardly currency enough left in Bengal to carry on any trade, or even to go to market for provisions and necessaries of life, till the next shipping arrives, to bring a fresh supply of silver. (Steuart)

If these shortages in capital were linked in any way to the high rates of interest, then one can perhaps also explain the fall in the second half of the seventeenth century. In this period the influx of European bullion to Bengal had increased dramatically and there must have been a simultaneous increase in the volume of commerce based on Om Prakash's argument that European trade had no displacement effect on the economy (Om Prakash 1991: 234–56). The benefit of the increase in trade was shared largely by the mercantile classes, but more particularly by the money-changers and bankers whose profit rose substantially with the transactions in money and credit. If this was true for Bengal, which had a developed money and credit market, then the trend in its interest rates could be linked, without any significant change in the credit structure, to the same broader movement which influenced the markets of Gujarat and Agra.

The case of Coromandel is interesting not only because it was a different currency zone but also because here the issue of tribute seems to have had an opposite effect on the interest rates, besides producing a dual impact on the monetary system of Golconda. The rates on the Coromandel coast and in Golconda in general were also high and there was a fall in the 1640s, a rise thereafter and a second fall in the 1670s. Golconda had a gold-based monetary system and the limited quantity of silver it received from overseas commerce was mainly used to pay for goods imported from the rupee areas of the Mughal empire. In 1635, Shahjahan led a campaign against the Deccan kingdoms, the outcome of which was the establishment of a tributary relationship between Golconda and the Mughal empire. The terms of the treaty signed between the two states included, among other things, the payment of an annual tribute and striking of rupees in the name of the Mughal emperor. By the 1660s, the need to remit the tribute in rupees and the establishment of a silver mint at Golconda began to encourage silver circulation in the region (*Selected Waqai*: 6, 15–16, 18). The introduction of the rupee into the economy of Golconda also proved beneficial to the silver importers who were able not only to obtain the coin locally but also use it in payment for the purchase of export goods.[18] Gradually, under the pressure of tribute and foreign commerce, the monetary system of Golconda began to turn bimetallic with the silver rupee and its fractional pieces (*ana*) making inroads into the exchange network of the region (Bodleian MS: 249b–250aff; Thevenot: 136, 140, 148; Bhimsen: 121; Ovington: 303; *Uytrekening*: 33, 44; Lockyer: 7–8). At the same time, the tribute also triggered a triangular bimetallic traffic in bill and money between Golconda, Aurangabad, the Mughal capital of the Deccan, and Gujarat. The Coromandel bankers lent huge sums in gold obtained from the state to the European factors and received payments in silver at Surat which was eventually transferred to Aurangabad to settle Golconda's obligations. This established a direct relationship between the supply of silver at Surat and the volume of credit at Coromandel while allowing, at the same time, the state of Golconda to contain the expansion of a competing currency in its coastal areas (Haider, forthcoming).

If the incorporation of Golconda's monetary economy into the larger network of silver movement commenced soon after 1635, it can offer some explanation as to why interest rates were relatively higher in the province before the 1640s and declined thereafter (Moosvi 1982: 377–78). The expansion in silver circulation, both in Gujarat and Golconda, allowed the total money supply to expand even when there was no substantial increase in the absolute level of gold money.

Contraction in Money Suply and the Volume of Credit

On the basis of an analysis of the temporal and inter-regional movement of interest rates, a case has been made out for a downward drift in the cost of borrowing resulting from an expansion in money supply in the seventeenth-century Indian economy. We now consider such examples where a contraction in money supply impinged upon the volume and cost of credit.

The first case is illustrative of the point that if the volume of credit and banking fluctuated within an acceptable range following a change in specie supply, it could not expand beyond the permissible limit. It was once reported that due to an acute shortage of metallic money (*kami i zar i naqd*), the bankers of Ahmadabad began to enforce the system of floating book credit by which transactions could be concluded and claims could be met without the intervention of specie.

The system was sustained by the bankers charging heavy discounts on converting bill money into cash (*anth*) (*Mirat:* 410–11). A conflict soon broke out between the banking and mercantile communities for the reason that, with no money in sight, merchants demanded payment in cash and refused to run their business on the basis of book transfer. Eventually, bankers were obliged to reduce the discount rate but not without a tempestuous showdown with the authorities.

The second case demonstrates the extent to which the volume of both currency and credit was susceptible to the increases and losses imposed by foreign trade. In the 1670s, a substantial fall occurred in the supply of silver in different parts of the Mughal empire due to the substitution of gold for silver in Spanish-American imports. The supply of silver to Gujarat from the Red Sea and the Persian Gulf also dried up during that monsoon. Isaac Lawrence, an English factor stationed at Surat in 1678, mentioned a 'great scarcity of money here, I meane rupees, which the like hath not beene known', and it was reported for Bengal that it received very little silver from the English in the past years and none at all from the Dutch (*Letter Book:* 54af). The acute shortage of silver brought about a steep fall in the gold price and induced gold to be brought out of reserves and hoards to make up for the shortfall in the monetary stock. The Mughal monetary authorities, in order to stretch the money supply, increased the mint price of silver by abolishing seigniorage, debased the rupee and reinforced the state monopoly on the sale of silver bullion to the mint (Haider 1996: 352–54). The adverse impact of monetary contraction on exchange economy was widely perceived and commented upon by contemporaries:

> These circumstances doe naturally produce a decay of commerce in the country; the rich moneyed men, who are the only support therof, chooseing rather to secure their estates then expose them in trade. (Foster, w 1925: 315)

> [The value of imported goods was lower than had ever been known], which has lately ruined many considerable persons in these parts, every few acquainting us with failing of one eminent shroff or another, which has made money so extremely scarce in Surat as has infinitely obstructed its usual course of trade. (*English Factories:* 228)

The two sets of evidence we have indicate that the paucity of money created an immediate deflationary effect on commodity prices and a fall in sales and profits. At the same time, the tightness of money was deepened by a contraction of credit and the capital available to finance commerce.

Conclusion

In this paper we put together scattered evidence to sketch the emergence of a monetized network of exchange supported by a system of credit and banking. We tried to show that credit had permeated the exchange sector of the Mughal economy ranging from the level of commerce in the urban centres to the process of production in rural areas. At each point, the lack of capital in the hands of manufacturers, merchants and consumers was redressed by a discernible class of bankers who made it their business to bring continuity to the process of economic exchange. Credit became organized and active as a result of the system of short-term loans and the extensive use of the bill of exchange (*hundi*) which functioned as a means of accumulation of banking capital, a mode of cash and credit remittances and a device to make payments and settle obligations. The negotiability of *hundis* guaranteed by endorsement and the use of *hundi* rupees to overcome currency diversity extended its commercial usage across provinces and mercantile groups. Through insurance and respondentia, this branch of commercial credit also provided protection to the moneylenders and speculators against default on debts and genuine losses incurred in the process of sharing risks with the debtors.

The seventeenth century brought considerable progress in the techniques of transferring capital and making payments. Inland commerce and long-distance maritime trade were now open to the massive participation of big and small merchants including the European companies. The continued influx of precious metals, particularly silver, provided the monetary basis upon which the credit structure rested. The function of credit instruments was to make existing money circulate more efficiently and take its place when it was not physically present. To that extent the scope and size of banking activities was also defined by the volume of metallic money. With the growth in money economy aiding specialization in commodity exchange and multilateral payment, credit also grew in proportion. It was both a symptom of the growing monetization and a factor which helped to bring it about. Interest rates signified this reciprocal relationship. When the circulation of money reached a point where it exceeded the demand for commercial capital, interest rates fell. The lowering of the cost of credit helped commercial investment and further broadened the parameters of monetized exchange.

Notes

[1] The first reference to banking is found in the Genoese notarial records of the twelfth and thirteenth centuries. By 1200, the *bancherius*, a term derived from the bench he used and reserved exclusively for the money-changer, was extending his activities from money-changing to deposit banking. There was however little specialization, and some bankers were merchants as well while some merchants dealt in foreign exchange. Forms of partnership developed with the bankers giving bonus to their customers out of their profit since it was not circumvented by any legal or theological restrictions. Testimonies relating to law suits in 1200 revealed other aspects of Genoese banking, mainly book transfer and credit creation. Cheques or written order of payments were first used in the fourteenth century whenever a customer was prevented from going to the bank. (1974: 200–05, 216–17). Roover argued (pp. 200–01) that the nucleus of thirteenth-century Genoese banking was money-changing and not moneylending, as was traditionally held by scholars such as Andre E. Sayous. Also see de Roover (1948); Lopez (1979: 1–24).

[2] For weekly markets (*peth*) held at the level of the *qasba* catering to the surrounding villages, see Lahori, *Badshahnama* (*Bib. Indica*, 1867–68: 345). For money-changers (*sarrafs*) visiting *qasba* markets for business, see *Selected Waqai of the Deccan* (AD *1660–1671*) (1953: 154). For village accounts of cash income and expenditure, see *Khulasat us Siyaq*, OIOC, MS Or. 2026, 64a–bff; *Dastur ul Amal i Alamgiri*, OIOC, MS Add. 6599, 46a–47ffa.

[3] Ibid., p. 247, verse 314. Almost all accountancy manuals of the Mughal period prescribed formulae to facilitate the calculation of interest on the principal amount. Munshi Nand Ram Kayasth Srivastavya, *Siyaqnama*, Lucknow, 1879, p. 15; *Lilavati*, OIOC, MS Add. 6641, 28a–bff.

[4] The artisans brought their products – cotton, silken stuff and other merchandise to the caravan *sarais* at Banaras from where the foreign merchants 'obtain them at first hand'. Tavernier, *Travels in India*, I, p. 97. Also *English Factories, 1618–21*, pp. 192–93 for the weavers bringing their products to the marts of Lakhawar and Patna.

[5] We are told about the Ahmadabad weavers that even the best of these did not 'possess a capital of 50 rupees'. Roques, tr. Indrani Ray, (1982–83: 88), fn 1.

[6] In 1621, when the governor of Patna, Muqarrab Khan, delivered money to the *sarrafs* to be remitted to Agra, the exchange rate became favourable to those borrowing money at Patna and paying at Agra. (*English Factories, 1618–21*: 236).

[7] Khachikian, (1966: 153–56, 173–74). Also see Manucci, (77–78) for an

Armenian merchant, Khwaja Safar, carrying a *hundi* from Agra to Patna to buy textiles.

[8] Several examples are available of state officials depositing sums of money with the *sarrafs for remitting tribute,* treasure or collections from their *jagirs.* Abul Fazl, *Akbarnama, Bib. Indica,* III: 762; *Selected Waqai of the Deccan:* 17; *Akhbarat i Darbar i Mualla,* MS. Royal Asiatic Society: 4 *safar,* 40th regnal year of Aurangzeb, and 28 Ramazan, 47th regnal year of Aurangzeb; Malikzada, *Nigarnama i Munshi:* 29, 30, 38. Cf. Habib, 'Banking in Mughal India': 11; Alam and Subrahmanyam, 'L'Etat Moghol et sa Fiscalite': 198– 99.

[9] For cases of depositors drawing upon their bankers see, B.L., Sloane MS 1910, 45bf; *Mirat i Sikandari* (eds), S.C. Misra and M.L. Rahman, Baroda, 1961: 504–05. Examples of deposit banking can also be cited for the eastern Deccan. When an official of the Golconda kingdom was harried by a subordinate to settle his outstanding salary claims, he wrote a note of payment on a *sarraf. Selected Waqai of the Deccan:* 10. Tavernier describes that the merchants buying diamonds at Rammalkota drew bills on the *sarrafs,* either at Rammalkota itself or at any other place, preferably Surat, where the diamond sellers themselves bought commodities. Tavernier, *Travels,* II: 47–48.

[10] Specimens given in an accountancy manual show that some *hundis* simply mentioned the name of the drawer (for example, Murlidhar Sahu) and the drawee (for example, Bhagwant Rai Sahu) with the amount and date. Bhaiyya Anand Ram [Mukhlis!], *Intikhab az Siyaqnama,* OIOC, MS. Ethe 2125: 147af.

[11] When an English merchant took up a bill on Ahmadabad drawn by a Mughal official at Jalore, it was discounted on the spot by a *sarraf.* Mundy: 290. Also see Bhandari: 25.

[12] See *Mirat i Ahmadi,* I: 410–11 for the classic description of the use of bill money. Habib, 'Merchant Communities in Precolonial India': 394.

[13] When the Agra factor of the Surat merchant, Virji Vora, intended to deduct a further 3 per cent from the *chalani* rupees while making payments to the English, the latter protested, claiming that these '*hundi* rupees' had always been current in payment for the bills of exchange. *English Factories, 1630– 33:* 154.

[14] *English Factories, 1642–43:* 140, 152. For a good discussion of how the Chettiar bankers of Tamil Nadu fixed interest rates in order to organize the flow of cash and credit see Rudner (1994: 90–92).

[15] Pivetti (1991: 8–9). In the debate in contemporary England over the determination of interest rates, the mercantilists emphasized the link between money supply and interest rates and argued that a fall in the latter was the direct result of an abundance of precious metals. They also considered it a positive factor for economic growth. Hume contested the mercantilist position by discounting the role of precious metals and put forward three causative factors namely, a) volume of demand for credit; b) volume of capital seeking investment; and c) the size of commercial profit.

In this analysis, both the phenomena – the abundance of money and low interest rate – were conditioned by one and the same factor, the expansion of trade and industry. Hume: 43, 45, 50–56.

[16] For an insightful remark that this may have been the case with the mercantile economy of the Mughal empire see Habib, 'Monetary System and Prices': 377.

[17] A good discussion of these opposite tendencies – known as the Gibson Paradox – can be found in J.M. Keynes, (1971: 177–78). Also see Wicksell, (1935: 168–69).

[18] *English Factories, 1665–67*: 329. For a description and illustration of the rupee minted by the Dutch at Pulicat (1666), see Tavernier, *Les Six Voyages,* II: 600 (Figs 5 and 6). Also see J. Brennig, (1978: 54–55).

References

Abdul Hamid Lahori, *Padshahnama,* 2 vols, 3 pts, Maulvi Abdur Rahim and Kabiruddim Ahmad (eds), *Bibliotheca Indica,* 1867–68.

Abul Fazl, *Akbarnama,* Bibhotheca Indiaca, III.

Abul Fazl, *Ain-i-Akbari.*

Akhtarat i Dartar i Mualla, MS Royal Asiatic Society.

Alam, Muzaffar and Sanjay Subrahmanyam, 'L' Etat Mughal etsa Fiscalite'.

Ali Muhammad Khan, (1761/1965), *Mirat-i-Ahmadi,* I.

Athar Ali, *Mughal Nobility Under Aurangzeb.*

Banarsidas, *Ardhkathanak,* Mukund Lath (ed. and tr.), 1981.

Bayly, C.A.A., 1983, *Rulers, Townsmen and Bazaar: North Indian Society in the Age of British Expansion 1780–1870,* Cambridge.

Bhaiya Anand Ram, Intikhab a2 Siyaqnama, OIOC, MS Ethe 2125.

Bhandari, *Khulasat ut Tawarikh.*

Bhandari, Sujan Rai, 1918, *Khulasat ut Tawarikh* (ed.), Zafar Hasan, Delhi.

Bhmsen, 1972, Tanikh i Dilkusha, tr. Jadunath Sarkar, V. Gkhonreller (ed.), Bombay.

Brennig, Joseph J., 1978, 'The Golconda Coinage of Shahjahan and Aurangzeb: A Mughal Tributary Courage', *Journal of the Andhra Historical Society,* xxxvii.

Bodleian MS Rawlinson A 302.

Chandra, 'Some Aspects of the Growth of a Money Economy'.

Cipolla, Carlo M., 1993, *Before the Industrial Revolution European Society and Economy 1000–1700,* London.

Dastur ul Ainal-i-Alamgiri, OIOC, MS Add. 65aa, 46a–47aff.

Day, John, 'Money and Credit in Medieval and Renaissance Italy', in *Medieval Market Economy.*

de Roover, Raymond, 1974, 'A New Interpretation of Banking', in Julius Kirshner (ed.), *Business, Banking and Economic Thought in Late Medieval and Early Modern Period,* Chicago.

de Roover, Raymond, 1948, *Money, Banking and Credit in Medieval Bruges,* Cambridge, Massachusetts.

English Factories, 1634–36.

Factory Records, Miscellaneous, OIOC, Vol. 3, 45–46ff.

Farmans and Sanads Granted to the East India Company, B.L., MS Add 29095, 1a–10bff.

Forster, George, 1798, *A Journey from Bengal to England, through Northern Part of India, Kashmir, Afghanistan and Persia and into Russia by the Caspian Sea*, 2 vols London.

Foster, William, 1925, 'Aurangzeb and the Treasure Hoard of Akbar', *Journal of the Royal Asiatic Society*, 15.

Habib, Irfan, 1964, 'Usury in Medieval India', *Comparative Studies in Society and History*, vi.

———, 'Merchant Communities in Precolonial India'.

———, 1972, 'The System of Bills of Exchange (Hundis) in the Mughal Empire', *Proceedings of the Indian History Congress*, Thirty-fifth session Muzaffarpur.

———, 1972, 'System of Bills of Exchange'. Sloane, B.L., 1910 (MS).

Haider, Najaf, 1995, 'Risk Sharing and Mercantile Credit in the Mughal Empire', Paper presented to the History Seminar, School of Oriental and African Studies, Unpublished London.

———, 1996, 'Precious Metal Flows and Currency Circulation in the Mughal Empire' in *Journal of Economic and Social History of the Orient* (JESHO), Vol. 39, No. 3.

———, 1999, 'The Quantity Theory and Mughal Monetary History', *The Medieval History Journal*, Vol. 2, No. 2.

———, *The Monetary System of the Mughal Empire*, forthcoming.

Hatcher, John, 1977, *Plague, Population and the English Economy, 1348–1530*, London.

Hume, 'Of Interest', *Writing on Economics*.

Keynes, J.M., 1971, *A Treatise on Money*, II, London.

Khachikian, Levon, 1966, 'The Ledge of the Merchant Hovhannes Joughayetsi', *JASB*, New Series, viii, 3.

Khwasat us Siyaq, OIOC, MS Or 2026, 64a–bff.

Kitab-i-Sikkaha, OIOC, MS Add 16855 15bf.

Letter Book of Isaac Lawrence, OIOC, Vol. 7.

Lilavati, OIOC, MS Add 6641, 289–6ff.

Lockyer, *Account of the Trade in India*.

Lopez, Robert, 1979, 'The Daron of Medieval Banking', in *The Daron of Modern Banking*, New Haven.

Malikzada, *Nigarnama i Munshi*.

Manucci, Niccolao, *Storia do Mogor*, 1656–1712, William Irvina Jr (ts.), 1907–08, London.

Mehta, Balmukund, *Balmukumdanama* (ed.) and tr. Satish Chandra, 1967, *Letters of a King Maker of the Eighteenth Century*, Aligarh.

Misra, S.C. and M.L. Rahman, 1961, *Mirat i Sikandari*, Baroda.

Moosvi, Shireen, 1982, 'The Mughal Empire and the Deccan–Economic Factors and Consequences', *Proceedings of the Indian History Congress*, Forty-Third Session, Kurukshetra.

———, 2000, 'The Indian Economic Experience 1600–1900: A Quantitative Study', in *The Making of History: Essays Presented to Irfan Habib* (eds) K.N. Pannikkar, Terence J. Byres and Utsa Patnaik, New Delhi.

Moreland, W.H., *Akbar to Aurangzeb.*

Mundy, *Travels in Asia.*

Nightingale, Pamcla, 1990, 'Monetary Contration and Mercantile Credit in Fourteenth Century England', *Economic History Review*, 2 ser xiii.

OIOC, *Original Correspondence no. 2071.*

Om Prakash, 1991, 'Sarafs, Financial International and Credit Network in Mughal India', in *Money, Coins and Commerce: Essays in the Monetary History of Asia and Europe (From Antiquity to Modern Times)* (ed.) E. Van Canwenberghe, Lenven.

———, *Dutch East India Company.*

Ovington, *Voyage to Surat.*

Pelsaert, *Remonstrantic.*

Pivetti, Massimo, 1991, *An Essay on Money and Distribution*, London.

Postom, M.M., 1959, 'Note', *Economic History Review*, 2, ser, xii.

Raychaudhuri, Tapan, 'Non-Agricultural Productiion' *Comparative Studies in Society and History.*

Risala-i-Ziraat, MS Edinburgh, 144, 10bff, 11a.

Roques, Georges, 1982–83, 'Of Trade and Traders in Seventeenth Century India: An Unpublished French Memoir by George Roques', Indrani Ray (Jr), *Indian Historical Review.*

———, *La Maniere de negotier dans Les Indes Orientalles de ice a mes Chers qnuis Et Confercs Les Engages de la Royalle Compagouge de France*, Bibliotheque Nationale, MS Fonds Francais 14614, 223–24ff.

Rudner, David West, 1994, *Caste and Capitalism in Colonial India, The Nattukottai Chettiar*, Berkeley.

Selected Waqai of the Deccan.

Spooner, Frank C., 1972, *The International Economy and Monetary Movements in France, 1493–1725*, Cambridge, Massachusetts.

———, *International Economy.*

Spufford, Peter, *Money and its Use in Medieval Europe.*

Srivastava, Munshi Nand Ram Kayasth, 1879, *Siyaqnama*, Lucknow.

Steuart, James, *A Collection of Miscellanies Relative to Coinage in India*, (n.p, n.d).

Supplementary Calendar.

Surat Documents, Suppl. Persan, 482.

Tavernier, *Travels in India.*

Thevenot, *Indian Travels.*

Usher, A.P., 1932–34, 'The Origins of Banking: The Primitive Banks of Deposit, 1200–1600', *Economic History Review*, iv.

van Santen, H.W., 1953, *De Verenigde Oast-Mdische Compaguie in Gujarat in Hindustan, 1620–60*, Leiden.

Uytrekening.

Waqai Sarkar Ranthambhor wa Ajmer, MS Asafiya Library, Hyderabad, transcript (nos 78–79), Centre of Advanced Study in History, Aligarh Muslim University, No. 78, 122ff, 326ff.

Wicksell, Knut, 1935, *Lectures on Political Economy*, II, London.

Yusuf Hussain (ed.), 1953, *Selected Waqai of the Deccan* (AD 1660–1671), Hyderabad.

A Note on Interest Rates in the Seventeenth and Early Eighteenth Centuries

Shireen Moosvi

A rudimentary history of interest rates in the Mughal period can be constructed almost solely from European accounts. Mughal sources that are rich in information on the system of coinage, bills of exchange (*hundi*) and the institution of *sarraf* have unfortunately yielded little on rates of interest.[1]

The data on interest rates from the English records were first collected by Irfan Habib (Habib 1964: 402–04). This collection was subsequently augmented by more data, notably relating to Gujarat (1622–33 and 1701–03) and other regions (Moosvi 2000: 337–38).[2] From the Dutch records, van Santen has given us rich information on Gujarat and Agra (van Santen 1953: 120, Table 13).[3]

The interest rates in the seventeenth and early eighteenth century can be seen, from their levels, to form four rather distinct zones, namely, Gujarat; northern India (mainly Agra), Bengal and Orissa, and Deccan and South India, and are set out in previous studies accordingly. The interest rates can be put on a graph (below), which shows both the common trends in movement and the disparities between their levels.

All the four graph-lines depict an unmistakable fall in the interest rates around the middle of the seventeenth century in all the zones, though the scale of decline varies.[4] In Gujarat the rate of interest fluctuated between 1 and 1.25 per cent per month from 1622 to 1650, barring the rate quoted for 1628 at Ahmadabad where the loan was procured against gold pledged with the lender at 0.5 per cent interest per month (Foster 1906: 239). Around 1650 there was a considerable fall: from 1651 on to 1703 the rates ranged between 0.33 to 0.8 per cent. At Agra, for which our information is rather meagre, a fall seems to have occurred during the course of 1647 when the cost of credit

84

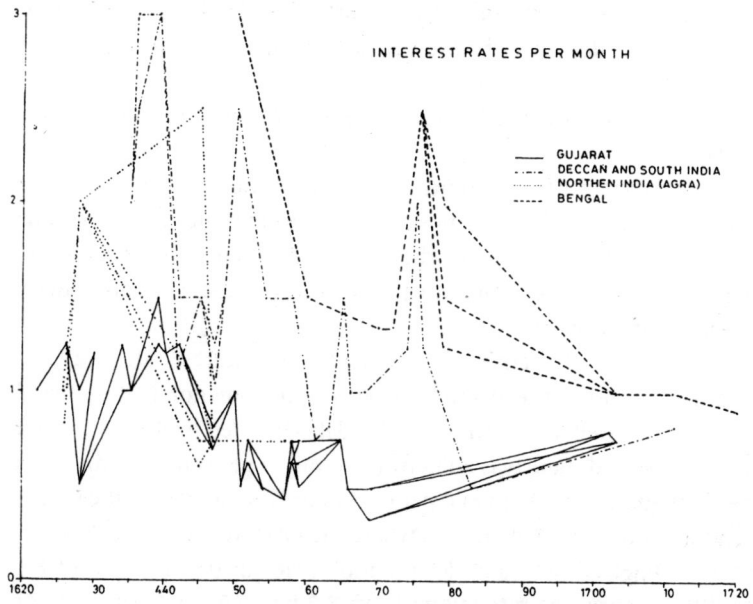

INTEREST RATES PER MONTH

———— GUJARAT
–·–·– DECCAN AND SOUTH INDIA
·········· NORTHEN INDIA (AGRA)
------- BENGAL

declined from 1–2.5 per cent to 0.625 per cent and did not rise above 0.75 per cent thereafter.

In the Deccan, on the other hand, the interest rates were high-er than in Gujarat and Agra. But as in the other two zones, a great fall in commercial interest rates seems to have occurred between 1639 and 1642. Before 1642 the rates seem to have always remained higher than 2 per cent, whereas after 1642 the interest per month appears to have varied between 1 and 1.5 per cent though in some years at Madras it fell below this level, while in the 1670s at Masulipatnam it even touch-ed 2 per cent.

The rates in Bengal for the first half of the seventeenth century are unfortunately not available and there is only one quotation from Bengal (or rather Balasore) for 1650. The subsequent quotations are much lower and a fall in the rates may be inferred for the 1650s. But the rates in Bengal still remained around 1.5 per cent. No information about rates is available for the last two decades of the seventeenth century but during the opening two decades of the eighteenth century these remained stable at 1 per cent per month. Thus, even after the decline of rates in Bengal, the interest rates there remained substan-tially higher than those at Agra and Gujarat. On the basis of information in the records of the Dutch East India Company, Om Prakash also infers that 'the average rate of interest in a money market such as Surat was lower – at times substantially lower – than in a somewhat less developed market such as Hugli in Bengal' (Om Prakash 1998: 161).

What do these trends in the movement of interest rates suggest? Not only does the noticeable fall in the rates in all the four zones around the middle of the seventeenth century call for some explanation, but the regional variations in interest rates also surely demand attention.

The seventeenth-century decline in interest rates was not confined to India; it seems to have been a phenomenon that occurred in Europe as well. It appears from the data collected by Sidney Homer that in England there was a fall from about 10 per cent per annum in the first quarter to less than 6 per cent in the last quarter of the seventeenth century. In Holland too, where the rates were in any case lower than in England, a steady decline took place in the first half of the twelfth century, the rate falling from 8.5 per cent to 4 per cent per annum, even taking it to below 4 per cent in the next half of the century: the only exceptions were the few years of war. A similar decline in rates also occurred in France and other parts of Europe about the middle of the seventeenth century (Homer 1963: 125–29, 139). Rates of interest appear to have registered steady decline in Italy (Genoa) from the last decade of the sixteenth century onwards, the dip becoming more prounced in the second decade of the seventeenth century during which these even dipped to below 2 per cent per annum (Cipola 1976: 227, 229).

It has been suggested that the 'increase in liquidity' which in itself was a result of 'greater supply of precious metal brought down the interest rates in some major financial centres of Europe' (ibid.: 229). The question arises whether the fall in the interest rates in India at about the same time was a consequence of similar developments. In a perfect market the interest rates should be determined simply by the supply and demand of money. In pre-modern times, prior to the introduction of paper currency, money supply would seem largely to have depended on the availability of precious metals. Here, however, one point must be clarified, since this seems to be missing in many texts where it is simply held that an influx of bullion should normally lower interest rates, in the belief that a rise in prices of commodities must result in a fall of value of money. But interest rates represent not prices of money but hire-prices of capital. Now if there is an influx of a precious metal, say, silver, and its supply is doubled, leading to a halving of its own price (the prices of commodities being doubled), capital would not really increase in real terms at all, since what was purchased by one kilogram of silver is now purchased by two kilograms. The rate of interest should then not fall at all, because in real terms no more capital has come into the market than before.

Seen in this light it is less easy theoretically to relate the fall of interest rates to the influx of silver during the sixteenth and seventeenth centuries from the Americas.

The silver influx by itself thus would not increase effective money supply and force a reduction in interest rates. If interest rates fall, this could mean either a fall in money demand, for example, through a fall in production, or market orientation. Alternatively, it could follow expansion in money capital in real terms, that is, an accumulation of silver in lenders' hands is greater, say, in gold value than before (if gold values remained steady).

The transfer of money-capital in large quantities from the Atlantic area to India, through various conduits, during the late sixteenth and seventeenth centuries, is well established and much has been written on it (Hasan 1969: 85–116; Moosvi 1987: 47–49; Haider 1996: 298–364). The imports of silver in the sixteenth and early seventeenth centuries, according to Irfan Habib, went mainly to replace the copper currency and was absorbed by increasing monetization of the economy through a cash-nexus. The value of silver thus did not fall in proportion to the influx of silver (Habib 1987: 139–60). Even after the replacement of copper by silver currency, during 1615–1705, the increase in prices of gold and copper in terms of silver works out at 33 per cent for gold and 110.4 per cent for copper (Moosvi 1987: 35). Now, if silver largely, merely served as the medium of payment, it would by the same token not add to capital at all, just as it did not until 1610 when the value of silver was reduced. In this case, then, there ought to have been no effect on the rate of interest until 1610. Since, unfortunately, we have practically no information on the movements of interest rates before 1610, this hypothesis cannot be checked with the available data.

The ideal situation would have been if we had with us at least approximate figures of gold, silver and copper stock in India, say, *c.*

1610, and their annual variations. We would then have been able to determine whether or not the variations in the relative values of the three metals were in proportion to the changes in their stock. Despite an attempt to establish the amount of stock of silver coins that I once bravely undertook (Moosvi 1987: 47–94), the exercise would be meaningless for our present purpose if there are no similar reconstructions of gold and copper.

We thus deal with the quantitative factor by considering possibilities. Let us begin with the supposition that though the price of silver fell after 1610 it did not fall in proportion to the increase in its supply. This could happen if there was a more-than-proportional increase in the consumption of silver for purposes of hoarding and of making ornaments. It must, however, be pointed out that the English factory records always relate the demand for silver in India to minting rather than to hoarding or ornaments. It is unlikely, therefore, that there was any large increase in silver-hoarding.

A much more important consideration is the difference in the interest rates between western Europe and India. The large margin of difference would be obvious from the rates in Europe we have already mentioned.

The rate of interest in England was reported to be only 4 per cent per annum in 1650, when at Surat (even after the fall in the interest rates) it was 7.5 to 9 per cent per annum according to the factors of the English East India Company, so that, the factors argued, the Company would gain by sending capital to India (Chaudhury 1975: 117). If this was so, then there would be a built-in pull for drawing silver to India from the Atlantic to South Asia merely for usurious purposes. Such transfers could exercise a downward pressure on the rates of interest in India. Indeed, in 1682 the Court of Directors of the East India Company claimed that by sending 'great stocks of money' to Surat they had forced down the interest rates prevailing there to as low as 6 per cent per annum (0.5 per cent per month) (Chaudhuri 1978: 159).

The matter requires more attention to be devoted to it than has hitherto been the case. It is to be borne in mind that it would not be necessary for money-capital to move directly from England, Holland or France to India; it could also move from the Mediterranean through the Levant to India, once the pull was there. Such transfers need to be studied in connection with the Ottoman empire (controlling the Red Sea) and Safavid empire (controlling the Persian Gulf). What we are arguing is that the exports of specie to India did not cover imports of Indian goods to Europe; these also represented, in part, a continuous export of money-capital. If this happened, then the supply of credit in India was bound to expand and force a fall in the interest rates.[5]

A second factor that could explain the fall in interest rates is one that has not so far been considered at all: an increase in the elements of liquidity, or, in other words, territorial and inter-sectoral mobility of money, which for Europe has been held to be a major causal factor in the process. In an early article, Irfan Habib pointed out that in the seventeenth century there were certain striking practices in Indian indigenous banking, in which the *sarrafs* played a key role; there was extensive deposit banking and insurance by the sarrafs (Habib 1960: 1–20), and also the use of *hundis* (bills of exchange). *Hundis,* being transferable (Habib 1972/73: 290–303), were crucial in increasing the liquidity of money-capital.

The problem here, however, is that we do not know if the practices were of recent growth. The fact that these were not evidenced earlier is not decisive when we remember that before Irfan Habib's paper of 1960, no one had noted the existence of deposit banking and insurance in the seventeenth century either.

We may close here with the problem of the regional differences in rates. The difference between North India (Agra and Gujarat) and the Deccan may at first sight be ascribed to the fact that the chief currency metal in the Deccan and South India was gold (since the basic coin for all price quotations was the *hun*), so that money supply in the Deccan was not likely to be affected as much by the silver influx as in northern India; not, that is, until after the Mughal annexations of Bijapur and Golkonda in 1686 and 1687. Gold supply would have become abundant (relatively) only in so far as silver replaced gold as currency metal in the peripheral areas of the Deccan (bordering the Mughal empire) or in some of the ports. Attractive as this argument may be, it encounters a serious objection in that we are concerned not with money supply but with supply of capital in real, not nominal, magnitudes; and this would not be affected by the South Indian coinage being in gold. Indeed, one may argue that, with Gresham's law operating, gold would be driven out of the Mughal empire as more silver flowed in to be minted into rupees; and there then might have been an actual gold influx into the southern states.

I should rather see the higher level of the rates in South India to lie in the lack of development of those financial practices of which we have spoken above. Arasaratnam, in his detailed study of seventeenth-century mercantile organization in South India, fails to record any institution of brokerage in South India (Arasaratnam). It can be seen that deposit banking in India was an extension of brokerage practices; so too, insurance. If so, we can perhaps consider whether a relative lack of liquidity is a better explanation of higher interest rates in South India.

The prevalence of high rates of interest in Bengal is rather more difficult to explain. One possibility is that there was a steady drain from Bengal in the form of revenues from the *khalisa* lands and *jagirs* of nobles sent up-country. If there was commerce of a sufficiently large volume by which the monetary circuit was completed by a corresponding amount of purchases, no large amount of specie (in the net) need have actually been transported out of Bengal. The loss of specie that Grant and Shore supposed to have occurred during the first half of the eighteenth century when, during some years, about a crore of rupees were annually remitted by the Nizams of Bengal to the Mughal Court,[6] need not really have taken place. We would then have to look for factors other than specie movements. One possibility is that the fall in interest rates to the levels of Agra and Gujarat was obstructed by the need for extra credit owing to the great expansion of silk trade, which made Bengal, in the latter half of the seventeenth century, into one of the great silk-exporting regions of the world (Chaudhury 1975: 114–25).

I should like to end by admitting that by the very nature of our evidence there is a great deal of speculation involved in all the points I have made; but, while our search for relevant data proceeds, there is also the need to seek clarity on the causative factors behind the economic processes of the seventeenth century. My purpose would be served if this note brings into focus the problems involved when one seeks to probe deeper behind observable facts, like the movements of interest rates.

Interest Rates

Notes

[1] Data on the principal and interest to be repaid on loans (*musa'adat*) given by Akbar to nobles is given in Abul Fazl (1867: 196), but there is no reference to interest rates on commercial loans.

[2] The data up till the end of Shahjahan's reign (1658–59) with full references are set out in Moosvi (1987: 373–74).

[3] Om Prakash (1998: 161, 4), also mentions the borrowings by the Dutch East India Company at Surat on interest and the differences in interest rates at Surat and Hughli, though he does not tabulate the interest rates.

[4] K.N. Chaudhuri (1978: 159) rather cursorily remarks that 'there was no long-term downward movement in interest rates in India'.

[5] This paragraph develops a suggestion made by me in Moosvi (1987: 374). *Economy of the Mughal Empire, c. 1595*, Delhi, 1987, p. 374.

[6] Fifth Report from the Select Committee on the Affairs of the East India Company with an Appendix and Glossary to the Report, 1812–13; Irish University Press, *Series of British Parliamentary Papers, Colonies: East India 3*, Shannon, Ireland, 1969, p. 321, lines 6–10, (Grant). Shore, in his Minute, agrees that the money must have come back by channels of trade; yet, he cites Grant for the figure of Rs 8.12 crore as being sent out to Delhi within a period of ten and a half years during Shujauddin Khan's viceroyalty; some more might have been sent, he says, to meet bills at Delhi (ibid., p. 183, paragraphs 133 and 134). Apparently, he supposes the specie to have been transported back physically to pay for Bengal exports.

References

Abul Fazl, 1867, *Ain-i Akbari*, Vol. I, edited by Blochmann, Calcutta.

Arasaratnam, S., 'Merchants Compromises and Commerce on the Coromandel Coast'.

Aziza Hasan, 1969, 'The Silver Currency Output of the Mughal Empire and Prices in India during the 16th and 17th Centuries', *Indian Economic and Social History Review*, VI.

Chaudhuri, K.N., 1978, *The Trading World of Asia and the English East India Company, 1660–1760*, Cambridge.

Chaudhury, Sushil, 1975, Trade and Commercial Organization in Bengal, Calcutta.

Cipolla, Carlo M., 1976, *Before the Industrial Revolution, European Society and Economy, 1000–1700*, London.

E. Foster, W. (ed.), 1906, *English Factories in India 1624–29*, Oxford.

Habib, Irfan, 1960, 'Banking in Mughal India' in *Contributions to Indian Economic History* (ed.), T. Raychaudhuri, Calcutta.

———, 1964, 'Usury in Medieval India', *Comparative Studies in Society and History*, Vol. IV, No. 4, The Hague.

———, 1972, 'The System of Bills of Exchange (Hundis) in the Mughal Empire', Proceedings of the Indian History Congress, Thirty-Third Session, Muzaffarpur, Delhi, 1973.

———, 1987, 'The System of Trimetallism', in *The Imperial Monetary System of Mughal India* (ed.), J.F. Richards, Delhi.

Haider, Najaf, 1996, 'Precious Metal Flows and Currency Circulation in the Mughal Empire, *JESHO*, Vol. 39, Part III.

Homer, Sidney, 1963, *A History of Interest Rates*, New Brunswick.

Moosvi, Shireen, 1987, 'The Silver Influx, Money Supply, Prices and Revenue-Extraction in Mughal India', *Journal of the Economic and Social History of the Orient (JESHO)*, Vol. XXX.

————, 1987, *Economy of the Mughal Empire—A Statistical Study*, Delhi.

————, 2000, 'The Indian Economic Experience 1600–1900: A Quantitative Study', *The Making of History: Essays Presented to Irfan Habib*, Delhi: Tulika.

Om Prakash, 1998, *European Commercial Enterprise in Pre-Colonial India*, (The New Cambridge History of India Series), Cambridge.

Series of British Parliamentary Papers, Colonies: East India 3, 1969, Shannon, Ireland.

van Santen, H.W., 1953, *De Gerenigde Dost-Indische Compagnie in Gujarat en Hindustan*, 1620–1660, Leiden.

Money and Banking under the Marathas

Seventeenth Century to AD 1848

A.R. Kulkarni

Agriculture being the only major way of life of people of medieval Maharashtra, the volume of monetary transactions of the region was quite limited. The Marathas, in their earlier phase of rule, did not introduce their own metallic currency as the coins in circulation could meet their requirements without much difficulty. Again, as it was the intrinsic value of the gold or silver coins that was the major consideration in exchange, they did not bother much whether the coin was minted by the Hindu, Muslim or Portuguese rulers. This situation did not change much as far as the currency was concerned; but with the increase in the scale of monetary transactions, new types of coins were minted to meet the requirements of trade.

The sources consulted for money and banking under Maratha rule are mainly drawn from the indigenous material supplemented by a few foreign ones. Among the indigenous sources, the accounts or ledgers of some major *sahukars* of the eighteenth century, besides a few state papers and family archives, throw much light on the subject under review. The travelogues of foreign travellers, particularly John Fryer, Careri, Thevenot, Tavernier and a few others, and factory records, particularly of the English, are useful in filling the gaps in information about the currency system of the Marathas.

It is proposed to take a brief review of the various aspects of money matters, like the mints, types of coins in circulation, the role of *sahukars* as moneylenders and bankers, the means of monetary transactions – the *hundi*, its varieties and operations – rates of interest and a few allied topics in this presentation.

93

Money
Mints

It is said that under Muhammad Tughluq of Delhi, every house had become a mint. However, the establishment of a mint, state or private, was a rare phenomenon in the early phase of Maratha power. Justice M.G. Ranade mentions that Shivaji had established his mint 'at Raigad, and copper and silver coins were issued from it', but it is not supported by any contemporary evidence.[1] However, it is very likely that Shivaji might have encouraged the medieval practice of establishing private mints by obtaining a regular licence from the government. For instance, a *sethi* (merchant) had applied for a licence for establishing a mint to issue *laris* (a silver coin) and it was granted for a period of five years on the condition that he would pay one *lari* per hundred *laris* struck and five *laris* for copper coins weighing one *maund*. Again, we find a reference to a term as a source of income in the *jamabandi* (rent-roll) of Aminabad of Cheul *prant* (Konkan), which is used perhaps to indicate the licence fee for minting coins (Kulkarni 1969: 129).

In the eighteenth century, the Marathas, who had adopted a policy of expansion in the north and hegemony in the south under the leadership of Peshwa Bajirao I (1720–1740) and his son Balaji Bajirao (1740–1761), involved themselves in continuous wars. Consequently, their demand for financing military operations and keeping the conquered territories under control increased beyond their expectations. This led to the establishment of more mints and the emergence of a new class of *sahukars* (moneylenders) who could meet the growing monetary requirements of the state. The *Selections from the Satara Rajas and the Peshwa Diaries* (SRPD)[2] give us plentiful information about the creation of new mints and the manufacture of several varieties of metallic coins – true, debased and counterfeit ones.

Permission was granted (1744–45), for instance, to one Balaji Bapuji to establish a mint at Nagothane to produce the *pice*, a copper coin of a specific weight, 10 *mashas*, for a period of three years, with a warning that violation of this condition would be severely dealt with. The mint-master was asked to pay Rs 50 for the first year, Rs 75 for the second and Rs 100 for the third year as licence fee. A mint was to be established at Mahuli fort (Satara district) in 1748–49 to strike copper coins like the *shivarai* (an *anna*) and *dhabbu*(double price) on similar conditions of payment as above (*SRPD*, Vol. II, No. 245, No. 246: 157, No. 247: 159).

Peshwa Balaji Bajirao (1740–61), who was a good administrator of finances, tried to regulate the functions of these private mints and bring them under state control. There were separate mints at Dharwad for producing coins of valuable metals like gold *mohurs* and *hons* and silver rupees. For some time they worked as per the conditions laid down by the state and produced true coins. But it was discovered later that the mint-masters, who were *zamindars* of the region, were misusing this facility and had started producing counterfeit coins. To check these fraudulent practices, the government decided to close all the separate mints and establish only one mint at Dharwad under the supervision of Pandurang Murar, to produce all three different coins, namely *mohurs, hons* and rupees. He was to collect six coins per 1,000 coins of each variety – *mohurs, hons* and rupees – produced in the mint and remit the amount to the royal treasury. He was also directed to see that the *hon* produced in the mint was of 3.5 *mashas* in weight, the *mohur* equal to the Delhi *mohur* in weight, and the rupee equal in weight to the Arcot rupee. This condition was put because all those coins were acceptable both to the state and the people.

The superintendent was also directed to keep the seals to impress on the coins in his possession; the artisans and employees of the mint were to be paid as per the earlier practice and increases in their salaries and privileges were to be made only after reviewing their work. As regards the salary of the superintendent, it was ordered that he should collect one extra coin of each variety per 1,000 coins from the *sahukars* who got them coined from his mint and remit the amount to the royal treasury, out of which his salary would be paid after reviewing his services. Similar orders were issued by the government to the other provinces under the Marathas (*SRPD*, Vol. II, No. 249: 164–65, year 1760–61).

The Peshwas had their mints at Pune, Chinchwad, Telegaon Dabhade, Vasai, Nagothane, Chandvad, Nasik, Daulatabad, Rahimpatpur, Dharwad and some other places. During the period of political instability, some of the mints were closed. When Peshwa Balaji Bajirao assumed power, he found that the financial position of the state was not satisfactory. He wanted Madhavrao Gosavi to establish a mint at Pune for issuing *patshahi* type of silver rupees and half-rupees to meet the immediate requirements of the state. He further ordered him that ornaments and other articles of gold and silver in the possession of the state, except those which were the property of deities in worship, be melted into bullion and used for producing rupees, half-rupees, *mohurs*, etc. The job of setting up of the Pune mint was entrusted to Dulabh Shet, chief *sahukar* of Pune city (Bhave 1935/1976: 405–06).

Three *sahukars* of Pune, namely, Dulabh Shet, Govindji and Govind Pandurang, requested the state in 1782–83 to grant them a *sanad* (permission) for setting up mints for striking *khurda* (fractional or copper) coins. The request was granted and an agreement was made with them containing some concessions along with instructions which they were to follow carefully. The most important instructions were as follows:

(1) A *nazar* (present) of Rs 12,001 should be paid to the government for this exclusive right given to them for the year 1783–84.

(2) Copper should be brought from Mumbai or other places, for which free movements of ships will be allowed.

(3) Copper coins should not be allowed to be brought into government territory from Alibagh and from the areas of the English. Any person acting in contravention of the rule should be fined.

(4) They can establish mints wherever it was possible, for which no money was charged. The areas recovered from the British would also be considered for establishing mints. In case the functioning of the mints was stopped due to political disturbances, a necessary extension of period would be given.

(5) The coins to be struck in these Konkan mints should be of following weights:

(a) Shivarai *paisa* . . . 9¼ *mashas*

(b) Alamgiri *paisa* . . . 13¾ *mashas*

(c) Dhabu *paisa* . . . 18½ *mashas* (*SRPD*, Vol. VIII: 240–42)

The problem of closing all the separate mints cropped up again in 1765–66. The superintendent Pandurang Murar represented to the government that the orders issued by the late Peshwa to abolish private mints, from which much-debased coins used to be issued, had remained a dead letter for various reasons. Immediately after its proclamation, disturbances prevailed for two years. The superintendent, therefore, appealed to the new Peshwa, Madhavrao (1761–73), to issue a supplementary *sanad*, and it was issued in 1765–66. It again directed to abolish all mints in the territory between the Krishna and Tunga-bhadra rivers and to establish a mint at Dharwad. Modified instructions were added to the earlier set of instructions. These were:

1. The *hun* was to be of 10 *kas* (strength) and 3½ *mashas* in weight.
2. The rupee *arkati phulcheri* (Pondicherry) was to be of one full *tola* in weight.
3. The *mohur* was to be 12 *kas* in weight.
4. Six coins of each variety should be paid to the government for every 1,000 coins issued; but as, owing to the large amount of debased coins now in circulation, persons changing old coins into new would be put to much loss, the above duty should not be levied for one year.
5. One *mohur* coin per 1,000 minted in addition to the above should be taken by the superintendent for himself. (*SRPD*, Vol. VII, 292–93, year 1765–66)

The attention of eleven *kamavisdars*, twenty-one *zamindars*, nineteen *sahukars* and twenty-one workers of twenty-one mints was drawn to the order regarding the abolition of all private mints and the establishment of one under government management at Dharwad. They were further directed to receive government dues in such coins only as might be issued from the new government mint at Dharwad (ibid.: 293–97).

When a *sanad* to establish a mint was granted, the details of establishment were also mentioned. For instance, one Lakshman Appaji, who was entrusted with the task of opening a government mint at Nasik in 1766–67, was allowed an establishment comprising a *karkun* (clerk) on Rs 20, two persons on Rs 6 each, and ten artisans, one blacksmith (*lohar*), five goldsmiths (*sonar*), two hammerers (*ghankari*), one engraver (*sikka*-maker) and a bellows operator (*bhatekari*), whose salaries could be fixed after making enquiries about the rates in the market. The rupee produced was to be of 11¼ *mashas* in weight or half a *masha* less than the quantity of silver that could be purchased for a rupee. The document also mentions the material required for striking coins, like iron, steel, coal, *takankhar* (bruce borax), *papadkhar* (impure carbonate of soda), *navasagar* (ammonium chloride), *chinch* (tamarind), etc., to be purchased from the market. It was expected that the profit from this mint for Rs 1,000 coined should be Rs 45 after leaving sufficient margin for wastages, wages of labourers and cost of material. The persons concerned with the mint were warned that this mint was being established by the government and that if any losses were incurred, enquiry would be made about it and wages and salaries would be paid in proportion to the losses.

When coins are manufactured on a large scale, fraudulent activities on the part of mint-masters are inevitable. Some mint-houses indulged in producing counterfeit, debased, lighter coins and thereby made profits by deceiving both the government and the public. It seems from the available documents that the Peshwas did not hesitate to take strong actions against those who violated the guidelines laid down in the *sanads* granted to them for establishing mints. Govind Naik Dewle, along with some goldsmiths in Pune, was fined Rs 2,000 by the government in 1748–49 for being involved in coining counterfeit rupees. Another goldsmith of Pune who manufactured counterfeit coins with the help of false impressions was not only punished for his crime, but his house was also attached and sold for Rs 1,100 (*SRPD*, Vol. II: 65–66; see also *SRPD*, Vol. VII: 301–02).

The government conducted an enquiry into malpractices in the mint at Chinchwad, a suburb of Pune, in 1766–67. It was found that the owners of the mint, Tuko Sonar and Moraji Sonar, were guilty of producing false rupees and *mohurs*. They were called to the office and the following instructions were issued to them. (i) Rupees of the Surat stamp should not be coined; the rupees should be of the Jayanagari stamp like the old *phulcheri* (Pondicherry), of full weight and good silver; the year on the stamp should be altered every year. (ii) The *mohurs* should also be of the Jayanagari stamp, like the old Aurangabad *mohur,* and of full weight and fine gold; the year on the stamp should be altered every year. Finally, the *sonars* were warned that any infringement of these conditions would be liable for punishment. A similar letter was sent to the owner of a mint at Telegaon Dabhade (*SRPD*, Vol. VII: 300–01).

In the year 1767–68, Anikar and Vatkar, the masters of the mint at Nasirabad (alias Dharwad) fort, maintained that they had held the privilege of minting coins for a long time including the period of Mughal rule over this region. They petitioned to the government that since the resumption of this region by the Marathas, another person, who had no *sanad* from any government, was issuing coins and that the government should enquire into this matter. After examining the records, the government accepted the right of the petitioner and confirmed the earlier *sanads* and granted him the privilege of minting coins on the usual terms (ibid.: 302–05).

In the year 1772–73, Tukoji Holkar requested the Peshwa to grant him a *sanad* to reopen the mint at Chandvad which was closed by the government as it was not producing true rupees of full weight. The request of Holkar was granted and he was asked to follow the pattern of Daulatabad in all respects. Tukoji Holkar was enjoined to be particularly careful that the coin turned out from the mint was of pure silver and of full weight (ibid.: 305).

When the Marathas surrendered to the British in 1818, the East India Company established its own rule, and with a view to bringing about some uniformity in the currency, abolished all the private and state mints in 1835.

Currency

Records of the seventeenth century show that a number of gold, silver and copper coins were in circulation in Maharashtra. Besides these metallic coins, *cowries* were used for smaller transactions, particularly in the rural areas.

The coins current in the Maratha country were mostly those of the Mughals, Bijapur, Golconda, the Portuguese and English, as well as the old coins of the dynasties that were no more in existence, for instance, the Vijayanagara empire. In addition to this, coins minted by private persons were also in circulation in the Maratha dominion.

It may be remembered that as there were no token coins in use, the market value of the coin depended on its metallic content or intrinsic value. Usually older coins of the same metallic content fetched lower values than the similar new coins. However, we sometimes find an old coin fetching a higher value than a current one for various reasons like weight, fineness, the policy of the bankers, the mode of payment fixed by the state and others.[3]

A striking feature of the South Indian currency was that the gold coin enjoyed the largest circulation and silver rupees were subsidiary to it, whereas in the north the silver rupee circulated widely and the gold coin was a supplementary coin (Ranade 1963: 217–18).

Classification of Coins

1. Gold coins: Information regarding the coins that were current under the Maratha rule in the seventeenth and eighteenth centuries can be collected and classified with the help of contemporary records such as chronicles, historical documents, state papers, individuals' records, particularly those of the *sahukars*, accounts of travellers, records of foreign merchants, and the factory records of the Dutch and English East India Companies.

Among the gold coins, *putali*, *mohur* and *hons* of various types were commonly used for state and individual monetary transactions. The *hons* are mentioned either by the names of the places or mints which coined them, like *Guti*, *Dharwari*, *Chandavari*, *Kaveripak*, *Vengurla*, *Vellori*, and so on; or by the names of rulers, like Rama-chandrarai, Shivarai, Achyutrai, Devarai, who were the Vijayanagara rulers. In view of the popularity of *hons* in the Deccan, the Muslim rulers of the Deccan also issued gold coins known as Padshahi, Muhammad Shahi, Ibrahimi Nisani *hons* and so on.

The gold coin is often referred to by foreign travellers as *pagoda*, which is an original Hindu coin called *varaha*, indicated by the symbol on it being that of an incarnation of Vishnu, which formed the crest of the Chalukyas and Vijayanagara (Rice: 301). *Pagoda* to Europeans meant a Hindu temple as it bore the image of a temple on it. However, they used the term *pagoda* to indicate the gold coin *hon*, which is a corruption of the Kannada word *honnu*, meaning gold.

The gold coin *shivarai*, also found among the coins of the Vijayanagara empire, is associated with the name of Shivaji, the founder of the Maratha power. The *shivarai hon* mentioned in the *Selected Waqai of the Deccan*, however, should not be confused with the Maratha *shivarai*, as it was a pre-Shivaji gold coin (*Selected Waqai*: 26). Whether Shivaji issued any gold coin in his name and that too in a large quantity is not conclusively established for want of documentary or physical evidence. One can therefore hardly agree with the statement of his chronicler Sabhasad, that there were four lakhs of *shivarai hons* in the treasury of Shivaji. There are numerous references to various other gold coins in Marathi records, but we hardly find any reference to *shivarai*, a gold coin supposed to have been struck by Shivaji, except in the chronicle of Sabhasad. Perhaps he made a confusion between the *shivarai* of the Vijayanagara empire and that of Shivaji.

G.H. Khare, a noted Maratha historian, maintains on the basis of an undated document preserved in the archives of the Chinchwad temple, that the *shivarai hons* of Shivaji were available in plenty in the seventeenth century. He ascribes this document to the period 1680– 1707. Another historian D.V. Kale discovered a gold coin in the possession of the descendants of Shivaji at Satara, bearing the legends 'Raja Shiva' on the obverse and '*Chhatrapati*' on the reverse side. From the available information on the gold coin of Shivaji, it can be said that Shivaji might have struck a few gold coins in his name called *shivarai* on the occasion of his coronation in 1674, to thereby proclaim his sovereignty. But he probably did not go beyond this; since a number of gold coins were already available and accepted by the people, Shivaji must have avoided the risk of putting his own coin in the market and making it acceptable.

The smaller denominations of the *hon* were *pratap*, *dharans*, *chavals*, *duvals*, *byals*, *falams* and *chakrams* – all minted in gold and current in medieval Maharashtra (Kulkarni 1997: 165–67, 2000: 216–18).

2. Silver coins: Among the silver coins current in Maharashtra, the most popular were rupees, *laris* and *takas*. Shahajani and Alamgiri Mughal rupees issued from Golconda were widely in circulation. The Abbasi (Persian) and Mahmudis (Gujarati) coins are mentioned in contemporary records. The rupee was a big heavy silver coin weighing generally 180 grams. Sometimes the rupees are mentioned as *chalani* and *khazana*. The current coin at any given time was known as *chalani* and was rated more than the older issues known as *khazana*, that is, old, debased and worn-out rupees, which were valued less than other rupees and were subject to discount (Hodivala 1928: 140–43).

Another silver coin was the *ashrafi* equivalent to the Portuguese *xerafin*. The *ashrafi*, in fact, is a term used for gold coin both in Arabic and Persian, but the Portuguese adopted it for their silver coin, *xerafin*, which they issued from Goa (Edwardes 1902: 109).

Lari was a silver coin of Persian origin, which was made of silver wire doubled somewhat like a hairpin, with inscriptions stamped on the prongs. The thick silver wire used for making a *lari* was more than three inches in length, doubled in the middle and slightly flattened to receive an impression of the stamp. It contained good and fine quality silver without any alloy. It assumed the name *lari* from the place Lar at the head of the Persian Gulf. It was first brought by the

Persian merchants to the Konkan and was accepted by the people and also by the Sultans of Bijapur. We therefore find different types of *laris* bearing the names of places where they were struck, like Dabholi, Chauli, Basra, Hurmuzi and so on (Kulkarni 1969: 243–47).

Taka was another important silver coin of the seventeenth century. Some scholars consider *taka* as merely a money of account and sometimes it is confused with the Mughal copper coin *tanka*. The records mention that forty-eight *rukas* (a small copper coin) make a *taka* and twelve *takas* generally make a *hon*; the *taka* therefore seems to be a proper silver coin actually in circulation and not merely a money of account (ibid.: 247–48)

The English East India Company also minted its own coins at Bombay, but they were not much used in the Maratha country as they were generally not considered equivalent to Mughal coins. The Company's Ambassador, Henry Oxinden, who attended the coronation of Shivaji at Raigad in 1674, mentions in his narrative that when Shivaji was requested to use the Company's coins along with those minted in his dominion, he refused to do so. His reply was that he neither forbade any coin from circulation in his dominion, nor forced his subjects to take a particular coin whereby they might be losers. He stated that 'if our [English] Coyne be of as fine an allay and as weighty as the Mogulls and other Princess, he will not prohibit its passing current' (Paranjape 1931: 374).

3. Copper coins: *Shivarai* or *chhatrapati, dhabbu, sajgani, tiruka, paisa, ruka, adka, jital* were the main copper coins current in the Maratha country for smaller transactions. Abbot had collected and examined nearly 25,000 such copper coins (*JBRAS*, Vol. XX: 123–24). Copper was consumed on a large scale in India for coinage. This metal was supplied by the English, as they considered it 'ready money'.

Below these copper coins bitter almonds and shells, called *cowries*, were used for small transactions, in Mughal areas more than in Shivaji's territories. However, Tavernier maintains that as they were current in the territory of Bijapur, we can take it for granted that they must be current in Shivaji's territories as well (Tavernier 1925: 29–30).

Eighteenth Century

The eighteenth century witnessed considerable changes in the currency system of the Marathas, mainly due to the growing demand for ready money to meet the expansion of the Maratha territories in the north and south. We have already noted the increase in the number of mint-houses under the later Maratha rulers. Another noteworthy feature of this period is the remarkable rise in silver and copper currency as compared to the previous century. *Hons* and *mohurs* are now rarely mentioned in our records, but we find innumerable references to different types of silver rupees and copper coins being minted and circulated during this century.

It is true that the circulation of gold coins, namely, *hons mohurs* and *putali*, was limited in the eighteenth century, but they were not altogether discontinued or withdrawn from the market. Our records mention the names of such *hons* as Ellori, Hyderi, Dharwadi, Sangiri, Vyankatpathi, Ekkeri, Durgi, Nagarpattani, Savanuri, Achyutrai, Plheghati, Sabdan Ali, Harpanhalli, Mahamadshahi, and so on, which were struck mainly in Karnataka. These *hons* were generally equivalent to Rs 3½ or 3¾ (Bhave 1976: 404; Chapekar 1937: 130).

Mohur was another gold coin that was in circulation from the seventeenth century onwards. A document of the year 1771–76 mentions a few *mohurs* with their exchange rates in rupees. The Delhi *shikka mohur* was exchanged at Rs 10-10-0, and Surati, Aurangabad, Banarasi, Kora Jahanabad, Machhli Bandar, Patani, Lahuri, Bhuranpuri *mohurs* were exchanged at Rs 13-12-0. A document of 1724–25 gives the conversion of different types of *mohurs* into rupees; the Aurangshahi Bahadurshahi *mohur*, for example, fetched Rs 12 (*SRPD*, Vol. VIII: 238–39; Parasnis 1900: 133fn). We also find *mohurs* bearing such names as Puneri, Ahmadabadi, Sheteshahi, Talegavi, Ahmadshahi, etc. (Bhave 1976: 404). However, we rarely come across the other gold coin *putali*, whose exchange value in 1774–75 was Rs 17.[4]

Silver Coins

The rupee was the most popular and widely circulated silver currency in the eighteenth century as compared to the seventeenth. There was a large variety of rupees with different exchange values which were used for various private and public transactions. They were: Rahimatpuri, Malkapuri, Chandvadi, Mirji Arcot, Chinchavadi, Hukkeri, Bagalkoti, Gajapuri, Talegapvi, Bhadochi, Surati, Panhali, Chatarsingi, Neelkandi, Saroli, Bahuti, Arcot-Ganjikot, Arcot-Phulcheri, Daulatabadi, Belapur, Badodi, Bhatvadi, Etav, Bavdi, Panali, Ankushi, Ekbanduki, Trishuli, Pharsi, Nagache, Turyache, Panchmela, Meete, Potechal, Vasaichal, Kalyanchal, Wai *sikka*, Hali *sikka*, Kasi *sikka*, Sipri *sikka*, Shahu *sikka*, Dehli *sikka*, Atiche, Bhunde, Alamgiri, Malharshahi, Muhammadshahi, Peth chalani, Bazaar *chalani*, Konkan *chalani*, Sarkar *chalani*, Dane *chalani*, Pune *chalani*, Hapis *chalani*, and so on (Chapekar 1937: 27, 33; Mahajan 1989: Appendix, 190–91). It is quite obvious from the above list that most of the rupee coins were known by the names of the places where they were struck.

The variety of silver rupees was mainly due to their acceptance in different parts of the region. It was therefore necessary to get the currency changed into one which was current in that market. This job of changing rupees was mainly done by the *sarafs* a goldsmith, or a *shroff*, a money-changer. The *batta* or commission charged by the *saraf* for changing Rahimatpuri into Chandavadi (AD 1798) was 4 annas per rupee, in addition to the government charge of 5 per cent. A person had to pay, for changing Rs 12-8-0 Rahimatpuri into Chandvadi, as that was the only coin acceptable into the royal treasury, as much as Rs 3-2-0 as the charges. Thus, of the Rahimatpuri Rs 12-8-0, the person could get Chandvadi Rs 8-14-6 only. Similarly, for changing Rs 50 Chandvadi into Malakapuri, a person had to pay 25 per cent *batta*. While making a purchase in the market, the customer had to pay at the rate current for his coin.[5] We therefore find such types of rupees as Dane (grain market) *chalani*, Peth *chalani*, Bazaar *chalani*, etc., mentioned in our records. 'Potechal' or 'Turechal' rupees were standard coins acceptable to the government. Kalyan *chal*, Pune *chal*, Vasai *chal* were rupees which were acceptable in those respective markets. The Arcot rupee, it seems, was quite current in Pandharpur, the centre of the cult of Vithoba or of the *varkaris* (devotees of Vithoba who visited Pandharpur at least twice a year), as it was required for feeding thousands of people. The Ankushi rupee bore the symbol of *ankush* (the weapon of elephant driver); the Farsi rupee, the symbol of an axe.

Coins of smaller denominations were *paisa*, *pavali*, *adheli*, two *annas*, one *anna*, etc., most of which were of copper, but *pavali* (¼ rupee) and *adheli* (½ rupee) were of silver (Chapekar 1937: 26–28).

Banking
Sahukars
The role of *sahukars* or *savkars* in the economic and political life of seventeenth and eighteenth-century Maharashtra deserve some special consideration. The term *sahukar* is used in Marathi documents

in the earlier period as merchant capitalist, but later on it denoted the moneylender, banker and, in a very limited sense, trader or entrepreneur. For instance, *Ajnapatra* (Royal Edict), a contemporary treatise on the polity of Shivaji's times, says:

> Sahukars (merchants) are the ornaments of the kingdom and the glory of the king. They are the cause of the prosperity of the kingdom. All kinds of goods which are not available, came into the kingdom. That kingdom becomes rich. In times of difficulties whatever money is necessary is available on credit. (Puntambekar 1929: 31)

The author of this *Ajnapatra*, Ramachandrapant Amatya, while writing on the 'commercial policy' of Shivaji, makes this observation particularly with reference to foreign merchants like the Portuguese, the Dutch, the Danes, the French and the English, and hardly to the *sahukars* under the Maratha rule, who were essentially moneylenders or bankers.

In the seventeenth century there were no organized banking institutions doing regular banking business, that is, accepting deposits and advancing loans, and these jobs were mainly done by the indigenous bankers, namely the *shets*, the *mahajans* (officers of the market), the *deshmukhs* and the *deshpandes* (officers of the village communities), and also by some brahmans (Kulkarni 1969: 252).

However, in the eighteenth century, perhaps because of the growing political activities of the Marathas, a new class of *sahukars*, mainly brahmans, emerged under the patronage of the Peshwas, which dominated the political and economic life of the Maratha country for several decades. Among the major banking houses, mention may be made of Tulshibagwale, Chiplunkar and Khasgiwale of Pune; Biwalkar of Kalyan; Dixit-Patwardhan of Nasik; and Vaidya of Wai (Satara). Bramhendra Swami Dhavadshikar (Satara district) – a saintly person – and some *gosavis* in charge of monasteries also advanced large sums to the Maratha kings, queens, Peshwas and numerous *sardars*. The records or account-books of these *sahukars* are available, and if properly researched, one would get a better and more authentic picture of the socio-economic and political history of eighteenth-century Maharashtra.

Besides their regular business of moneylending to private persons, they advanced money on a large scale to the Peshwas and other dignitaries for their personal expenditure for various religious, social, and family functions. They supplied the money needed for military expeditions in various parts of the country, to the Maratha chiefs including the Peshwas.[6]

Banking Functions
Loans

Advancing money to needy persons on certain terms, such as rate of interest, time and mode of payment, was the main function of banking. Private persons borrowed money from the moneylender for various purposes, such as subsistence, performance of various family functions like marriage, religious and social activities, defraying the expenses of litigation, paying ransom, and very rarely for commercial purposes.

During periods of distress, famine, drought and similar unforeseen calamities, people either left their houses and migrated to some other place in search of jobs, or remained at home and borrowed money at exorbitant rates and hard conditions for their bare maintenance. Whenever an advance was taken on condition of returning it after harvest time, it may be presumed that the loan was taken for subsistence and usually in kind. Usually such transactions were made within the village, but when a deal was made with an outsider, the recovery was made with vigour (Rajwade 1915, letters 15, 19).

Watan being the most important institution, determining the status of the person in the village, the watandars fought strongly to preserve it perpetually in their families. We find the village and pargana watandars like deshmukhs, deshpandes, kulkarnis and others borrowing heavily, sometimes at ehorbitant rates, from the local moneylenders for this purpose (Sardesai 1938, letter no. 48).

Sometimes loans were taken to pay a ransom. One Siddi Khan raided Rajapur in south Konkan and carried away some members of a Kunbi family. The Kunbi agreed to pay Rs 210 to the Khan for getting his sons released. For this he had to request a shenvi (broker) to stand as security for him, and the borrowed money from a moneylender for a short term by paying him some additional money. Similarly, a Maratha sardar, Bajaji Naik Nimbalkar of Phaltan, who was suspected as an ally of Shivaji by the Bijapur kingdom and therefore arrested, was released when he pleaded his innocence and agreed to pay a ransom of 60,000 hons, which he borrowed from two moneylenders (Kulkarni 1969: 253–54).

Money and Banking under the Marathas

The Peshwas seem to have been the principal borrowers from the *sahukars* of Pune. Large loans were mostly for unproductive purposes and often remained unpaid in the stipulated time. The ledger-books of most of the *sahukars*, some of them either officers or relatives of the Peshwas, show large sums borrowed for marriages, giving presents, feeding brahmans, religious and social functions, annual allowances, temples, festivals, pilgrimages and several other things in which their families or relations were involved.[7] Sometimes money was spent on superstitions. For instance, the brahmans of Pandharpur reported that the *kamavisdar*, the inauspicious touch of a lizard, to the body of God Vithoba could be propitiated only by performing certain ceremonies and feeding a thousand brahmans. A sum of Rs 400 was borrowed for this ceremony (*SRPD*, Vol. VIII: 255).

The Peshwas being brahman by caste, enjoyed a privileged position in the society, which brought them many social, political and monetary advantages. One peculiar institution called *ramana* was developed by the Peshwas through which distribution of *dakshina* – money rewards – to brahmans in the month of *Shravan* was organized on a large scale; for this the royal treasury was depleted and to fill it, and even for making payments to the civil and military servants, money was borrowed from the *sahukars*. In 1796–97, Rs 245,990 were distributed as *dakshina* among 3,851 brahmans at various gates of the city, including the royal palace. The next year (1797–98), the amount became almost double, that is, Rs 441,066, and 54,413 brahmans assembled in Pune to receive it. A deity was worshipped for getting more rains for nearly 121 days by performing various ceremonies and feeding brahmans, which involved an expenditure of Rs 10,117 in 1795–96 (*SRPD*, Vol. V: 227–35, 247–51).

Earlier, the Peshwas used to raise money for financing their military expeditions by contracting loans, on the terms of the *sahukars*, heads of monasteries and many other persons. For instance, an expedition against the Nawab of Savnur (Karnataka), undertaken in 1753, shows an expenditure of Rs 214,776 in the ledger-book of Tulshibagwale. The *Diaries of the Peshwas* have recorded the public debts incurred by them for administrative and military purposes. A loan of Rs 332,631 was taken from a *sahukar* named Raste in 1763–64, and Rs 100,000 and Rs 200,000 from other *sahukars* in 1767–68. A document gives a list of forty *sahukars* from whom the Peshwa received loans in cash or cloth to the tune of Rs 1,622,292-15-0 in the year 1763–

64 (Chapekar 1937: 81–82; *SRPD*, Vol. VII: 306–11). A document of this year gives a long list of *sahukars*, the amounts borrowed by Peshwa Balaji Bajirao from them at varying rates of interest, that run into a crore and a half of public debt during 1740–61. This was a period full of military activities, leading to the third battle of Panipat (*SRPD*, Vol. II: 170–80). Peshwa Bajirao I, who had borrowed from many people, wrote to his principal creditor Brahmendra Swami, that his forehead was practically worn out by rubbing it at the feet of his creditors.[8]

Besides the Peshwas, many *sardars* also borrowed money to fulfil their military assignments. The money so raised was called *nalbandi*. *Nal* literary means 'a horseshoe', and *nalbandi* means horseshoe-money, or money raised for the equipment of cavalry for the field, or an advance made to a military captain whose troop was sent on military service. The *vaidya sahukars* paid Rs 1,600 to a servant of Raghuji Bhonsale, Senasahed Subha of Nagpur for *nalbandi* in 1734. There are several references to the advances made by the *vaidyas* to Raghuji Bhonsale for military purposes. For instance, he received Rs 35,000 from the *vaidya* in 1744 to obtain the release of Chandasaheb of Trichinapally from French custody.[9]

State Loans

We hardly get adequate information about state loans, that is, money advanced to cultivators and traders for encouragement or promotion of their respective vocations, both in the seventeenth and eighteenth centuries in Maharashtra. We find, however, a circular letter of Shivaji addressed to the *subhedar* of Prabhavali in Konkan, giving us details of Shivaji's plans of granting interest-free *tagai* loans to cultivators for purchasing the equipment necessary for agricultural operations, or for their maintenance during the period of distress. The money thus advanced was to be recovered in easy instalments according to the convenience of the cultivator, and under no circumstances was any amount in excess over the principal advanced to be exacted (BISM, *SCS*, Vol. IX, letter 55, 5 September 1676).

The practice of *tagai* loans both in cash and kind continued in the eighteenth century. We find a *sanad* being issued by Peshwa Balaji Bajirao to a *kamavisdar* in 1751–52 to grant all sorts of concessions to cultivators affected by calamities. The letter says:

It has been represented that the Pargana has been reduced to poverty, therefore if some *tagai* advances can be made to the ryots, improvment might be expected. You are, therefore, directed to make advances to the extent of two–three thousand rupees as may be necessary with a view to securing the best cultivation. The advances to be recovered next year in due time. (*SRPD*, Vol. III: 238, letter 382)

Modus Operandi

How the bankers conducted monetary transactions under Maratha rule, deserves some consideration.

1. *Karja Rokha*: When the terms of the loan were agreed to by both parties, namely, by the *dhanko*, the creditor, and *rinko*, the debtor, a document called *karja rokha*, also referred to as *karja katba*, *kharja khat* or *kharja patra*, was prepared and signed by both parties and witnesses. The *karja rokha* mentioned the necessary details such as the names of creditor and debtor, the purpose of loan, the amount of loan or principal, the rate of interest, the mode of payment and the period of return, and the penalties if the principal with interest was not returned within the stipulated time as mentioned in the agreement. Sometimes the moneylender advanced money to the debtor not directly but through a surety who assured him of the payment of money with interest. The name of such a surety was specifically mentioned in the *karja rokha*. The creditor often insisted on surety, particularly the pledging of some immovable property. The Naik Nimbalkar of Phaltan was in immediate need of Rs 2,000, for which he agreed to pledge his elephant, whose market value according to him was Rs 9,000, but according to others, not more than Rs 7,000. In the agreement it was made clear if the payment was not made within three months including interest, the mortgaged property would be confiscated. Nimbalkar also agreed to keep a servant who would look after feeding the elephant at his cost (*Vaidya*, Vol. III, 1 March 1741: 8).

No document was complete without the signatures of witnesses, whose numbers varied from two to nine or even more, depending upon the nature of the property involved in the deed. If it was an ordinary loan, generally the village officers, namely, the *patil* and the *kulkarni* or some permanent resident of the village concerned, acted as witness. But when a *miras in'am* was pledged, along with the perquisites attached to it, the number of witnesses was quite large. The *miras* land being a hereditary holding and not that of an individual, it was necessary to give notice to such other persons in the village who may have had any interest in the transactions. The debtor had to mention specifically in the document that he had contracted and signed the deed on his own account and willingly without any restraint (Kulkarni 1969: 252–53).

The format of the *karja rokha* did not undergo any major changes in the eighteenth century. A document of 1737, for instance, mentions the name of *dhanko* (creditor), followed by that of *rinko* (debtor), purpose of the loan, amount in figures and words, rate of interest, the period of repayment of both principal and interest, surety of the Peshwa and another person – all the details required for a legal deed (*Vaidya*, Vol. I: 35–36, 36–37).

Interest

During the period under review, loans were generally advanced for a short period, of six months to one year, or for an even shorter period. This was particularly so when a loan in cash or kind was made to an agriculturist for his maintenance and agricultural operations. In such cases, the principal with interest was often collected immediately after the harvest. It was perhaps due to this practice of short-term advances that the rate of interest was usually mentioned as per month per hundred. When the money was borrowed for purposes of litigation or for military expeditions, which were very common in the eighteenth century, the time limit for repayment was often longer.

In the seventeenth century the normal rate of interest on secured loans was 15 per cent per annum, but in the case of unsecured loans the rates went up to 60 per cent per annum. Again, the rates charged from brahmans were less than those of the other communities (BISM, *SCS*, Vol. IV, Letter 722, 23 February 1655).

The normal rates of interest in medieval Maharashtra were higher than those of ancient times. Though we do not find records showing different rates being charged to different classes, occasionally we come across a distinction being made on the basis of the status of the debtor. The purpose was to consider the solvency of the debtor rather than his position in society.

The rate of interest depended upon the nature of the loan and the economic position of the debtor concerned. We find the rate of interest rising to 37½ per cent per annum in one case and as much as 60 per cent per annum in another case (Kulkarni 1969: 255).

Sometimes a loan is not taken for any fixed period. In such cases, the rate of interest for the first month seems to have been higher than for the subsequent months, probably with a view to inducing the debtor to keep the loan for a longer period. It is quite likely that the creditor, in the absence of good avenues of investment, might have induced a solvent party to keep the loan for a longer period even at a lower rate (*MIS*, Vol. XX, No. 15). Loans in kind were advanced to the cultivators for a minimum period of six months on the condition that they should repay the amount in double. Sometimes the creditor received a favour when the loan was returned in kind. A *kamavisdar* was ordered that the creditor *vaidya* should get corn towards the payment of his debt at a rate one *seer* cheaper than the Satara rate.

If a debtor failed to repay his debt as per the agreement within the stipulated time, he was severely penalized and was often made to pay double the original amount. The repayment of debt was considered as a moral duty and failure to do so was equated with the sin of killing a cow, the murder of a brahman at Varanasi, or having illicit relations with one's own mother (*Peshwa Daftar*, Vol. XXXI, letter 48).

This general picture regarding the rates of interest, its mode of payment and the consequences of non-payment did not change much in the eighteenth century. The only difference is that we get voluminous source material through the ledger-books of *sahukars* mentioned earlier.

The normal rate of interest, which was known as *shirasta* or as per practice, was one rupee and two *annas* per month per hundred, that is, 13½ per cent per annum. For instance, Bajirao I had borrowed Rs 50,000 from the *vaidya* at this rate in 1740 (*Vaidya*, Vol. II: 16–17).

The rates are generally mentioned in rupees per month per hundred, like *ekotra* (Re 1), *duhotra* (Rs 2), *adichotra* (Rs 2½), *barotra* (Rs 12), and so on. Sometimes some concession was given in the interest. Whether the concession in interest was given or not was mentioned in the *karja rokha* itself, as *vaja soot* (minus deduction) or *veena soot* (without deduction). It seems that 1/35th part of the interest was also deducted from the total and the rest was mentioned in the deed itself (*Vaidya*, Vol. I, letters 35, 38, 56; *SRPD*, Vol. II: 168–69). Sometimes the *sahukar* charged a premium or bonus above the stipulated interest, called *manoti*. For instance, on a debt of Rs 2,000, *manoti* at the rate of Rs 2 per hundred was charged (Chapekar 1937:

123). Sometimes the interest became more than three times the principal (*Vaidya*, Vol. V: 49, letter 45).

Recovery

Recovery of loan was a matter of much difficulty for the *sahukars*, particularly of loans advanced to the royal families, Peshwas, *sardars* and other officials. As *watan* land was most dear to the officers, the *sahukars* demanded the custody of a part of the *watan* land along with the perquisites attached to it. When *miras* land was pledged for a loan and the loan was not repaid on time, there was always the threat of appropriation of the *miras* (Kulkarni 1969: 256–57).

In the eighteenth century, as the volume of loans increased, debtors began to induce the *sahukars* by assigning the collection of revenues of some *mahals*, villages, etc., towards the repayment of loans. In the family archives of the *vaidyas*, we come across several such revenue assignments made to the *vaidyas* from time to time for recovery (*Vaidya*, Vol. I, letter nos. 9, 12, 16, 17, 19, 25, 31, 42, 66).

The Maratha government of the eighteenth century imposed a levy called *karja pati*, a cess for the liquidation of debts. This *karja pati* was collected mainly from the northern powers who were under Maratha control, like the Rohillas of Bhopal, who were under the Holkars between 1754 and 1760–61.

A document of the year 1754–55 mentions that the amount of *karja pati* to be levied from Amarshing Raje and Jagatraj Raje of Bundele was fixed at Rs 6¼ lacs and 5 lacs respectively for the year 1754–55. It was decided to levy *karja pati* on *kamavisdars*, *karkuns*, *darakdars* and other officers enjoying land assignments for their remuneration, village officers, and others of Gujarath, Khandesh and other places.

Sometimes the contribution by officers was equal to their annual income. The *zamindars* sometimes collected their share from the people under their jurisdiction. However, when some *zamindars* imposed the *karja pati* on the *mahars* serving in the forts, they represented their case to the government and got exemption from *karja patti* (*SRPD*, Vol. III: 341–52). In the year 1776–77, *karja pati* was levied on bankers, traders and gentlemen of independent means. Even the Bhopes, worshippers of the goddess of Saptashringa, were obliged to contribute an amount equal to their one year's gain towards *karja pati* in 1779–80. If they failed to do so, it was ordered that their income for one year should be confiscated and remitted to the treasury (*SRPD*, Vol. VI: 301–03).

If the debtor, even after several requests, refused to repay the loan, the *sahukars* resorted to the ultimate weapon, that is, fasting at the gates of the debtor. This is called *dharane* and the urging for payment is called *tegada* in our records. Brahmans were hired for the fast. The fasting at the debtor's residence was called *kshetra* and the brahmans were counted for getting the necessary payment for each *kshetra*. When a brahman fasted at the gate it was embarrassing for the debtor to dine, and so he often persuaded the brahmans to give up the fast and eat with him. Sometimes, with a view to humiliating brahman debtors, people of other castes were hired for the *dharane*. Sometimes the *sahukar* himself with his entire family performed *dharane*.[10]

Hundi

Hundi is a bill of exchange; when it is official it is called *varat* (*barat*); all other types of *hundis* are private in nature. During the period of Maratha rule, most of the banking functions were carried out through *hundis*.

Varat means an order upon a treasury to pay. Shivaji used this instrument for making payments to his officials. Sabhasad, the contemporary chronicler of Shivaji, writes that to the *sarnobat* (military commander), the *majumdars*, the *karkuns* and members of his personal staff, salary was paid by orders on the various treasuries of the state (Joshi 1929: 24). However, the English factors, it seems, were not very happy with the payments made by *varats* for the purchase of their goods by Shivaji. From the correspondence it appears that it was not easy to collect the money due on *varat* on a treasury, and that if and when paid, the payment might be spread over two to three years. They preferred, therefore, payment in silver coins to *varat*, which, according them, was 'uncertain money'. This system created a class of brokers who charged a commission, called *hundanaval*, for realizing the money mentioned in the *varat* (Paranjape 1931: 114, 99, 48).

In the eighteenth century, Pune was a big centre for exchange of all types of *hundis*, and customers often preferred *hundis* to the banking houses of Pune. Tulshibagwale, Chiplunkar, Dixit-Patwardhan and Khasgiwale were some of the leading *sahukars* who were connected with other parts of the country dealing with the operations of *hundis*. Sometimes the term *hundi chitti* or simply *chitti* (that is, note for *hundi*) is used to indicate the regular *hundi*. For instance, a document mentions that the Holkars of Indore issued a *chitti* to the firm of a person called Kasikar (Chapekar 1937: 127). There are various types of *hundis,* such as *shahjog hundi,* which means a bearer cheque, that is, the person who holds the *hundi,* and *dhanijog hundi,* which means a *hundi* which mentions the name of the person who purchases it in the name of some other person and the name of the person who is supposed to pay the amount mentioned therein. It is, in other words, a *darshani hundi,* which is payable at sight, or in modern terminology, a demand draft. *Pedh hundi* means a duplicate *hundi* issued in the event of loss of the original *hundi.* There is one more type of *hundi* called *lahani hundi* or *hundiche lahane.* It means that a person issuing a *hundi* to some other person with whom he has no credit, but with a view to getting his *hundi* honoured, sends either cash or a *hundi* from his professional friend so that 'his' *hundi* is honoured. *Bhalavan hundi* means an assurance from the *sahukar* that he will pay the amount in a particular type of currency (Chapekar 1937: 138, 135–39). *Jaga hundi* means a *hundi* from a particular place.[68]

The major centres at which the *hundis* were issued or honoured are mentioned in our records. Among them, besides Pune, Shrirangpattan, Bundelkhand, Mumbai, Paithan, Satara, Kashi, Konkan, Aurangabad, and several other places are found frequently mentioned. These *hundis* were sent to different places through an emissary called *jasud* who was paid travelling expenses called *masala,* which were recovered by the *sahukar* from the addressee (Chapekar 1937: 134–38). Pune being the chief and perhaps more reliable centre for *hundi* transactions, people sometimes insisted that the payment be made in Pune only. For in stance, the agent of *vaidya* writes that out of the two *hundis* brought from Nagpur, the person concerned was paid one *hundi* in Pune, but in spite of much persuasion, he insisted that he would receive the second *hundi* also from a Pune banker (*Vaidya,* Vol. II, No. 59: 65–66, in the year 1740).

The commission charged for *hundis* by the *sahukars* was called *hundanaval* and its rates varied between 1 and 3 per cent or even more. Nominal charges were collected for small amounts. *Dhanijog hundi* rates were higher than for other types of *hundis.* For instance, a *sahukar* charged Rs 200 extra for a *hundi* of Rs 500 (*Vaidya,* Vol. IV, No. 20: 15, in the year 1744). When a *hundi* was accepted, a commission called *sakarai* was taken while paying cash, and even when he rejected the *hundi*, he charged a fee called *nakarai*.

The *vaidya sahukars* who were the financers of the Bhonsales of Nagpur and other Maratha chiefs like the Pant-Sachiv of Bhor, Pratinidhi of Aundha, Patwardhan of Sangli, Miraj and others, amassed large fortunes from moneylending. They used to keep this money safe in secret parts of their mansion at Wai in metal pots and big vessels of copper, and in places like *deoghar* (room for family deities), kitchen, middle room, and even bathroom (*Vaidya*, Vol. V, No. 6: 4–5, in the year 1750).

From this brief résumé of money and banking under the Maratha rule, it can be said that most of the monetary transactions of the *sahukars* were for unproductive purposes and we rarely come across documents sanctioning even petty amounts for commercial purposes.

Notes

[1] Ranade (1963: 218). Ranade confuses Rajgad with Raigad, the fort capitals of Shivaji. Shivaji shifted to Raigad only after his escape from Agra in 1666. Secondly, Ranade's statement is based on two observations of Grant Duff: '(He) first assumed the title Raja and struck coins in his name' (p. 156) and 'Shivaji who had long back struck coins and styled himself Raja and Maharaja' (p. 204). S.M. Edwardes, the editor of the sixth edition of *A History of the Maharattas*, Oxford University Press, 1921, has challenged this view in his footnote on p. 156.

[2] This series in nine volumes was prepared by G.C. Vad with the help of D.B. Parasnis, B.P. Joshi and K.B. Marathe, under the auspices of the Deccan Vernacular Translation Society, Pune, 'printed and published with the permission of Government of Bombay' between 1901 and 1911. Justice Ranade had initiated this series, but the government did not allow the Society to publish his introduction to the *Peshwa Diaries*. It was read before the Bombay Branch of Royal Asiatic Society in June 1900 and later published separately.

[3] Kulkarni (1979: 233–35). For more details, see also Khare (1933) and Maheswari and Wiggins (1989).

[4] *SRPD*, Vol. VII: 291. For the exchange values of the coins see Mahajan (1989: Appendix I and II, 186–89).

[5] Chapekar (1937: 139). *Batta* means difference or rate of exchange. It was operated in two ways. *Baherbatta*—here the difference of value is added, whereas in *antabatta* it is deducted. *Bajarbatta* means the rate of exchange at which various coins are current in the market with reference to a standard currency.

[6] For a detailed account of the *sahukar* families, see the following:

(a) Chapekar (1937: 2–10).

(b)Parasnis (1900).

(c) Vaidya, S.L. (ed.), *Selections from Vaidya Daftar*, in five volumes, covering a period from 1641 to 1755 and published between 1944–51 from Pune. This voluminous published and unpublished record, still unexplored, deserves much attention from scholars interested in the economic history of the eighteenth century. Jadunath Sarkar, while reviewing the fifth volume of *Vaidya Daftar*, writes, 'These Brahmans were not medicine men (*vaidya*) but bankers and advisers to Chhatrapati Shahu, the Peshwa. . . . Hence they not only give precise information on the indigenous banking of South India, but also throw unexpected light of a purely political character. . . . Bengal is specially interested in the report of a *vaidya* agent who visited Murshidabad and Siraj-ud-daula's Court two months before the battle of Plassey' ('A Noble Historic Family', *Modern Review*, July 1951).

(d) Dixit Patwardhan came to Pune from Nasik in Bajirao's times. A number of unpublished account-books of the family are deposited in the *Bharat Itihas Samshodhak Mandal*, Pune. For details see, Kulkarni (1973).

[7] Chapekar (1937): A number of documents are cited in this respect in his book; see pp. 46–60 of the Introduction for details, and the relevant documents cited therein.

[8] Parasnis (1900, Letter No. 32 of 1734: 41). Grant Duff translated this letter thus: ' I have fallen into that hell of being beset by creditors and to pacify soucars and sillidars, I am falling at their feet till I have rubbed the skin from my forehead' (Vol. I: p. 390 fn).

[9] *Vaidya Daftar*, Vol. II, p. 3, for *Nalbandi* and p. 28 for Raghuji Bhonsale. See also Sardesai (1953: 270).

[10] Chapekar (1937: 123, 126, 127, 130–31). *Dharane* literally means dogged sitting in restraint at the door of a debtor by the creditor or his agent to enforce the payment of his dues, and *tagada* means urging for payment.

References

Bhave, V.K., 1935, *Peshwekalin Maharashtra*, Pune; reprint Delhi: ICHR, 1976.

Central Records Office, Hyedrabad Govt., *Selected Waqai of the Deccan* (AD 1660–71).

Chapekar, N.G. (ed.), 1937, *Peshwaichya Sawalit*, Pune: BISM.

Edwardes, S.M., 1902, *The Rise of Bombay: A Retrospect*, Bombay.

Edwardes, S.M. (ed.), 1921, A *History of the Marathas*, Oxford University Press.

Hodivala, S.H., 1928, *Historical Studies in Mughal Numismatics*, Calcutta.

Joshi, S.N. (ed.), 1929, *Sabhasad: Shivaa Chhatrapati Chaitra*, Pune: Chitrashala Press.

Khare, G.H., 1933, *Mandalatil Nani* (Marathi), Pune: BISM.

Kulkarni, A.R., 1969, *Maharashtra in the Age of Shivaji*, Pune: Deshmukh Prakashan.

Kulkarni, A.R., 1997, *Shivakalin Maharashtra* (Marathi), Pune: Rajhansa Prakashan.

———, 2000, *Shivajike Samayka Maharashtra* (Hindi), Delhi: Grantha Shilpi.

Kulkarni, G.T., 1973, 'Banking in the 18th Century: A Case Study of the Poona

Bankers', *Artha Vijnana*, Vol. XIV, No. II, Gokhale Institute of Politics and Economics, Pune, June.

Mahajan, T.T., 1989, *Industry, Trade and Commerce during the Peshwa Period*, Jaipur: Pointer Publishers.

Maheswari, K.K and Kenneth W. Higgins, 1989, *Maratha Mints and Coinage*, Nasik: Indian Institute of Research in Numismatic Studies.

Paranjape, B.G. (ed.), 1931, *English Records on Shivaji (1659–1682)*, No. 486 dated 13 June 1674, Part I, Pune: BISM).

Parasnis, D.B., 1900, *Brahmendra Swami Dhabadshikar*, Bombay: Babaji Sakharam.

Puntamabekar, S.V., 1929, *A Royal Edict* (Translation of *Ajnapatra* in Marathi), Madras; reprinted from the *Journal of Indian History*, Vol. VIII, Parts I and II.

Rajwade, V.K., (ed.), 1915, *Marathyanchya Itihasachi Sadhane (MIS)*, Vol. XX, Dhule.

Ranade, M.G, 1963., 'Currencies and Mints under Maratha Rule', in *Rise of the Maratha Power and Gleanings from Maratha Chronicles*, Bombay: Bombay University.

Sardesai, G.S. (ed.), 1938, *Selections from Peshwa Daftar (PD)*, Vol. XXXI, Poona.

Sardesai, G.S., 1953, *New History of the Marathas*, Mumbai: Phoenix.

Sarkar, Jadunath, 1951, 'A Noble Historic Family', *Modern Review*, July.

Selections from the Satara Rajas and the Peshwa Diaries, referred to as *SRPD*.

Tavernier, J.B., 1925, *Travels in India*, London: Oxford University Press.

Vaidya, S.L. (ed.), 1944–51, *Selections from Vaidya Daftar*, 5 vols, Pune.

Indigenous Banking and Commission Agency in India's Colonial Economy

Rajat Kanta Ray

The rise of an organized European-dominated corporate sector in the Indian economy in course of the nineteenth century created an unprecedented division of the economic space between *le blanc et le noir*. The pre-existing indigenous system of trade and finance was subordinated to western banks and corporations, and out of this process the subordinated Indian part of the commercial system emerged in a new form, and was redefined as the bazaar. The corporate sector, almost entirely white in the high noon of imperialism, seemingly had in this obscure dark under-space, its incomprehensible other. But in fact, both the corporate sector and the bazaar represented interlocked forms of capital seeking to penetrate a chronically deficit, monsoon-driven agricultural economy in which there was a hiatus between the fixed system of rural, exploitative credit and the forms of mobile credit represented by banks and corporations, and by *shroffs* and *arhatiyas*.[1]

The process of colonial expansion earlier in the nineteenth century had brought about large demonetizations and contractions of credit and consumption. The Maratha territories of Poona and Nagpur after the annexation of 1818, the Kaveri valley after the dispersal of the Maratha court of Thanjavur in 1855, and the fertile realm of Awadh after its occupation by the British in 1856, all exhibited clear evidence of contraction in coinage, aristocratic–military consumption, artisan manufacturers and commercial credit. In the second half of the nineteenth century, the better means of communications, especially railways and telegraph, brought about the beginnings of a reintegration of India's domestic commercial economy. At the turn of the twentieth century, the process gathered momentum and the integrative commercial devices called *hundi* and *arhat* quickened the financial operations of the bazaar. These devices had existed in the old Indian

118

economy. For carrying *hundis* Indian bankers had their own special couriers since they distrusted the European post, and it was believed that their couriers conveyed information long in advance of the government mail (Cooke 1863: 21). The railways, cables and the telegraph changed all that, and the space in which indigenous bankers and commission agents operated was absorbed as a subordinate sphere in the wider imperial economy of the late nineteenth century (Hoey 1880: 63).

In the re-drawn economic space, the upper sphere belonged to a small set of exchange banks and European managing agencies operating on a high profit margin, and the lower sphere to a mass of 'native' bankers and commission agents conducting a large volume of small transactions at a low profit margin. A US consular official advising American businessmen on prospects of business with India told them, 'The main thing to be considered about Indian trade is that with most articles purchased by the masses of people it is not a question of how good but how cheap.' He distinguished this mass market from a small market for high-class goods catering to something like one million people whose standard of living was substantially higher – the European population of merchants, missionaries, civil administrators, and officers and soldiers of the British army, the Indian princes, large landowners and merchants, the Parsee community of Bombay and the Eurasian element – with western tastes. 'Such people are all patrons of department stores and shops where substantially the same qualities of goods are sold as in Europe and America.' These people made up an important though limited market for high-class goods, but their number was insignificant compared to the mass of the Indian population. The adviser put the American businessman's problem succinctly: 'to sell goods suitable not only for the comparatively small upper and middle classes, but goods cheap enough and simple enough to be within the reach of over 300,000,000 people who belonged to the poor and illiterate classes of society'. It was here that the shroffs and *arhatiyas* of towns and *mandis* and the *beoparis* and *mahajans* operating in the country stepped in. The consular official reflected:

> In doing business with the upper and middle classes it is possible to secure a rather wide margin of profit, but the sales must be comparatively small. In doing business with the great masses of the people the margin of profit must be extremely small; however, the

sales and collective profits may be enormous. (Baker 1915: 14–15; U.S. Department of Commerce, Special Consular Report No. 72)

In effect, there were two markets in India and the rates of money prevailing within these markets were hardly affected by one another. One was the western money market; the other was the bazaar. As a former finance secretary of India who worked after retirement as general manager of the P & O Banking Corporation said, in a talk at the Royal Society of Arts, the business of the shroff was to invest funds, whether his own or that deposited with him by other parties in *hundis*. 'As Banks do not compete with him for the purchase of traders' *hundis*, the *hundi* rate in the bazaar has little relation to the Bank rate and is determined by the shroffs themselves' (Gubbay 1928: 14).

European business ploughed the field which it had reserved for its oligopolistic operations and seldom bothered with the bazaar rate. The organ of European business in India, the *Capital*, reported every week: (1) the Bank of Bengal's bank rate, (2) the Bank of England's rate of interest, (3) council bills and telegraphic transfers, (4) specie shipments, (5) government paper, (6) share prices, and (7) exchange rates in London. These were the rates European business houses were concerned with. Its report on the money market did not include the bazaar rate or the *hundi* discount rate of the Presidency Banks of Bengal, Bombay and Madras (*Capital*, 6 November 1888, 6 July 1889). Those rates did not concern the Europeans. The unconscious assumption of separateness comes out in the *Capital*'s report on the wheat market in Bombay on 26 January 1901: 'The position of this article remains unchanged, the little speculation going on being wholly confined to the bazaar' (*Capital*, 31 January 1901). Evidently, European businessmen were dismissive of the bazaar. Only in extraordinary conditions, such as plague or famine, might they sit up and glance at the bustling world of native monetary operations around them. Thus, in the famine of 1901, when dullness appeared as 'the characteristic feature of our markets' and the scarcity of money had the effect of 'limiting trade operations', the *Capital* reported that the Bank of Bombay had raised its discount rate to 9 per cent, 'and money in the bazaar cannot be had under 10 to 12 per cent, partially owing to many of the shroffs and Marwaris having left the city' (*Capital*, 28 February 1901).

And yet enquiries in extraordinary times, such as the disruption of silver currency in the last years of the nineteenth century, might reveal that the rates in the bazaar might not be so contemptible after all. Henry Fowler, the Chairman of the Currency Committee, asked Allan Arthur, President of the Bengal Chamber of Commerce, on 7 June 1898: 'You have told us about the high bank rate. Has the rate been as high as the discount in the bazaar?'[2] Arthur immediately negated the unconscious assumption that the bazaar rate had been higher than the bank rate:

> No, my experience is that the rate of discount in the Calcutta bazaars has not been so high as the bank rate. During the recent period of stringency I know I had some bills to discount and I went and asked the rates of discounting them, and I was quoted in the bazaar 8 per cent. I was quoted by the Bank of Bengal 13½ per cent. I did not discount the bills but these were the quotations that were given to me.

The Fowler Committee's initial assumption that the bazaar rate would always be higher than the bank rate – an assumption not borne out when official reports on the bazaar rate began on a regular basis – arose from their confusing the moneylender's fixed-book credit rates with the mobile credit rates of the shroffs who discounted bills of exchange. The *Capital* expressed this prejudice in that very year in an article on 'The Indian Trader and His System of Commerce' (*Capital*, 28 April 1898). The 'Indian trader', in its perception, was typically a 'mahajun' who ran a business monopoly detrimental to the European and the *ryot* alike. By making an advance to the *ryots* for the purchase of bullocks, ploughs and seed grains, he got an iron grasp on their crops, always endeavouring to avoid paying out in money; 'and to further this purpose, every Rs 100 collected goes to purchase a bar of gold, and it would not be committing oneself to say that every mahajun's strong-room is verily a gold mine composed of gold bricks'. This, despite the Calcutta mint master's official report, as early as 1870, that hoarding of gold was a practice among the native chiefs and wealthy *zamindars*, but not of the wealthy traders:

> Such men employ their money to the utmost, and do their utmost also to keep up their credit by fostering the popular idea of buried wealth: whatever they hoard is only their working balance, and is in their peculiar stronghold, but their money is used truly well and

economically, and of late years from some parts of India largely in speculations. (Hyde 1870: 6)

The last remark by the mint master is an indication that by 1870, the business of the shroffs and *arhatiyas* was being extended from spot transactions to forward transactions with the help of the new communications. Needless to say, hoarding would have made it impossible for them to extend either type of transaction. The business of the Indian banker and commission agent was different from that of the proverbial moneylender.

The distinction between the two types of business was clearly spelt out by the Lieutenant-Governor of the northwestern provinces and Oudh in his evidence to the Fowler Committee in 1898. 'There are', he said, 'two [kinds] of loan transactions up country. There is the loan by the *bunneah* or village money lender, who deals with his own money alone, and there is the loan by the *mahajan* or banker, who deals with other people's money as well as his own.'[3] The moneylender operated with his own capital. The banker in the larger centres of commerce, on the other hand, was into credit-generating *hundi* operations and he thus dealt with other people's capital, mobilizing it for commercial rather than agricultural operations. The moneylender financed the cultivator by advancing him money for the purchase of seed, plough-cattle and ornaments, and got the money back in grain by hypothecating the crop. The banker did not enter into this type of petty commodity production. He financed trading operations between market towns and seaports, either by financing commission agents (*arhatiya*) who guaranteed long-distance deliveries or by acting as commission agents themselves. In this type of operation, the general credit of the country, the state of trade, export conditions, and the question whether credit was good or bad, figured importantly – considerations that did not enter into the moneylender's more restricted business (*Parliamentary Papers* 1898: 695–96, 698, 700). The moneylender's rates were necessarily much higher than the rates at which the banker discounted traders' *hundis*.

Banks and shroffs constituted distinct monetary circuits through which capital moved far and wide, but moneylenders were outside the orbit of these movements of money. The impetus behind the monetary movements derived from 'busy' season and 'slack' season, which were closely linked to the agricultural calendar. The

Treasurer of the Bank of Bengal told the Fowler Committee: 'There is always a great difference between the commercial demand for currency during the busy season and during the slack season because the moment the rainy season commences there is a great stoppage of trade'.[4] Accordingly, both bank and bazaar rates climbed in busy season and sank in slack season, but moneylenders' rates, which were fixed according to the credit of the individual borrower, did not go through such fluctuations. The distinction between these rates were specified by the Deputy Controller of Currency in northern India who reported, in 1922, that apart from the bank rate, there were three distinct rates in his circle: (1) as between shroff and shroff 5 to 9 per cent according to seasons, (2) as between shroffs and traders on demand promissory notes, ornaments, etc., 2 or 3 per cent above the bank rate, and (3) as between the village *bania* and the *zamindar* for small unsecured advances, 12–24 per cent (MacWatters 1922: 28). Of these rates, the bank rate, the inter-shroff loan rate (at 5–9 per cent, this was no higher than the usual bank rate) and the discount rate of traders' *hundis* by shroffs fluctuated from season to season, but the interest rate on loans by moneylenders to *zamindars* and *ryots* did not undergo such seasonal variations and usually ruled twice or thrice higher. The rates ruling in the bazaar were thus distinct from the bank rate on the one hand, and the moneylender's rate on the other.

The seasonal variations in the bazaar rates were linked to large movements of money from one end of the country to the other. As early as 1866, just before his credit was shaken in the busy month of April, the well-known speculator Premchund Roychund of Bombay raised big amounts of money on the Calcutta bazaar. 'I sold', he told the Bombay Bank Commission after his failure, which brought about a general crash in Bombay, 'three lakhs of my bills on Calcutta in half an hour in the bazaar and I could have sold twenty lakhs'.[5] This indicated the tentative beginnings of a process by which Bombay and Calcutta would emerge, after the connecting up of the two towns by the East Indian Railways and the Great Indian Peninsular Railways, as the nodal points of the integrated bazaar. The Marwadi Chamber of Commerce informed the Bombay Provincial Banking Enquiry Committee in 1930: 'Bombay and Calcutta are the two clearing houses of India. Delhi, though in a lesser degree, performs a similarly important function. In any town of any consequence in terms of trade and commerce, *hundis* on Bombay and Calcutta can be sold and purchased in an unlimited measure.'[6] Evidence collected by the United Provinces Banking Enquiry Committee[7] at the same time indicated that indigenous money markets in *mofussil* towns were linked to important money markets, such as Cawnpore, Calcutta, Bombay and Delhi, through two mechanisms: (1) through *arhatiyas* who had principals in important towns for whom they purchased grain, cotton, or other commodities, and from whom they ordered finished goods for sale in the *mofussil*, and (2) through correspondents or agents of indigenous bankers to whom they forwarded the *hundis* which they purchased on those towns or on whom they issued *hundis*.

As European banks began springing up in the Presidency towns and other inland centres of commerce in the high noon of imperialism following the Mutiny, the chief of Bank of Bombay expressed the hope at a directors' meeting on 7 March 1864: 'The vast busi-ness hitherto monopolized by the Shroffs and Soucars will, I think, ere long fall into the hands of the large banking establishments' (*Parliamentary Papers* 1869: 86, 269). This did not quite happen. The development of forward transactions (*vayade ka sauda*[8]) and the expansion of spot transactions (*hajar ka sauda*), enabled domestic bankers and commission agents to expand their *hundi* and *arhat* business along the lines of the railways and the telegraph, and to come to a mutually advantageous accommodation with the European banks and firms. The expansion of the indigenous banking business went on right through the First World War and the post-war years, until the great depression halted it. On the eve of the great depression, *hundi* rates in the Delhi bazaar were as low as 2¼ per cent in slack season and 6 per cent in busy season,[9] indicating a plenitude of cheap accommodation for wholesale merchants and commission agents. By the year 1920, the critical role of this credit in the functioning of India's domestic economy was so well appreciated that the Controller of Currency started quoting bazaar rates regularly, unlike the *Capital* of yesteryears.

His report of that year showed in a diagram 'the course of the various Bank rates in comparison with the average rates of accommodation in the bazaar'. The latter figures were obtained from Calcutta in 1920 and the rate shown was 'the average rate at which shroffs were prepared to discount traders' bills' (MacWatters 1921: 29). The report for 1921 cited bazaar rates from Bombay for the first time and from then on the Controller of Currency, and later on the Reserve Bank of

India (1935), regularly reported Calcutta and Bombay bazaar rates along with the bank rate (MacWatters 1921: 28; Reserve Bank of India 1940: 29). These annual reports identified three critical money rates: the bank rate, the Imperial Bank *hundi* rate and the bazaar rate. 'The bank rate', spelt out the report for 1927,

> is the rate at which the Imperial Bank will ordinarily advance money against government securities, while the Imperial Bank *hundi* is the rate at which the Imperial Bank will discount or rediscount first class trade three months' bills. The bazaar rates are those at which the bills of small traders are discount by shroffs. The rates for bills of large traders and shroffs are not given separately as they follow very closely the Imperial Bank *hundi* rate. (Denning 1928: 17)

The banks and the shroffs had a link through the discounting of shroffs' paper by the Presidency Banks of Bengal, Bombay and Madras, and afterwards the Imperial Bank of India.[10] Nevertheless, the business of the shroffs remained quite distinct from that of the banks. This was evident enough to the officials of the Presidency Banks when, in the crisis of 1898, the official rate rose abnormally high, and yet the rate in the bazaar stopped at 7 or 8 per cent, though the Presidency Banks' rate might rise to 10 or 12 per cent. Officials who were asked to explain this to the Fowler Committee pointed out that the shroffs, who financed nearly the whole of the internal trade of India, rarely, if ever, discounted European paper, and never purchased foreign or sterling bills. Neither did they lend money on government paper or similar securities, but confined their advances to the discount of *hundis*. There was an invisible segregation here, which would explain both the subordination and resilience of the shroffs within the colonial economy. The *hundis* they purchased were mostly those of traders, especially commission agents, at rates of discount varying from 9 to 25 per cent depending on how big or small the traders were. But the *hundis* that they bought and sold to each other, which were chiefly the traders' *hundis* bearing the shroff's own endorsement, ruled the rates in 'the native bazaar' and were usually negotiated at from 5 to 8 per cent in the busy season. They also discounted their endorsements 'pretty largely' with the Presidency Banks when rates were low and discontinued doing so when they rose above 6 per cent.[11] This explains why the bazaar rates were quite independent of the bank rate. The more so because the banks themselves never issued *hundis* and did not engage in the *hundi* business except in the way of discounting bankers' endorsements.

Hundi and *arhat* were the twin instruments in the great expansion of the bazaar from 1858 to 1929, powerfully aiding the thrust into the futures trade (*vayade ka sauda*). Without these two indigenous devices, the railways and telegraph by themselves would not have fostered the long-distance inland trade and its integration through the development of futures. *Hundi*, or the inland bill of exchange, was supposed by C.N. Cooke to have been a corruption of the word *Hindwi* or Hindoo, 'a word which is Persian, and, therefore, evidently given to them by the Mahomedan conquerors' (Cooke 1863: 21). Actually, the word was a modification of *hundika*, a Sanskrit word derived from the verb *hund*, that is, to collect (see Apte 1959: s.v. *Hundika*). This bill also served as an instrument for credit, and as its use proliferated in the prosperous years before 1929, it largely became the instrument through which bankers raised funds from pensioned people and widows who purchased it for the interest it offered. The *hundi* was thus a substitute for the deposit, which, as far as shroffs were concerned, was evidently contracting in this period.[12] *Arhat*, too, was an indigenous word, meaning 'agency for selling someone else's goods by charging commission' and also 'the godown where such goods are stored' (Prasad, Sahay and Srivastava 1943: s.v. *arhat*). The *arhatiya* gave a guarantee in a transaction between the buyer and the seller who might be at a great distance from each other, and he therefore charged a higher commission than an ordinary broker (*dalal*) who simply brought the buyer and seller together.[13] The acceptability of the *hundi* as a bill of exchange and a credit instrument over the longer distances of the railway network required the generation of trust, and trust was predicated on the commission agency system which now came into its own.[14] For the use of merchants, annual directories were published, which detailed hundreds of market towns (*mandis*) along the railway routes, with a list of commission agents and banks at each *mandi*.[15] The banking communities that typically specialized in the business of discounting *hundis* usually doubled as commission agents and perhaps also combined this business with wholesale trade on their own account. The Marwari bankers of Bombay and Calcutta did this, but the Multani bankers of Bombay acted only as commission agents and never as wholesale traders.[16]

The bazaar, unlike the modern corporate sector, did not constitute an impersonal market but functioned through communities that regulated the newcomer's entry into their respective businesses. In the market towns of upper India, such as Agra, Hathras and Khurja, bankers, grain dealers and cloth merchants belonged to joint families that had carried on the business for generations, and an initiation ceremony was known by which a new firm would be admitted into that circuit. The young man would bring out his would-be account-book, physically display the capital he intended to invest in the business, and the invitees, who were established bankers and merchants, would put their names down in the book if they were favourably impressed, also sometimes putting down the amount to which he would be accommodated. Without this accommodation, a new banker, cloth merchant or grain dealer would not be able to draw *hundis* on others and would not find it possible to do business with other towns through bills of exchange. The acceptance of the firm's *hundi* by the community of bankers and merchants was essential for its successful operation.[17] The entry-control mechanisms were by no means absolutely exclusive, but every market, each line of business, including the banking business of discounting *hundis*, was visibly dominated by certain hereditary groups. In that sense the bazaar, though a part of the expanding *gesellschaft* of colonial India, was still ensconced in clusters of *gemeinschaft*.

In the 1930s and 1940s, modern corporate forms of business took hold over India's vast domestic market, and Indian merchants and businessmen increasingly adopted these new forms. Banks attracted deposits and issued pro-notes in inland centres of commerce, and companies won public confidence through published balance-sheets. In these altered circumstances, *hundi* and *arhat* no longer played the role they did earlier in the expansion and integration of the inland trade after the coming of the railways. The business of *hundi* banking gradually atrophied and Marwaris, Multanis, Natukottai Chettiars and other banking communities went into other types of business.

Notes

[1] These distinctions have been set out in Ray (1995) and Ray (1988).

[2] *Parliamentary Papers*, Minutes of Evidence before the Currency Committee Part I, C.9037, 1898: 469ff. See also Bagchi (1997: 42–50), and Rajat Kanta Ray's review of Bagchi in *Economic and Political Weekly*, 9 August 1997, pp. 2029–30. Bagchi made the important suggestion, and I concurred, that the inter-shroff borrowing rate within the inner circle was lower than other rates in the bazaar. This privileged rate might have been more or less consistently lower than the bank rate too.

[3] *Parliamentary Papers*, Minutes of Evidence before the Currency Committee Part I, C.9037, evidence of Sir Antony Patrick Mac-Donnel, Lieutenant-Governor, NWP and Oudh, 4 July 1898, p. 694.

[4] *Parliamentary Papers* Minutes of Evidence before the Currency Committee Part I, C.9037, evidence of Alexander Martin Lindsay, deputy secretary and treasurer, Bank of Bengal, pp. 595–96.

[5] *Parliamentary Papers HC*, Vol. 15, 1868–69, *Bombay Bank Commission, Report of the Commissioners Appointed to Enquire into the Failure of the Bank of Bombay*, London, 1869, evidence of Premchund Roychund, 5 August 1868, p. 126.

[6] *Bombay Provincial Banking Enquiry Committee*, Evidence, Vol. IV, Calcutta, 1930, p. 523.

[7] *Report of the United Provinces Provincial Banking Enquiry Committee 1929–30*, Vol. II, Evidence, Allahabad, 1930, p. 61.

[8] For an explanation of *vayad* (futures), see Barjatiya (n.d.: 78).

[9] *Banking Enquiry Committee for Centrally Administered Areas 1929–30 Vol. IV, Evidence Taken in the Delhi Province*, Calcutta, 1930, p. 137.

[10] Hence arose the Imperial Bank *hundi* rate. Other banks also kept up regular lists of shroffs whose paper they discounted, with credit ratings against each. The practice went back to the old Bank of Bombay before it crashed in 1867 in the Premchund Roychund fiasco. See evidence of James Blair, *Parliamentary Papers* HC, Vol. 15, 1868–69, *Minutes of Evidence taken in England*, p. 231.

[11] Evidence of J.H. Sleigh, secretary and treasurer of the Bank of Bombay, 1898, cited in *Punjab Provincial Banking Enquiry Committee 1929–30*, Evidence, Vol. II, Lahore, 1930, p. 691.

[12] Oral evidence of Shikarpur Shroffs' Association, *Bombay Provincial Banking Enquiry Committee*, Vol. IV, pp. 353–54.

[13] Shakir Jan and Aulum Jan, Appellants, V. Ahmud Ollah, Respondent, 1 August 1806, *The Indian Decisions (Old Series) Sudder Dewanny Adawlut Reports, Bengal*, Madras, 1912, pp. 145–47.

[14] Thus we learn in Kanji Devji V. Bhugwandas Narotamdas, 1904, that upcountry merchants, being unacquainted with Bombay shroffs and merchants, did not deal with them, 'but deal with well-known Bombay firms, who, on that account, are known as pukka adatiyas' (1911: 552–53).

[15] One such directory, listing grain and grocery commission agents, was

published from Gujranwala from 1922 onwards. *Beopari Arhat India 1958–59*, n.d., Kamla Nagar, photo page.

[16] Joint memorandum on Indigenous Banking in Calcutta by Mr Kasturchand Kothari, proprietor, Sadasukh Gambhirchand, Mr Balmukund Daga, Manager, Bansilal Abirchand, and Mr. Dipchand Poddar, Partner, Tarachand Ghanshyamdas, *Report of the Bengal Provincial Banking Enquity Committee 1929–30*, Vol. II, Evidence Part I, Calcutta 1930, pp. 421–25; Oral evidence of Shikarpur Shroffs Association, Bombay Provincial Banking Enquiry Committee, Vol. IV, Calcutta, 1930, pp. 353–54.

[17] Replies and oral evidence of B.G. Bhatnagar, lecturer in Rural Economics, University of Allahabad, *Report of the United Provinces Banking Enquiry Committee 1929–30*, Vol. IV, Evidence, Allahabad, 1931, pp. 466–75.

References

Apte, Vaman Sivaram, 1959, *The Practical Sanskrit-English Dictionary.*

Bagchi, Amiya Kumar, 1997, *The Evolution of the State Bank of India, Vol. 2, The Era of the Presidency Banks 1876–1920*, New Delhi.

Baker, Henry D., 1915, *British India with Notes on Ceylon, Afghanistan and Tibet*, Washington D.C.

Banking Enquiry Committee for Centrally Administered Areas 1929–30, Vol. IV.

Barjatiya, Mohan Lal, n.d., *Bharat Ka Vyaparik Itihas* (a Hindi Language History of Indian Trade), Bhanpura, Indore.

Beopari Arhat India 1958–59, n.d., Kamla Nagar.

Bombay Bank Commission Report of the Commissioners Appointed to Enquire into the Failure of the Bank of Bombay, 1869, London.

Bombay Provincial Banking Enquiry Committee, Vol. IV, Calcutta, 1930.

Cooke, C.N., 1863, *The Rise, Progress and Present Condition of Banking in India*, Calcutta.

Denning, H.C. (Controller of Currency), 1928, *Report of the Controller of Currency for the Year 1927–28*, Calcutta.

Evidence Taken in the Delhi Provinces, Calcutta, 1930

Gubbay, M.M.S., 1928, 'Indigenous Indian Banking: A Paper Read at the Royal Society of Arts', London, with a discussion by Sir Henry Strakosch *et al.*, Bombay.

Hoey, William, 1880, *A Monograph on the Trade and Manufactures in Northern India*, Lucknow.

Hyde, A., 1870, *Report on Metallic Currency*, Calcutta.

MacWatters, A.C., 1922, *Report on the Operations of the Currency Department, the Movement of Funds on the Resource Operations of the Government of India for the Year 1921–22*, Calcutta.

Parliamentary Papers HC, 1868–69, Vol. 15.

Parliamentary Papers, 1888, Minutes of Evidence before the Currency Committee Part I, C.9037.

Prasad, Kalika, Rajvallabh Sahay and Mukundilal Srivastava (eds), *Vrihat Hindi Kosh*, 1943, Banaras.

Punjab Provincial Banking Enquiry Committee 1929–30, 1930, Lahore.

Ray, Rajat Kanta, 1988, 'The Bazaar: Changing Structural Characteristics of the ildigenous Section of the Indian Economy before and after the Great Depression', *Indian Economic and Social History Review*, Vol. 25, No. 3.

————, 1995, 'Asian Capital in the Age of European Domination: the Rise of the Bazaar of 1800–1914', *Modern Asian Studies*, Vol. 29, No. 3.

————, 1997, 'Review' of Bagchi (1997), *Economic and Political Weekly.*

Report of the United Provinces, Provincial Banking Enquiry Committee 1929–1930, 1930, Vol. II, Allahabad.

Reserve Bank of India, 1940, *Report on Currency and Finance for the Year 1939–40,* Bombay.

Roy, Sripati, 1911, *Customs and Customary Law in British India,* Calcutta.

The Indian Decisions (Old Series) Sudder Dewanny Adawlut Reports, Bengal, Madras, 1912.

U.S. Department of Commerce, Bureau of Foreign and Domestic Commerce, Special Consular Report No. 72.

Rise of Modern Banking in the Princely States of India
The Case of the Bank of Baroda

Dwijendra Tripathi

Historical studies of business instrumentalities in India are few and far between; those focusing on the princely states are even less. In proportion to the total number of banks that existed in the country on the eve of independence, the number of those that had originated in princely India was by no means small. And yet, practically all the available banking histories – their number is not very large anyway – deal with institutions that developed in British India. Accounts of developments in areas under the princely order provide perspectives and insights that may supplement, even modify, the understanding gained from analysing situations in territories under the direct governance of the British Crown.[1] The rationale for the present paper is precisely this.

Our choice of the subject has several justifications. For one, the Bank of Baroda is today among the oldest of such institutions floated by Indians; most banks established before it came into being either on the initiative of British officials working in India or were branches of British exchange banks (Reserve Bank of India 1954: 6). Secondly, this was the first major banking institution set up in princely India that survived and flourished.[2] Thirdly, this was the only banking company originating in a princely state that retained a distinct identity after independence; all the others became subsidiaries of the State Bank of India. And lastly, Baroda state, where the bank was born and consolidated its position, was among the largest states in princely India, and some of its rulers were counted among the most progressive of the native princes. Sayajirao Gaikwad III, whose reign witnessed the birth of the bank and its rise to a position of some consequence, was known for his enlightenment, liberality and reformist zeal. He is still remembered with gratitude for a series of measures he adopted to promote the welfare of his people and modernize the administration of his king-dom. How this set-up affected the fortunes of the Bank of Baroda, is the principal focus of this study.

I

A brief description of some relevant aspects of the financial management of Baroda state before Sayajirao III came to the helm may provide a useful backdrop for our study. Prior to 1802, when the Gaikwads entered into subsidiary relationship with the English East India Company, the revenue collection machinery of the state centred around the so-called *potedari* system – a system that prevailed in some form or the other in practically all the successor-states of the Mughal empire. The revenue rights of a village or a group of villages were assigned by the Gaikwad rulers to a rent collector, known as *ijardar*, who undertook to deposit in the royal treasury an amount fixed by the state. The state thus could manage without an elaborate revenue col-lection apparatus, although the system gave a free hand to the rent-collectors. To simplify the matter still further and to avoid dealing with a host of intermediaries, the Gaikwads positioned a group of five merchant moneylenders, or *sahukars*, between the state and the *ijar-dars*. These *sahukars* were known as *potedars*. Whenever the gov-ernment needed money, it would issue to one of these *potedars* a money warrant accompanied by a letter of credit, known as *varat*, enjoining upon some *ijardars* to reimburse the *potedar* from the revenue of villages farmed out to them. Not only did the state borrow directly from the accredited *sahukars*, the latter also directly settled the claims against the state, if authorized to do so. The *potedars*, thus, functioned as some sort of a bank, and the state warrant was in the nature of a cheque drawn against the security of land revenue.[3]

Despite their critical position in the financial system of the state, the *potedars* remained reconciled to their subservience to the political authority as long as the Gaikwad rulers were in absolute control of the kingdom, for the *potedars* had no other power to look up to for protection. The rise of the British as a force to reckon with in western India around the end of the eighteenth century altogether changed the situation. Now the *potedars* were not ready to honour the government's warrants for money unless the East India Company pledged its authority as a guarantee for repayment. The Company agreed to the proposition, provided the state joined the subsidiary system. The financial position of the state in the meantime had become so precarious that the Gaikwads had little option but to submit to the British condition. With the state joining the subsidiary alliance in 1802 the subjugation of the kingdom was complete, and its *potedars* became the Company's guaranteed merchants. A trilateral system, with the British providing the most crucial link, took the place of what until then had been a purely bilateral arrangement between the Gaikwads and their shroffs.[4]

The state's liabilities, however, continued to mount and the shylockian grip of the *sahukars* over the government finances continued to tighten, at once strengthening the British–*potedar* axis and weakening the political authority of the *de jure* power. As the British power consolidated itself, the guarantee arrangements became less and less relevant for the Company. The guarantees given to the local merchants, therefore, were gradually withdrawn on one pretext or the other. This gave an opportunity to the Gaikwad rulers to take some effective steps to loosen the *potedar* noose around their neck.

The credit for initiating the process of cutting the *potedars* down to their size goes to Sayajirao II (1818–1867), unquestionably the most indomitable of the Gaikwads in the first half of the nineteenth century. At the first stage, he began issuing money warrants to merchants other than the state's *potedars*. At a later stage, he set up as many as four private banks of his own, which, in due course, began to function as additional *potedars* to the state, reducing considerably the shroffs' hold on the financial system. Sayajirao's four successors, who occupied the throne before Sayajirao III (1875–1939) came to the helm, pursued this policy relentlessly, with the result that the new king inherited a financial system under which all the *potedari* rights were vested in the banks privately held by the ruling princes. The accredited shroffs had already lost the privileges they had been accustomed to ever since the inception of the Gaikwad state, much before Sayajirao III appeared on the scene.

II

By any standard, Sayajirao III can be regarded as the modernizer of Baroda state. With his ascension began an era of reform, the like of which the state never experienced in its entire history. No sphere of life remained untouched by the reform programme – be it political, economic, educational or cultural. In the realm of financial management, the outmoded system of land settlement and revenue administration yielded to a more equitable and less exploitative arrangement, modelled after the one prevailing in Bombay Presidency. The method of revenue collection underwent a complete reorganization. The *potedari* system, or whatever was left of it, was given a statutory burial and the banks established by Sayajirao III's predecessors and functioning under their private control were abolished. All financial transactions with the state would henceforward be conducted through the state treasuries (Sargent 1928: 188–96, 252–56; Desai 1929). Concern for economic development had a special place in the Maharaja's scheme of things. Realizing the inadequacy of the existing credit facilities to accelerate the process of economic change, a financial institution under the name of the Baroda Pedhi Company Limited was set up on the initiative of the state. The Pedhi had a share capital of Rs 3 lakh, 50 per cent of which was subscribed by the state. The Pedhi started functioning in Baroda from 1 February 1884. A similar institution was set up in Visnagar which functioned under the control of the district collector.

The Pedhi as well as the Visnagar bank were modest institutions. Given the economy of the state, dominated overwhelmingly by agriculture and with very little industry in sight in the mid-1880s, the planners could not have conceived anything more ambitious. These institutions did not achieve much[5] and made very little impact on the economic scene of the state, with the result that more than a decade after they came into being, 'the difficulty of procuring capital for industrial or agricultural improvement' was reported from every district (Government of Baroda 1897: 8). In the meantime, the government had appointed an industrial commission, the first ever in India, to explore the industrial potential of the state and recommend a plan of action. The commission submitted its report in 1896. Regretting the absence of credit facilities, the commission recommended the setting up of government banks in each district primarily to help agricultural development.

As for the needs of commerce and trade, the commission expressed the hope that the Baroda Pedhi could be restructured and strengthened to develop into a full-fledged commercial bank (ibid.: 8–10). But in the light of the performance of the Pedhi, few shared this optimism. At least the Maharaja did not. On his suggestion, his government approached, in 1906, the Bank of Bombay, one of the three Presidency Banks in the country having very close links with the colonial administration, to open a branch at Baroda. However, the conditions on which the bank was ready to act on this suggestion were such that the state government could not accept. Another Bombay-based institution, the Indian Specie Bank, was far less stringent in its demands and wanted nothing more than the freedom to move funds between its branches elsewhere and the one proposed to be opened at Baroda. This appeared to be a pretty innocuous and perfectly justified condition and the state government was willing to accept it. But the financial elite of Baroda, particularly the erstwhile *potedars*, felt alarmed. They felt that the proposed branch would 'develop into nothing short of a feeder to Bombay, and that in the near future it would suck up all the resources of the state and its people to the lasting benefit of the trade and industries of Bombay only' (Government of Baroda 1930: 187–88). It is quite possible that the *swadeshi* spirit sweeping the country in the wake of Lord Curzon's ill-conceived plan to divide Bengal, shaped to some extent the reaction of the Baroda elite.

Luckily for them, the opponents of Indian Specie Bank's proposed entry into the Gaikwad kingdom found a friend and guide in the economic advisor to the Maharaja. An American by nationality, Ralph C. Whitenack had just entered upon his duties but had already developed a close contact with the city's gentry, including the shroffs opposed to the Specie Bank proposal. Their representatives had several discussions with him before they met formally in his office on 29 January 1907 and pledged their cooperation in setting up a state bank for Baroda.[6]

Whitenack apprised the Maharaja of his discussion with the shroffs and with the Maharaja's permission, drafted a comprehensive proposal in consultation with the leaders of the local business community and heads of various departments of the government. Suggesting that the proposed institution be called the 'People's Bank of Baroda', he explicated in the minutest details the manner in which the capital would be raised and management would be organized. While pleading for state patronage to the proposed institution at least during its infancy, he explicitly stipulated that the state should have no share in the capital and in no way supervise or interfere with the management. Whitenack, however, wanted the state to guarantee a minimum annual dividend of 4.5 per cent on the capital employed at least during the first five years.[7]

Under pressure from the Maharaja's council of ministers, the guarantee proposal was dropped. The council also did not favour the inclusion of the word 'People's' in the name of the proposed institution. With compromises on some other points between the council, Whitenack and the Baroda shroffs led by the House of Haribhaktis, the draft proposal was placed before the Maharaja for his orders. While giving his assent to the proposal, the Maharaja added a very important concession, binding the state to maintain with the proposed bank an interest-free deposit of Rs 2.5 lakh or one-fourth of the paid capital of the bank, whichever was less, for the first fifteen years. Another deposit of Rs 7.5 lakh or three-fourth of the paid capital, whichever was less, maintained for the same period, would earn an interest of 4 per cent per annum from the bank.[8] In view of the fact that the paid-up capital, at least during the initial stages, was visualized to remain limited to Rs 10 lakh, the net effect of these two concessions taken together was that during the first fifteen years, the amount placed by the state at the disposal of the bank, with or without interest, would be equal to its entire paid-up capital. This was substantial encouragement indeed.

The Maharaja's sanction cleared the decks for drafting a detailed prospectus. To underline the fact that the operations of the proposed institution would not be confined to the boundaries of the state only, the government and the local promoters considered it appropriate to associate with the project some leading businessmen from Bombay and Ahmedabad, the two prominent business centres in the neighbourhood of Baroda. The persons selected – Sir Vithaldas Damodar Thackersey, Sir Lalubhai Samaldar (both from Bombay), Ambalal Sankarlal Desai and Chamanlal Nagindas (both from Ahmedabad) – were highly respected in business circles; all of them had close relations with the state and its ruler; and all were known for their nationalist views. It was this group that now took over the leadership of the project, relegating the Baroda shroff to the background.

This created no problem as the local promoters, quite conscious of their own limitations, readily accepted the leadership of the distinguished outsiders. The state bureaucracy, however, was much less awed. For some strange reason, the accountant general and the legal remembrancer, who had earlier raised no objection to the concession relating to the state maintaining a deposit of 10 lakh with the bank, now expressed reservation on the ground that the bank had no security to offer. Another of their arguments was that the bank's likely investments out of the state might implicate the government in lawsuits in British India in the event of possible legal action to recover the dues.

These arguments had little validity, as Whitenack pointed out. He reminded these two officials that the bank's paid-up capital would be a sufficient guarantee for the state deposits and that the state already had considerable investment in railway companies and large deposits in Bombay banks that were not subject to the Baroda courts.[9] As the officials remained unmoved, Vithaldas and Samaldas threatened to dissociate themselves from the project saying that they had 'a name to lose' if the bank failed, which would surely happen if the deposits in question were not made. A similar ultimatum came from Maganbhai Haribhakti, the leader of the local shroffs. Whitenack was so furious that he bluntly wrote to the *dewan* that if the government failed to back 'this institution . . . within the bounds set by reason and business principle', he would not assume any further responsibility for industrial and economic improvement of the kingdom.[10] Unable to withstand these combined pressures, the bureaucracy relented and the Maharaja finally accorded his approval to the bank's prospectus on 16 December 1907, observing: 'The Bank is not designed to assist the Baroda government . . . by providing loans . . . but to help the people in their industrial pursuits.'[11]

He made a similar observation while addressing a public meeting held on 19 July 1908 to educate the common people about the significance of the project. Welcoming the birth of the bank, 'built on the solid foundations of private capital and private enterprise', he emphatically declared that his government had no immediate need of such an institution'.[12] The next day the Bank of Baroda was registered under the Baroda Companies Act of 1897. Its prospectus, issued shortly afterwards, referred to it as a public limited company organized 'under patronage of and largely supported by the Government of H.H. the Maharaja Gaikwad'. The names of prominent shroffs and financiers of the state along with the four promoters belonging to Bombay and Ahmedabad appeared on the board of directors headed by

Vithaldas Thackersey. The board also included the accountant general of the state, a member of the royal family and Whitenack, serving in his personal capacity.[13]

The board lost little time to put together an operational team headed by a general manager. Charles E. Randle, an Englishman serving as a senior executive in a Bombay bank, was appointed to this post on a salary of Rs 700 per month along with attractive perquisites. Though the *dewan* would have preferred an Indian for the post, most others including the Maharaja and his economic advisor favoured a European on the ground that it would add to the prestige of the bank.[14] All other employees except the accountant and assistant accountant belonged to the clerical category, and their monthly salary ranged between Rs 30 and Rs 150. With few rules and regulations constraining his administrative style, Randle would preside over this simplistic structure like a lord, making a mockery of the principle of job security for his Indian subordinates.[15]

If the promoters of the bank thought that with the registration of the bank and setting up the nucleus of an operating team their problem with the state bureaucracy was over, they were sadly mistaken. Soon after the bank was launched, a major crisis erupted. Its origin lay in the manner in which the share capital was to be raised. According to the articles of association, the authorized capital was Rs 20 lakh divided into 20,000 shares of Rs 100 each. Assuming that the public enthusiasm for investing in a somewhat unfamiliar enterprise would be lukewarm, at least initially, the board had decided to call up only Rs 50 against each share of Rs 100, and this too was to be paid in a phased manner spanning over a period of three months. The fear of the directors turned out to be entirely correct as only 13,000 shares were taken by the beginning of October 1908, the Maharaja himself taking the largest block of 900. As per the board's decision, the first instalment to be paid against each share was of Rs 20 only. Consequently, the bank had Rs 260,000 in its capital account by the end of October. Randle now asked the government an equal amount – one-fourth of it interest-free and the balance bearing 4 per cent interest – in accordance with the concessions granted.[16]

The accountant general and the legal remembrancer were up in arms once again. Giving a strange interpretation to the concessions, they maintained that the state was not bound to deposit the amount in question until all the shares were fully paid up. Obviously, they were confusing paid-up capital with paid-up shares. This revived the old controversy that had earlier threatened the birth of the bank. The infuriated directors were in no mood to accept the erroneous interpretation which, if acted upon, would cripple the bank even before it stood on its own legs. Whitenack lambasted the bureaucracy in no uncertain terms, lamenting the 'unwarranted official obstacles with which the Bank has had to contend' right from the beginning. No one could predict where the stalemate would lead to, but the timely and sage intervention of the acting *amatya* C.N. Seddon saved the situation. Without leaving any doubt that in his own view the bureaucracy was wrong and the directors right, he gave a more persuasive reason for accepting the latter's interpretation. Even if the board was wrong, he argued, its interpretation was one that 'very many people will concur in accepting. . . . Capital is so shy of Native States that we must avoid the slightest suspicion of breach of faith.'[17] Another ugly episode in the short career of the bank, thus, passed off into history.

In comparison with these major crises, the bank faced only minor problems in its dealings with the state bureaucracy in the next two years. The state agreed without much hitch, in 1910, to transfer its treasury work to the young institution and keep a balance of Rs 5.5 lakh in interest-free current account. These facilities, however, were to be available only after the Rs 50 called up against all the 20,000 shares was fully paid up. By the end of April 1910, when the above contract was signed, this amount had been paid against 13,000 shares only. To help the bank once again the Maharaja took another 2,000 shares, paying Rs 50 against each. The remaining 5,000 shares were underwritten by Vithaldas Samaldas, a prominent financier of Bombay and Lallubhai Samaldas's brother. The stipulated conditions for the contract having been fulfilled, the bank took over from the treasury the task of receiving and paying money on behalf of the state, and began to operate as the banker of the state with effect from 15 June 1910 ('Note on Bank's History', Note 21).

All this helped the bank stabilize its position and survive the banking crisis that, beginning 1913, gradually engulfed the entire land. By 1917, as many as 87 banks with aggregate paid-up capital of nearly Rs 200 million failed, causing serious depletion of public confidence in the modern system of banking (see Ray 1938: 221–31; Shinaz 1919: 365–68). If the Bank of Baroda emerged unscathed from the crisis, it was in no small measure due to its close links with the Gaikwad state.

III

The bank, however, had to pay a heavy price for this. With the added financial stakes of the Baroda state in the institution, the bureaucracy began to look upon it almost as a department of the government, and official interference in its working increased. Soon after the decision to transfer the treasury work to the bank, Randle was asked to change its working hours so as to conform to the working hours of the government offices, on the ground that the bank was 'subsidized by His Highness' Government so liberally' (Government of Baroda 1909, Vol. II: 104), but he somehow withstood the pressure. But when the Maharaja himself began to use the bank as a convenient instrument to further his personal financial interests, it was an altogether different matter. Whatever his other virtues, Sayajirao III lagged behind none of his predecessors in his love for money. One of the ways through which he sought to augment his financial gains was to invest in business concerns located in British India, investment opportunities in the state being limited. But this could involve him in legal complications in the courts in British India, a thought he could not entertain. The bank offered an easy way out. For, it could become a safe conduit for his investments in other parts of the country. The Maharaja found Randle a willing ally in this enterprise. The general manager possessed an acute understanding of the share market and was no less interested in speculation. The banker and the king naturally became very close to each other. As an unofficial advisor to the Maharaja on his investments in shares, Randle aided and abetted in the misuse of the bank to serve the personal interest of the ruler. Two examples will bear this out.

The first relates to a transaction dating back to 1912 when a loan of Rs 25 lakh was advanced to a Madras-based firm, Messrs Tawker and Sons, against the security of some jewelleries. Only one-fifth of the amount belonged to the bank. The balance came from the personal funds of the Maharaja and all negotiations were conducted by the state accountant general, Anant Narayan Datar. All documents were executed in the name of the bank which, through a separate agreement, acknowledged having received a sum of Rs 20 lakh from the Maharaja. The jewelleries taken in pawn, however, were to remain in the possession of His Highness, and an agent enjoying his confidence was to have control over them. To complicate the matter still further, the bank, on the Maharaja's suggestion, surrendered its power to enforce the rights and remedies exercisable under the contract to Datar through a power of attorney which could not be revoked except at the request of and with the consent of the king. This meant that in case of default, the management of the bank could take no action against the debtors unless Datar was willing to oblige.

Datar, however, proved to be a treacherous officer. When Tawker and Sons failed to honour the payment schedule as agreed to in the contract, he started selling the pawned jewelleries with the help of the state jewellers, Messrs Lalbhai Kalianbhai Zaveri and Co. The bank had no reason to worry, however, because it continued to receive regular payments against its share of the loan, and Datar and not the bank maintained the account of the Maharaja's share. In 1922, however, the bank received no payment either from Datar or from Zaveri and Co., and when the board conducted an enquiry in 1924, it was discovered that a part of the proceeds from the sale of the jewelleries was not accounted for at all. This set off a series of investigations. By 1927 it had been established beyond doubt that Datar, in collusion with the state jeweller, had cheated both the bank and his master. The Maharaja, however, blamed the bank which he thought was the trustee of his money, whereas Randle faulted the Maharaja for placing so much trust in an unscrupulous officer.[18]

Exactly when this episode was vitiating the relations between the king and the banker, the skeletons of another ill-advised transaction were slowly coming out of the cupboard. This related to a series of loans given to one Charles J. Smith who owned a number of collieries in Bagidigi village of Dhanbad district in the province of Bihar. Between 1912 and 1919, a sum of Rs 8 lakh had been advanced to Smith from the bank, though the bulk of the funds actually came from the king. Then Randle devised a circuitous route for the bank's credit – a large part of which again was Maharaja's money – to flow to Smith. He persuaded one Edward Villiers, an employee of Smith having close connections with high British officials in India, to establish a managing agency firm under the name of Villiers Limited, and to promote a number of companies with the funds advanced by the Maharaja through the bank. Now all loans to Smith began to flow through Villiers or his companies.

Unfortunately, all this was happening at a time when the coal industry was about to enter a prolonged period of slump that was to last almost till the onset of the Second World War. As the condition deteriorated and Smith lost all hopes of liquidating his debts, he was forced to mortgage his entire property to the bank and appoint Villiers Limited as the managing agents of his concern in the hope that under its management the collieries would turn the corner. This, however, did not happen, and by 1924 it became clear to Smith that he had been cheated by his own erstwhile employee. To extricate himself from his clutches he filed a suit, but the documents he had signed in innocence were against him. He therefore thought it expedient to settle the matter out of court, forfeiting the mortgaged property to the bank. The amount outstanding against him, according to the bank authorities, was then close to Rs 17 lakh. The Bagidigi collieries, thus, became the property of the bank. In normal times, it would not have been a bad bargain, but in view of the prevailing depression in the coal industry, the property was a liability rather than an asset. The Maharaja once again held Randle responsible for this fiasco and the bank suffered a huge loss as the collieries could fetch only a mere pittance of Rs 4 lakh when they were auctioned off about a decade later.[19]

The transactions with Tawker and Sons and Charles Smith created a wide gulf between the king and the banker. Randle was obviously wrong in involving the institution in sordid affairs, but given the political set-up of the state, he could not have done otherwise without anatagonizing an extremely popular ruler. Having joined the bank on a modest salary of Rs 700 per month, he had risen successively in his career and was drawing a staggering sum of Rs 6,000 per month by the end of the 1920s, attractive perquisites apart.[20] Admittedly, he had been a cautious banker on the whole and steered the Bank of Baroda safely through an extremely difficult period in the history of Indian banking, but his achievement and efficiency alone could not have earned these enviable rewards for him, had he not purchased royal favour at the expense of a public enterprise of which he was the custodian. If he had any illusion, this was dispelled soon after the Tawker–Smith episodes.

His appointment, according to the contract, was to end on 1 July 1933. Almost a year before this date, he informed the management that he would not like the contract to be renewed any further. The board, however, requested him to continue till July 1934, when the silver jubilee celebrations of the bank would conclude. In case Randle chose to retire earlier, he was assured of a special remuneration of Rs 1,60,000 in appreciation of his long and meritorious service. It was also resolved to instal his marble bust in the head office building at Baroda and an oil portrait at the Bombay branch office. Touched by the singular recognition, the English banker agreed to put off his retirement, as suggested by the board.

Randle could not have been unaware of the changed attitude of the Maharaja towards him, but he grossly misjudged the mood of the ruler, or else he would have turned down the request of the board. In fact, everything was apparently going well for him when all of a sudden a communication was received from the accountant general in October 1933 asking the board to retire Randle with effect from 1 January 1934, with nothing more than normal benefits. The suggestion was a direct interference in the internal affairs of the bank and thus a gross violation of the undertaking given by the state. Also, strangely enough, no reason was given by the state officer for his action. Yet the management could not resist the pressure from the palace. Not only was the banker relieved of his duties as desired by the accountant general, an enquiry was also instituted into the affairs of the institution during his tenure. The only thing that the committee found against the former manager was that he had secured loans for himself on different occasions in the name of fictitious persons without the approval of the chairman – a practice which was not uncommon among the bank executives in those days. Under ordinary circumstances, the board might have condoned these lapses without batting an eyelid, but the situation now was anything but ordinary. On Randle's failure to offer an acceptable explanation, the board resolved to treat him as having been 'dismissed' with effect from 1 January1934, and his provident fund amounting to Rs 1.45 lakh was attached as a penal measure.[21] An officer who had done so much for the institution in spite of many failings on his part, thus, bowed out of the scene in utter disgrace simply because he had lost royal favour.

IV

Most studies of economic development of India, or of institutions associated with such tasks, during the British rule emphasize the role of the colonial basis of governance and the racial character of the governing class to explain the country's economic backwardness. Bagchi's observation about the Bank of Bengal that it 'was very much a part of the framework of imperial rule and the latter impinged on the substance and style of the functioning of the Bank in numerous ways'

(Bagchi 1987: 137) may reverberate through most of the studies in one way or the other. Our account of the Bank of Baroda too, though functioning in a native state and under Indian management, reveals similar characteristics. On the one hand, the bank probably would not have come into being or even achieved a reasonable degree of consolidation but for the active interest and assistance of the Maharaja. On the other hand, even such an enlightened and progressive monarch as Sayajirao III could not control his temptation to put to illegitimate use what essentially was a private-sector firm, with a view to furthering his own interests. And his liberality and reformist outlook did not prevent him from using his privileged position to interfere in the working of an institution he and his government had promised to keep outside their control. No wonder that the Bank of Baroda realized its full potential only after the end of monarchy.

If this was happening under a progressive ruler, what would have been the situation in less fortunate states? We would have some idea only if we undertake more studies relating to the Indian native states. But at least the limited experience of the Bank of Baroda suggests that along with the impact of colonialism on the economic system, we should also take into account the effect of the unresponsive character of governments in princely India. If the native states lagged behind imperial India in economic development, it was primarily because their rulers, with no meaningful check on their system of governance, did not use the limited powers available to them in the imperial set-up to give a better deal to their people, or only used them for personal aggrandizement.

Bagchi has also referred to the 'racialist basis of the governance' of the Bank of Bengal. Our account of the Bank of Baroda suggests that even though the governing board of this institution was dominated by persons of nationalist persuasion, there were obvious racial overtones in its governance. One of the reasons for appointing an Englishman as the executive head was his racial background. His fat salary, Rolls Royce car and horse-drawn buggy, luxurious mansion, pompous lifestyle, and above all, ostensible proximity to the Maharaja, must have created a huge gulf between him and the rest of the employees whom he treated as no better than vassals and trusted but little. Apparently, nobody objected to his style of functioning until he became *persona non grata* to the Maharaja for reasons that had nothing to do with Randle's administrative behaviour. And the management's faith in European superiority was so great that the person selected to succeed him, William G. Groundwater, was also an Englishman, despite the disappointment with Randle towards the close of his tenure. Indians themselves, even the informed ones, seem to have reinforced, though perhaps unwittingly, the racial environment prevailing in Indian organizations during the colonial era.

Bagchi refers to the wide variance between the salaries of he European and Indian staff in the Bank of Bengal, functioning essentially under a European management. As we have seen, the salaries of the Indian staff in the Bank of Baroda were a pittance in comparison with Randle's emoluments, even though it functioned under Indian supervision. Perhaps such gulfs prevailed in other Indian-controlled banks too.[22] Unjust and arbitrary as it may seem today, the gulf between the salaries of Indian and European staff working in Indian banking institutions was perhaps more a function of demand and supply rather than of racial considerations. Indigenous expertise in modern banking was woefully scarce at that time, making the European personnel almost indispensable and raising their market value.

This brief account of a banking firm based in a native state seems to offer these perspectives – and correctives. More of such studies may offer even more.

Notes

[1] Among the histories of Indian banks, Bagchi (1987), Bagchi (1997) and Bagchi (1989) are the most comprehensive. R.K. Seshadri (1982) lacks historical rigour, while Prakash Tandon (1989) is more of a personalized account. The only history of a bank originating in princely India published until now is Tripathi and Misra (1985).

[2] The Bank of Rahilkhand, set up in 1862 with the active support of the Nawab of Oudh, was the first bank in princely India, but it had a short-lived existence. Cooke (1863: 379).

[3] Desai and Clark (1923, Vol. II: 3–8, 403–06); Government of Baroda (Financial), 'Papers Dealing with the Transactions with State Bankers and State Banks', Bundle Nos 1–93, Baroda Records Office, Baroda; Government of Baroda, *Historical Selections from Baroda State Records*, Vols. III to VI, published between 1936 and 1941, contain letters exchanged between the government of the state and various *potedars*, as also specimens of the pay orders issued by the state.

[4] For details of Gaikwad–*potedar*–British relations, see Desai and Clark (1923, Vo. I: 485–503); also Gense and Banerji (1934).

[5] Baroda Pedhi Company, *Memorandum of Association and Articles of*

Association, Baroda, 1892. A copy is available in Baroda Records Office, Baroda.

[6] Government of Baroda (Political), Miscellaneous Department, Section 47, 'Personal File of R.C. Whitenack', File No. 70, State Records office, Baroda.

[7] Government of Baroda (1909: 1–2); Whitenack's Memoranda to Maharaja, 28 February 1907 and 7 March 1907 (ibid.: 6–37).

[8] Whitenack to Haribhakti, 27 June 1907 (ibid.: 51).

[9] For opinions of the accountant general and legal remembrancer and Whitenack's reply, see ibid.: 61–74.

[10] Thackersey and Samaldas to Whitenack, 29 August 1907 (ibid.: 66–98); Haribhakti to Whitenack, 4 September 1907 (ibid.: 74–76); Whitenack to the *dewan*, 17 September 1907 (ibid.: 79–80).

[11] Huzur Order, 16 December 1907 (ibid.: 120–21).

[12] Government of Baroda, *Speeches and Addresses of His Highness Sayajirao III Maharaja of Baroda*, London, 1928: 221–23. The volume says that the speech was delivered on 9 July 1908 on the occasion of the 'opening of the New Bank of Baroda'. Obviously the date is misprinted as the same has been published in the *Bombay Gazette* of 22 July 1908 along with the speeches delivered by others in the meeting. The *Times of India* approvingly commented on the Maharaja's speech in its issue of 23 July 1907.

[13] Bank of Baroda, *Prospectus*, Baroda, 1908, Bank of Baroda head office, Baroda; also Whitenacks's *tippan*, 7 September 1908, in *Bank of Baroda Records*: 144.

[14] Bank of Baroda, 'Minutes of the Board Meeting', 16 August 1908, head office, Baroda.

[15] Author's interview with S.J. Ashlot who had joined the bank in 1920s and was until recently the oldest employee living. Also Bank of Baroda (1958: 1–8). An incident that Ashlot related to the author is revealing of Randle's style of administration and the nature of job security the employees had. Once an employee, who was on sick leave, was spotted on the road by Randle. The very next day the employee was dismissed on the ground that he had given false reason to secure leave. Another old employee told the author that Randle sanctioned leave with extreme reluctance.

[16] Government of Baroda (1927 33); Whitenack's *tippan* of 14 November 1909 in *Records of the Baroda Government*: 161–69. Also see an untitled, unsigned typescript relating to the history of the bank (henceforth 'Note on Bank's History') available among the confidential files of the chairman at the head office, Baroda.

[17] Accountant general to manager, Bank of Baroda, 8 October 1908 and 13 October 1908, *Records of the Baroda Government*: 150–52; opinion of Legal Remembrancer, 3 September 1908 (*Records of the Baroda Government*: 155–56); Randle to Whitenack, 27 October 1908 and Whitenack's *tippan*, 14 November 1908 (*Records of the Baroda Government*: 161–69); *Amatya's* opinion (ibid.: 170–75).

[18] Government of Baroda (1927: 67–69); also a typed document entitled 'Note on the Responsibility of the Bank of Baroda Ltd. For the Loss of His

Highness the Maharaja Saheb in the Loan of Rs 20 lakhs to Messers Tawker & Sons of Madras', preserved among the chairman's confidential papers at the head office of the Bank of Baroda. The note was prepared on the orders of the ruler, most probably, by Randle himself.

[19] The Villiers–Smith episode is thoroughly documented in Government of Baroda (1927–28); also see Smith's plaint, filed in the court of subordinate judge at Dhanbad, preserved among the chairman's confidential papers at the head office of the Bank of Baroda at Baroda; Bank of Baroda, 'Minutes of the Board Meeting', 27 January 1938, head office, Baroda.

[20] Author's interview with J.S. Ashlot at Baroda. This is also clear from the minutes of several board meetings which fixed Randle's emoluments from time to time.

[21] Bank of Baroda, 'Minutes of the Board Meetings', 1 December 1932, 28 December 1933, 21 March 1934, 29 June 1934, 27 November 1937; also Dwijendra Tripathi's interview with J.M. Mehta at Baroda. Mehta, who died recently, had served as a member of the Baroda Banking Enquiry Committee and was a nephew of the *dewan* during the 1920s.

[22] In the Indian Bank, for instance, run by Indians and employing no Europeans, the salary of the highest executive office in 1912 was Rs 750. The three officers next to him drew between Rs 220 and Rs 100; all others drew between Rs 55 and Rs 4. Seshadri (1982).

References

Bagchi, A.K., 1987, *The Evolution of the State Bank of India*, Bombay.

———, 1989, *The Presidency Banks and the Indian Economy 1876–1914*, Calcutta.

———, 1997, *The Evolution of the State Bank of India*, New Delhi.

Bank of Baroda Records.

Bank of Baroda, 1908, *Prospectus*, Baroda: Bank of Baroda head Office.

Bank of Baroda, 1958, *Fifty Years of Service and Achievement*, Baroda.

Cooke, C.H., 1863, *The Rise, Progress and Present Conditions of Banking in India*, Calcutta.

Desai, G.H., 1929, *Forty Years in Baroda: Being Reminiscences of Forty Years Service in the Baroda State*, Baroda.

Desai, G.H. and A.B. Clark, 1923, *Gazetteer of the Baroda State*, Bombay.

Gense, J.H. and D.R. Banerji (eds), 1934, *The Gaikwads of Baroda*, Baroda.

Government of Baroda, 1897, *Report of the Industrial Commission*, Baroda.

———, 1909, *Selections from the Records of the Baroda Government: The Bank of Baroda*, Baroda.

———, 1927, *Report on the Khangi Investments*, Baroda.

———, 1927–28, *Report of the Villiers Investment-Enquiry Committee*, 3 vols, Baroda.

———, 1928, *Speeches and Addresses of His Highness Sayajirao III Maharaja of Baroda*, London.

———, 1930, *Baroda Banking Enquiry Committee Report*, 1929–30, Baroda.

Ram, Ramchandra B., 1938, *Present Day Banking in India*, Calcutta.

Reserve Bank of India, 1954, *Banking and Monetary Statistics*, Bombay.

Sargent, Philip W., 1928, *The Ruler of Baroda*, London.

Seshadri, R.K., 1982, *A Swadeshi Bank from South India: A History of the Indian Bank, 1907–1982*, Madras.

Shinaz, Finlay, 1919, *Indian Finance and Banking*, London.

Tandon, Prakash, 1989, *The Banking Century: A Short History of Banking and the Pioneer – Punjab National Bank*, New Delhi.

Tripathi, D. and P. Mishra, 1985, *Towards a New Frontier: History of the Bank of Baroda*, New Delhi.

The Depression Years

Indian Capitalists' Critique of British Monetary and Financial Policy in India, 1929–39

Aditya Mukherjee

The Depression

With the onset of the depression years the situation in India changed drastically and many of the apprehensions about the Indian economy expressed in India in the previous years now acquired much greater urgency. World prices, especially those of primary produce, plummeted and India's export earnings collapsed. With agricultural prices so low (in the Punjab, wheat was selling at less than one-third of its normal pre-war value), the government was unable to collect full revenue (Schuster to Irwin, 1 June 1931, L/PO 269).[1] Also with the fall in export earnings there was great difficulty in securing remittance to meet India's sterling obligations or the Home Charges amounting to about £35 million per year (ibid.). With both revenue and remittance in jeopardy, the colonial government was in the throes of a major financial crisis.

India's gold reserves were once again commandeered (by issuing Reverse Council Bills against them), but that there were political and economic limits to the expedient of drawing on the currency reserves to meet remittance was evident (ibid.). The other alternative of resorting to sterling loans in London also got exhausted, as could be judged from the failure of the sterling loan in 1931 (ibid.). Under continuous pressure from London,[2] the Government of India sought to ease remittance by ultimately resorting to severe deflation, contracting currency repeatedly and thus causing havoc in the Indian economy, especially in the money market.

However, a total breakdown of the remittance mechanism was averted by the massive export of gold from India that occurred in this period. The gold exports were crucial in compensating for the drastic drop in India's export surplus on commodity transactions

149

(Bannerji 1963: 22, 27; Subramanian and Homfray, 1946: 45–46; Birla 1944: 17). Gold was now offered for sale because the rural population, badly hit by the depression, was forced to use its savings to meet its revenue obligations and consumption requirements (ibid.). Also, the massive deflation pushed gold prices in India below world prices, thereby encouraging its export.[3]

Privately, some British officials like Schuster, the Finance Member, now began to recognize that 'the British government has been alone responsible for the state of affairs in India and for a policy which – wrongly perhaps but nevertheless in fact – the whole Indian public has resented and opposed'. He wrote to Irwin, the Viceroy, in June 1931: 'No one . . . can deny that the position would be much easier today if the rupee had not been stabilized at 1s 6d in 1927. And we are asking a new responsible Indian Government to take on that legacy' (Schuster to Irwin, 1 June 1931, L/PO 269).

Schuster, being aware that 'we are on the brink of a crisis which may mean absolute disaster – not only for India but for Britain also', suggested some conciliatory moves towards Indian financial and political opinion. For example, he suggested the announcing of a credit of about £50 million or better still, the return of the £100 million war gift (made by India to Britain) by the British government to enable India to tide over the present crisis and give her enough resources to set up a Reserve Bank immediately. He pointed out how the currency policy of the Government of India was 'one of the most important factors in the whole anti-British political movement' (L/PO 269). The need to give concessions on this point to the commercial community, who were seen to be 'probably the decisive factor' in the Civil Disobedience movement was also argued.[4]

However, it appeared that Schuster's was a lone voice within the government. Also, it was difficult to say as to 'where Schuster's regime ended and where India Office dictation prevailed'.[5] There was, as a result, little change in government policy regarding finance.

The Indian exchange continued to be shored up and maintained at 1s 6d through monetary and fiscal deflation and continued gold exports. When Britain went off the gold standard due to the financial crisis at home, the rupee was not allowed to adjust itself *vis-à-vis* gold but was forcibly linked to sterling. This was also the period when, as I have shown elsewhere, the prolonged discussions on the proposed Reserve Bank and its final establishment in 1935 took place in a manner that lay bare the basically unchanged nature of imperial policy (Mukherjee 1992: 229–34; Mukherjee 1994: 301–400). Despite protests during the constitutional discussions in the Round Table Conferences and constant pressure through other forums, it was not possible to budge the British on this key area of financial and monetary policy.

This then was the context in which the Indian response to British financial and monetary policy in this period was framed. Indian capitalist leaders and the Federation of Indian Chambers of Commerce and Industry (FICCI), which broadly represented the Indian capitalist class, spearheaded the Indian critique, as they did for most of the economic issues that arose *vis-à-vis* the colonial government in the twentieth century, after the First World War. (The FICCI was established in 1927.) By this time however many Indian capitalists were convinced that merely protesting against British economic policy would not do and a solution was seen in the move towards self-government. As will be seen below, their position now coincided with much of what contemporary nationalist economists and even the leaders of the National movement were saying.

These capitalists, responding perhaps more sharply than on any other economic issue so far, argued that the government financial policy, especially that of maintaining a high exchange through deflation was the root cause of the depression being felt more intensely in India than in other countries of the world.[6] The world depression itself was said to be man-made and caused by the 'exploitation of the less powerful by the more powerful', by 'one politically powerful nation holding the other in subjection and having the best to itself'.[7]

The sophisticated critique that Purshotamdas Thakurdas (a leading light among Indian businessmen) and others had made earlier (in the late 1920s) of the impact of artificially maintaining a high exchange rate of the rupee and of the policy of deflation on agriculture, industry and trade, was again invoked (Mukherjee 1989: 99–124). The great increase in the intensity of this impact was now emphasized. They particularly highlighted the deteriorating condition of the agriculturists as the most distressful development. The sharp fall in prices had hit them hard, especially as export prices fell by 36 per cent, while import prices fell only by 16 per cent between September 1929 and December 1930.[8] The sharp turn in the terms of trade against primary produce affected the 'agriculturist . . . with special severity'.[9] 'The value of India's export trade tumbled from Rs 319.15 crores in 1927–28 to Rs 132.27 crores in 1932–33, the nadir of depression, and even in 1936–37 was only Rs 196.13 crores' (Birla 1944: 17). Not surprisingly, 'the burden of rural indebtedness rose from Rs 900 crores in 1928–29 to Rs 1200 crores by 1933 which in real terms amounted to Rs 2200 crores, assuming that no repayment of debt or payment of interest was made' (ibid.).

G.D. Birla outlined the depressing economic scenario in a letter to J.M. Keynes and sought his support in what he thought was the only remedy to relieve the agriculturist – 'an immediate settlement of political trouble and a *50 per cent rise in prices*' (emphasis added).[10] The Currency League in a press note on 22 November 1933 asserted that the 'crying necessity of today is a rise in the prices of commodities and particularly of primary products and the only way . . . to bring it about is to devaluate the rupee which is being wrongly and unjustifiably maintained at 18d sterling in the face of continuously dropping prices in the country'.[11] It was pointed out that 'the sensational depreciation in the dollar' (by a possible 50 per cent) as well as the depreciation of the currencies of other sterling group countries like Australia and New Zealand (by about 10 to 25 per cent), while the rupee was kept at an unnaturally high level, was leading to Indian produce losing out to that of these countries in the world market.[12]

Further, the critics pointed out that the deflationary policy followed by the government, leading to the withdrawal of 'about 133 crores of rupees from circulation mainly through borrowings' (for example, the recent announcement of the Government of India treasury bonds at 6½ per cent), was leading to extreme tightness in the market. Bank rates shot up to about 7 to 8 per cent in Calcutta and Bombay when money had been 'available in other financial centres at 2 per cent or 1½ per cent'. No funds were available for trade and industry and even 'the marketing of crops . . . maturing in the fields' was becoming difficult.[13]

The high exchange was also depleting India's gold resources, 'threatening the inconvertibility of the currency' and reducing a basic precondition for the starting of a Reserve Bank. The FICCI repeatedly complained that the government, in order to maintain and cheapen remittance, was persisting with a high exchange despite the fact that it exacerbated the economic crisis in India, as it led to the depressing of prices, pushing up of the value of taxes and debt, depletion of gold resources, flight of capital, and a rapid growth in national debt and debt services.[14]

The British Prime Minister's offer in June 1931 of financial aid to India in the form of credit was not received with much enthusiasm, though Schuster had hoped that it would be seen as a conciliatory move (Schuster to Irwin, 1 June 1931, L/PO 269). Such loans, it was said, were only 'temporary palliative(s)' and could not go on for a long time and therefore were not a solution to the problem. Besides, it was 'undesirable' to resort to such methods because not only had the loans to be repaid but the interest services would involve an additional burden, further exacerbating the problem.[15]

The capitalists warned the government of the danger of political upheaval if they continued to pursue the existing monetary policies. There was increasing discontent among the middle class and a definite encouragement of 'Bolshevik tendencies' among the agriculturists and the 'ignorant masses'. The peasant was making persistent demands for land revenue remission and was unable to pay rent or interest charges, and 'almost a blood feud between the zamindar and the tiller of the soil' was developing in many provinces.[16]

Given this context, therefore, the capitalists repeatedly urged the government to bring in reform in the financial sphere. However, while continuing to urge reform, they were increasingly showing awareness of two significant aspects. First, that it was not enough to go on passing resolutions asking for reform; some stronger sanctions were necessary (R.K. Sidhwa in FICCI, *A.R.*, 1931: 106–07). The Congress taking up the sterling ratio question and Gandhiji putting a lower sterling ratio as one of his eleven points were therefore welcomed by them (FICCI, *A.R.* 1931: 105). Second, it was realized that the ultimate solution was political, as the 'economic and financial restoration of India' would occur only when the 'management and control of Indian Currency and Finance' was handed over 'to the elected representatives of the people'. Just as, conversely, 'the substance of self-government' would be achieved only with complete 'fiscal and financial autonomy for India'.[17]

A review of some of the other major issues regarding public finance and monetary policy that came up in these years will provide an indication of how and why some leading capitalists arrived at this position.

The Rupee–Sterling Link

The decision of the Government of India, under the direction of the Secretary of State, to link through an ordinance the rupee to sterling (September 1931), once Britain herself went off the gold standard, met with strong criticisms by the Indian capitalists. The 'arbitrary and despotic action of Sir Samuel Hoare . . . completely ignoring not only the wishes of the Legislative Assembly and the Round Table Conference but also the declared intentions of the Government of India' was described as the 'last straw on the camel's back and the death knell of that intolerable constitution' which gave the Secretary of State such powers.[18] Referring to the earlier British refusal to grant India a proper gold standard and the bringing in instead of the gold exchange standard as a mechanism for introducing a link with sterling through the backdoor, Purshotamdas Thakurdas said that, since September 1931, 'back door became the front door', as the rupee was completely de-linked from gold and firmly linked to the sterling.[19]

However, despite widespread protests, the government remained firm on this point and the rupee remained linked to sterling, giving indirect control over Indian exchange to the Bank of England and the Secretary of State. This link was to continue till as late as April 1947 when, consequent on India joining the International Monetary Fund, the link of the rupee with the sterling was at last severed and the latter became a foreign currency.[20]

The Indian capitalists generally had opposed the link with sterling and argued in favour of the rupee being left free to find its own level. The divorcing of the rupee from sterling was expected to lead to a considerable fall in the rupee in terms of gold, a fall which, as argued repeatedly, would help agriculture and industry and meet the most immediate need of raising prices and give a fillip to exports.[21] By linking the rupee to sterling the government missed the opportunity 'to undo the wrong perpetrated on India by overvaluing the Rupee' (Resolution in FICCI, *A.R.* 1952: 48). The FICCI, in its strongly worded resolution passed in the 1932 annual meeting, listed some other substantive objections to the linking of the rupee to sterling:

> (a) Future management and fate of sterling are and must remain outside the control of the Government of India.
>
> (b) The new valuation of sterling in terms of gold will be determined in accordance with considerations affecting the economic and

financial conditions of the United Kingdom, and may possibly prove detrimental to the economic and financial interests of India.

(c) Any claim of any measure of stability being secured by link to sterling is neither material nor real as sterling itself, under the present conditions, is, not only fluctuating but most unstable.[21]

Further,

had the rupee been allowed to remain linked with gold, as recommended by the Hilton Young Commission and as laid down by the Act of 1927, the obligations of the Government of India in sterling would have cost, when converted, lower and lower in terms of rupee as the sterling depreciated in gold value.[23]

Also, it was said that it was impossible to conceive of a Reserve Bank's reserves held in sterling, as the Government of India seemed to propose. 'There is no certainty when sterling would be stabilized and even if it is stabilized there is no guarantee that Britain will not again abandon Gold Standard.' It was pointed out that the 'National Bank of Egypt had to abandon Gold Standard when Britain abandoned it because it had most of its reserves in sterling.' The rupee, therefore, 'should not remain linked with sterling but should be allowed to find its natural level and then should be independently linked with gold and for that purpose Government of India should acquire gold.'[24]

The apprehension expressed by the FICCI that 'one inevitable consequence of linking the Rupee to Sterling would be the diversion of all Gold and Dollar credits accruing to India for the bolstering up of the value of Sterling' was to turn out to be painfully true, particularly during and immediately after the Second World War, when India was, through the empire dollar pool, 'deprived of many millions of dollars which should, in the normal course, have been made available to her'.[25] I have, in another place, while discussing the sterling balances and the empire dollar pool, commented at length on this question of how the rupee–sterling link was used by Britain to her great advantage at considerable cost to India (Mukherjee 1990: 229–51).

Lastly, in the discussions on Indian financial questions held at the India Office (as part of the Round Table Conference talks) in October 1931, G.D. Birla (another pre-eminent leader of the capitalist class) strongly argued that 'the Ordinances of the Government of India *have not even linked the rupee to sterling,* they have simply stopped the exchange below 1/6d . . . i.e., you allow the exchange to go higher than 1/6d but you do not allow it to drop below 1/6d'.[26] Sir Henry Strakosch, the financial expert from the India Office, was forced to concede that the rupee was actually 'pegged at the lower sterling point', though he added that this was only a legal point and he doubted 'whether the rupee will go of its own accord above 1/6d'.[27]

Quite significantly, in these discussions at the Round Table Conference, Gandhiji, using more or less the arguments put forward by the capitalist leaders, took a firm position in favour of a lower exchange, highlighting the plight of 80 per cent of the population, that is, the agriculturists.[28] The Indian Merchants Chamber and FICCI welcomed this support and conveyed their 'respectful thanks' to the Mahatma for protesting against the policy followed by the Secretary of State.[29]

Gold Exports

Another issue taken up by the capitalists in a big way was the unprecedented level of gold exports from India during the period of the depression. Between 1931–32 and 1939–40, the total value of gold exports was a stupendous Rs 383 crore (Birla 1944: 17). In the initial years of the depression the gold exports were particularly high. 'Practically a couple of gold mines' were put 'at the disposal of England and the world at large',[30] with the shipment of four months alone equalling 'more than one-third of the annual world supply of new gold'.[31]

India had a large export surplus in commodities between 1920–21 and 1930–31, enabling a substantial net import of treasure. However, since 1931–32, in a total reversal of the situation, the export surplus in commodities shrank drastically, and India began to export large amounts of gold. Between 1931–32 and 1938–39, on average, more than half (about 55 per cent) of the total visible (positive) balance of trade (that is, balance of transactions in merchandise and treasure) was met through the net exports of treasure, with the exports of gold increasing sharply in years when the commodity balance of trade was particularly low. For example, in 1932–33, *gold exports constituted about 95 per cent of the total visible positive balance of trade.*[32]

The crucial role of gold exports, therefore, in India's continuing to meet her remittance requirements or 'sterling obligations' – the Home Charges as well as other invisibles such as profits, dividends and interests earned on foreign investments – was evident. And the capitalists repeatedly accused the government of allowing such huge gold exports to continue, despite constant protests, because it wanted precisely to maintain a smooth flow of this remittance.[33] The government was also accused of allowing gold exports with the intention of shoring up the rupee exchange and maintaining it at the inflated rate of 1s 6d, at a time when the falling balance of trade was putting a downward pressure on the rupee.[34] The government's restriction on import of silver and its sale of silver were also said to be leading to the contraction of currency and thus, through deflation, maintaining the bloated value of the rupee at 1s 6d.[35]

More importantly, the capitalists argued how India's gold exports were crucial for British interests at home. At a time when Britain was facing a balance of payments crisis these exports played a major part in *strengthening the value of sterling vis-à-vis gold* and other currencies.[36] 'The help', said N.R. Sarkar, was so 'timely and material that sterling showed a tendency to sag as soon as gold exports from India began to slow down'.[37] The gold exports were also said to have enabled Britain to repay war debts to the US and the 'credits advanced by the Federal Reserve Bank of New York and the Bank of France without drawing upon her (own) gold' (Sarkar, FICCI, *A.R.* 1932: 13–14; Parikh, FICCI, *A.R.* 1933). In fact, argued Sarkar, 'it was most unlikely that if Indian gold were unavailable England would have been able to repay America. In all probability, she would have been forced to default or raise a loan in America' (FICCI, *A.R.* 1933: 27ff).

It was small wonder then that the gold export was one issue on which the British Home government remained very firm. The Governor of the Reserve Bank of India, Osborne Smith, had apparently to resign partially because of his taking a position on this question which was far too independent of the India Office and the Finance Department. His support for the capitalist and the nationalist demand (for devaluation of the rupee to prevent outflow of hoarded gold from India) led to an extraordinary tiff between him and the government, with some choice abuse being traded.[38]

The government put forward several arguments in favour of gold exports – arguments that were systematically countered by the capitalists. N.R. Sarkar, the President of Bengal National Chamber of Commerce, criticized the 'laboured' argument that India's gold exports 'would enable the countries who have gone off the Gold

Standard to return to gold, and that if this did not happen gold might soon depreciate in value and inflict incalculable loss upon the holders of gold in India'. He argued that such an eventuality (was) extremely remote', and besides, if countries like America and France with such large holdings of gold, who

> would stand to lose most from any possible depreciation in the value of gold . . . did not think it necessary to part with any of their gold just in order to help other unfortunate countries to return to the gold standard, it is almost ironical to ask India to step in to do a good turn to a sinking world.[39]

Sarkar also criticized the basic fallacy in the Finance Member Schuster's argument that, given the shrinkage in India's exports, gold exports were necessary to maintain the level of imports. The arguments, he said, assumed that maintenance of imports was necessary for India while actually a decline would give relief to indigenous industry. Besides, if exports could not support the imports, the natural thing to do was not to begin selling gold but to follow the path taken by other countries including England when faced with such a situation, namely, raise tariffs to curtail imports, depreciate currency to stimulate exports and put an embargo on export of gold (Sarkar, FICCI, *A.R.* 1933: 23ff).

Schuster's argument that gold exports would increase the purchasing power of foreign countries who in turn will buy more from India, was ridiculed by Sarkar as a very 'novel' way of pushing exports. He posed a counter-question: since England was in great need of customers and India was one of her greatest customers, 'would Sir George Schuster suggest to England that she should export her gold to India so that it may increase India's purchasing power and enable her to buy more from England?' The need, he said, was not to increase the purchasing power of India's customers but that of India, by retaining Indian gold in India and making it a basis for her currency (Sarkar, FICCI, *A.R.* 1933: 23ff; Mehta FICCI, *A.R.* 1933).

Two other arguments put forward by the Finance Member were also sharply countered. First, the argument that, if gold was not sold to buy sterling, it would result in the government not being able to maintain its statutory obligation to maintain the rupee–sterling ratio. It was pointed out by Sarkar that other countries including the UK were abandoning the basis of their currency system for the sake of preventing an efflux of gold, and besides, he said, 'Sir George (Schuster) . . . could well have assured himself that the disavowal of the Government's obligation to maintain the ratio would be welcome to the commercial community in India who have consistently been complaining against the over-valued rupee' (FICCI, *A.R.* 1933: 26).

Second, Schuster's refusal to restrict the export of gold on the basis of his political philosophy which 'forbids him from interfering with the private liberty of individuals' was also shown to rest on dubious grounds. Making an obvious reference to the political suppression of the second Civil Disobedience movement, A.D. Shroff pointed out that the Finance Member could not invoke *laissez-faire* or non-interference in one sphere, when he himself was an

> important part of the present Government of India, who is responsible not only for suppressing the ordinary liberties of the citizens of this country but whose policy makes impossible, if I may say so, the very exchange of confidences between husband and wife under clause 4 of the Emergency Powers Act which has become the law of the land. (FICCI, *A.R.* 1933: 35ff)

A point that the capitalists repeatedly made was that while so many arguments were given for maintaining India's gold exports, other countries including England were doing exactly the opposite. Since Britain and Japan went off the gold standard, Britain 'allowed its exchange to go down rather than export gold' and Japan 'has prohibited the export of gold by decree'.[40] In fact, far from losing gold, most countries, like England, France, USA, Netherlands and Switzerland, were conserving and actually acquiring gold, while India continued to export gold out of 'considerations other than Indian interests' and was being 'made a pawn in the larger game of imperial finance'.[41]

The capitalists' demand on this question was fairly clear and unequivocal. Through speeches, petitions and resolutions in the FICCI and other chambers of commerce they demanded, year after year, an embargo on the export of gold.[42] They urged that the government use the opportunity of 'distress' gold being available in the market in the present conditions to purchase gold and build up adequate currency reserves, paving the way for the easy establishment of a Reserve Bank in India.[43] This policy, they said, would also lead to the expansion of currency in a 'more natural and safer way' and would provide crucial relief by raising prices to some extent.[44] Interestingly, contemporary nationalist economists V.K.R.V. Rao and P.A. Wadia, in a letter to FICCI, congratulated the body for taking up these demands and urged them to further mobilize public opinion to compel the government to change its policies.[45]

Capitalists like Purshotamdas who had been leading the agitation against the government's financial policy were, however, getting weary of taking part in a movement to stop gold exports, because 'under the present constitution' it may 'mean knocking one's head against a stone wall', as the India Office continued to do the opposite of the general public opinion in India. The 'only remedy' seen therefore was 'to insist on responsibility at the centre in matters currency and financial' in the new constitution.[46] Similarly, Sarkar saw a solution only in the 'establishment of a true national government in India'.[47] There were others who suggested that rather than appealing to the government the capitalists should intervene directly and persuade firms dealing in purchase and export of gold to desist from doing so (Santanam, FICCI, *A.R.* 1933: 44).

Government Budgetary Policy

We have seen above how the government, in order to maintain the 1s 6d ratio and ease remittance, resorted to monetary deflation or contraction of currency in circulation, through measures such as the issuing of Reverse Council Bills, depletion of currency reserves, excessive government borrowing, etc. (Sri Ram, FICCI, *A.R.* 1931: 6). The rapid repatriation of sterling public debt which occurred in this period also had a deflationary effect, causing a further squeeze in the financial situation.[48]

Apart from the monetary deflation, the government also resorted to such 'savage' financial and fiscal deflation, mainly through drastic cuts in expenditure, especially capital expenditure,[49] that the government revenue account showed a surplus for most of the depression years (barring 1930 and 1931), despite a substantial fall in revenue receipts in these years (Bagchi 1975: 45–47, 64–65; Thomas 1939: 496–97). The heavy cuts in government expenditure seriously aggravated the crisis in the economy caused by the depression, by further reducing effective demand. The government, however, continued to defend its orthodox financial policy in the name of 'sound finance' and a 'balanced budget'.

The capitalists also saw the necessity of retrenchment in government expenditure. Some prominent Indian capitalists, including Purshotamdas Thakurdas, were members of the Indian Retrenchment Committee of 1922–23 (Bagchi 1975: 44, 426). However, the position of Indian capitalists on how and where retrenchment was to be done suggests that they did not entirely 'acquiesce' in a policy of 'financial orthodoxy' followed by the 'British rulers', as suggested by A.K. Bagchi in his major work, *Private Investment in India* (Bagchi 1975). A major change in their views and positions appears to have occurred since the 1920s (not, perhaps, taken fully into account by Bagchi), and in the 1930s their difference with the government view became quite evident.[50]

The capitalists almost unanimously argued[51] that, if India was unable to meet her *Home Charges and other sterling obligations,* then the solution lay not in resorting to currency and financial manipulations, export of gold or increased taxation, but in cutting/reducing these obligations themselves. Year after year, through every possible forum, their leading lights argued that the government must considerably cut its expenditure, some arguing for a cut of up to one-third.[52] The areas where they demanded cuts were government civil and military expenditure, and *not capital expenditure* on railways, irrigation or public works. The bureaucracy, it was said, was top-heavy and paid far beyond the financial resources and taxable capacity of India. Hence salaries and pensions should be considerably reduced and further recruitment from Britain should stop.

Much stronger arguments were put in favour of cutting military expenditure. Statistics were given to show how India's defence expenditure as a proportion of total expenditure was the highest in the world, much greater than even countries like the USA, Great Britain, France, Belgium Japan, Canada and Australia. In fact, the actual defence expenditure in India was said to be much higher than that specifically set aside for this purpose in the budget, as expenditure on other items such as strategic railways belonged strictly under the head of defence expenditure.[53] Further, most of the defence expenditure was incurred not directly for India's defence but to meet Britain's world-wide imperial interests – India serving as the proverbial 'milch cow of the British empire' (Purshotamdas, FICCI, *A.R.* 1933). It was therefore demanded that not only should defence expenditure be drastically cut, *inter alia* by replacing British troops with Indian recruits, but that

Britain should share a 'legitimate' proportion of the burden.

In a note circulated at the Round Table Conference in 1933 by Purshotamdas, 'the financial difficulties of India during the last fifteen years' were 'attributed to a large extent to the enormous monetary contributions direct and indirect made by India' (estimated at Rs 305 crore) 'towards the expenditure on the Great War'.[54] The huge 'unproductive' public debt was also said to have accumulated to a large extent to meet British imperial, primarily military, interests. Consequently, in 1932, the FICCI, in a resolution which was reminiscent of the AICC report brought out a few months earlier,[55] demanded 'the appointment of a tribunal for an impartial and thorough investigation into the financial obligation between Great Britain and India'.[56] During the Second World War, with the phenomenal increase in defence expenditure, the demand for a fair allocation of the expenditure came up again in a big way, and the Indian capitalists began endorsing the additional demand for popular control over defence expenditure.[57]

As mentioned earlier, while the capitalists demanded a reduction in civil and military expenditure, they were opposed to cuts in capital expenditure (Lalbhai, FICCI, A.R. 1935: 14). In fact, the argument precisely was that cuts in the former would release funds for 'nation-building departments'.[58]

It was with this perspective that the capitalists looked forward to provincial autonomy as then more funds could be made available to the provinces which would use them for developmental expenditure.[59] The Otto Niemeyer report on financial adjustment between the Government of India and provincial governments was criticized for not recommending cuts in expenditure of the central government, especially military expenditure, thus leaving provincial governments 'no elbow room' for developmental expenditure without resorting to additional taxation.[60] Also, the FICCI urged the government to secure a re-division of the burden of imperial military expenditures at the Imperial Conference so that India may get some relief and 'immediately make available to Provincial Governments considerable sums towards the expenditures of nation building departments'.[61]

Clearly, it was not 'financial orthodoxy' which led the capitalists to argue for cuts in expenditure. They wanted cuts in those areas that they thought were wasteful and not in India's interests, and that created an excuse for financial and monetary manipulations of the government, causing further damage to the Indian economy. For developmental purposes or 'productive' expenditure, they argued, shortage of finance was not a bottleneck, provided the 'fad' or 'fetish' of 'balanced budgets' indulged in by the government was given up and urged that *deficit financing* or *public loans* could help to meet shortfalls in revenue, that if used for productive purposes, 'they do not necessarily prove any inherent weakness in government finances' (Sarkar, FICCI, *A.R.* 1934: 10–11; Birla, FICCI, *A.R.* 1934: 175–76). G.D. Birla argued that even the gold standard reserve could be 'used for economic advancement of the country rather than keeping it invested where it does not benefit India in the least' (FICCI, *A.R.* 1934: 174). Interestingly, the capitalists, who had always opposed the depletion of gold reserves or government borrowing to meet remittance or as a method of deflation, had no hesitation in suggesting that the reserves or government borrowing be used for productive developmental expenditure. Examples were given of how the United States, Japan and Germany under Hitler were using huge deficit budgets or raising large loans for developmental public expenditure.[62] A clear preference was thus expressed for the modern Keynesian conception of finance rather than for the 'orthodoxy of Schuster' (Sarkar FICCI, *A.R.* 1934; Birla FICCI, *A.R.* 1934).

Rather than merely 'wailing for improvement in the world economic situation', the path urged by G.D. Birla in 1934 for recovery from the depression was the adoption by the government of a '*bold reflationary policy* by undertaking a scheme of public works expenditure specially in rural areas' (emphasis added).[63] Further, N.R. Sarkar and others argued that 'the initiation of a vigorous capital programme would prove to be an effective way of stimulating the demand for industrial goods, inducing greater purchasing power in the masses and relieving industries suffering from a dearth of demand and plethora of stocks', and also of finding 'much needed employment for the huge army of unemployed'.[64] The days of 'undiluted *laissez-faire*', it was said, 'are gone for ever' and while all other countries, including England, were giving it up, the government continued to apply it to India (Sarkar, FICCI, *A.R.* 1934: 5, 14).

Clearly, the capitalists saw the necessity of active intervention by the state in wide-ranging areas to enable a basic restructuring of the economy. Planned 'mass action' and 'Government intervention' with the 'cooperation of the people', was necessary if India was to be lifted from the economic morass and achieve 'substantial rise in our standard of living'. 'Half-hearted' tariff protection, quotas, price restriction or other similar tinkering by the government will not 'take us anywhere' unless 'they form links in a chain' with a planned 'purpose behind it' (Birla FICCI, *A.R.* 1934: 167–68). And, as G.D. Birla was to argue repeatedly, 'financial orthodoxy' and the 'fetish of balanced budget' was not to be allowed to come in the way of planned economic development. He asserted that 'those who (brought) in the question of capital', that is, of the shortage of financial resources for developmental expenditure, 'simply wanted to dodge the issue' (Birla, FICCI, *A.R.* 1934: 175–76).

In their criticism of British policy, Indian capitalist circles were naturally bound by their own interests, and could not naturally demand the 'adoption of a framework of socialist planning', which, as Bagchi argues, was necessary 'for the removal of the basic obstacles to industrial development in India'. However, neither were they quite satisfied with 'mercantilist platitudes' contenting 'themselves by demanding tariff protection' (Bagchi 1975: 426–27). Their vision of Indian economic development, though within bourgeois parameters, in some ways even anticipated the innovations brought about in the world capitalist system in the years to come.[65]

Notes

[1] Schuster, Finance Member, to Irwin, Viceroy.

[2] George Schuster, the Finance Member, wrote to Viceroy Irwin on 1 June 1931: 'We have been getting the usual telegrams from London trying to force us to contract, contract, contract and put up the bank rate – in their own words "to create a money famine", which will make it impossible for people here to get rupees to sell for sterling. They say if you only do that you will get remittance.' L/PO 269.

[3] Speech of N.R. Sarkar, BNCC President, 5 Febrary 1932, *Purshotamdas Thakurdas Papers* (hereafter *PT Papers*), press clippings, fl. 11, Nehru Memorial Museum and Library, New Delhi.

[4] See Viceroy, Willingdon, to Samuel Hoare, Secretary of State, 14 March 1932, attaching a note by Schuster, L/PO 271.

[5] Review of Schuster's work in the last five years by the financial expert and major capitalist leader Purshotamdas Thakurdas, 5 May 1934, *PT Papers*, fl. 76. See also Schuster's speech in FICCI defending the 1s 6d ratio, denying the role of currency policy in the depression and attributing India's depreciated credit abroad to the Civil Disobedience movement (Federation of Indian Chambers of Commerce and Industry, *Annual Report*; hereafter referred to as FICCI, *A.R.*: 1931).

[6] C.B. Mehta in *Free Press Journal*, 20 September 1931, *PT Papers*, press clippings, fl. 13; Sri Ram, President, FICCI, *A.R.* 1931: 6.

[7] Purshotamdas, *Free Press Journal*, 20 September 1931, *PT Papers*, press clippings, fl. 13.

[8] G.D. Birla's letter to *Manchester Guardian*, 2 October 1931, *PT Papers*, fl. 111, pt 1.

[9] Memor. 'On the Rs./stg. Ratio', 19 September 1933, enclosure to G.D. Birla to Purshotamdas, 20 October 1933, *PT Papers*, fl. 145.

[10] 28 May 1932, *PT Papers*, fl. 107, pt II.

[11] *PT Papers*, fl. 145; see also Purshotamdas to Schuster, 24 November 1933, *PT Papers*, fl. 145.

[12] A.D. Shroff to Sir Osborne Smith, 22 November 1933 and Memor. 'On the Rs./Std. Ratio', 19 September 1933, *PT Papers*, fl. 145; Purshotamdas, Notes on Minutes of Dissent on the Report of the Committee on Indian Reserve Bank Legislation, 1 September 1933, *PT Papers*, fl. 189.

[13] G.D. Birla, *Manchester Guardian*, 2 October 1931; Purshotamdas, Note dated October 1931, *PT Papers*, fl. 111, pt 1; Jamal Mahomed, President, FICCI, to Schuster, 9 September 1931, *Walchand Hirachand (WH) Papers*, fl. 8, pt II; Purshotamdas in *Bombay Chronicle*, 3 September 1931, *PT Papers*, press clippings, fl. 11; President, FICCI, *A.R.* 1937: 8ff.

[14] Jamal Mahomed, President, FICCI, to Schuster, 9 September 1931, Press Statement by Jamal Mahomed 9 October 1931, *Walchand Hirachand Papers*, fl. 8, pt II. For a general criticism of a high ratio and the demand for a lower ratio also see, FICCI resolutions on currency and exchange in FICCI, *A.R.* 1930, 1931, 1934, and Purshotamdas's reply to Schuster in FICCI, *A.R.* 1930: 118ff.

[15] Jamal Mahomed to Schuster, 9 September 1931, *Walchand Hirachand Papers* (hereafter *WH Papers*), Nehru Memorial Museum and Library, fl. 8, pt II.

[16] Purshotamdas to the Viceroy, Willingdon, 18 June 1931, *PT Papers*, fl. 106; Purshotamdas in *Bombay Chronicle*, 3 September 1931, *PT Papers*, press clippings, fl. 11; Currency League of India, press note, 24 November 1933, *PT Papers*, fl. 145.

[17] Purshotamdas in *Bombay Chronicle*, 26 September 1931, *PT Papers*, press clippings, fl. 13 and in FICCI, *A.R.* 1932: 56; D.P. Khaitan in FICCI, *A.R.* 1931: 97–98.

[18] Resolution, FICCI, *A.R.* 1932: 49; press statement by President of FICCI, Jamal Mahomed, on exchange and currency policy of Government of India, 9 October 1931, *WH Papers*, fl. 8, pt II; FICCI telegram to Secretary of State, 24 September 1931, FICCI, *Proceedings of the Executive Committee* (hereafter *Proc. of E.C.*), 1931: 14–16.

[19] Article by Purshotamdas called 'Currency and Exchange' in a volume published by the American Academy of Political and Social Science, USA, May 1944, *PT Papers*, fl. 280.

[20] *Free Press Journal*, 22 January 1947, *Times of India*, 17 April 1947 and Speech of Indian Merchant's Chamber President, May 1947, *WH Papers*, fl. 92: 1.

[21] See G.D. Birla's note to Gandhiji during the Round Table Conference (RTC) discussions, October 1931, and Purshotamdas in the Discussion of Indian Financial Questions held at India Office, 16 October 1931, *PT Papers*, fl. 111, pt. II.

[22] FICCI, *A.R.* 1932: 48–49. See also telegram by Indian Merchant's Chamber to Government of India, Finance Department, 22 September 1931, *PT Papers*, fl. 111, pt II.

[23] Indian Chamber of Commerce, Great Britain, to the Secretary of State, 1931 (no date), *PT Papers*, fl. 111, pt 1 and resolution passed by public meeting organized by Indian Merchant's Chamber, Bombay, 25 September 1931, *PT Papers*, fl. 111, pt II.

[24] C.B. Mehta of Bombay Bullion Exchange in FICCI, *A.R.* 1933: 34.

[25] Press Communique, FICCI, *Correspondence Volumes* (hereafter *Corresp.*), 1944: 43.

[26] 6 October 1931, *PT Papers*, fl. 113.

[27] Discussion at the India Office of Indian Financial Questions, 6 October 1931, *PT Papers*, fl. 113.

[28] Gandhiji's note to Strakosch, 23 October 1931, *PT Papers*, fl. 111, pt II and report of discussions at India Office, 16 October 1931, *PT Papers*, fl. 113.

[29] Resolution passed at Public Meeting organized by the India Merchants' Chamber (IMC), Bombay, 25 September 1931, *PT Papers*, fl. 111, pt II, and telegram from FICCI committee to Gandhi, 24 September 1931, FICCI, *Proc. of EC*, 1931: 14–16.

[30] Purshotamdas, Note on Schuster's Work over the Last Five Years, 5 May 1934, *PT Papers*, fl. 76.

[31] Speech of N.R. Sarkar, President, Bengal National Chamber of Commerce (BNCC), 5 February 1932, *PT Papers*, press clippings, fl. 11.

[32] The above figures have been computed from Subramanian and Homfray, 1946: Table XII, 45–46. C.B. Mehta of Bombay Bullion Exchange cites similar figures for 1931 to 1938, FICCI, *A.R.* 1938: 46–50. See also Kasturbhai Lalbhai, President, FICCI, *A.R.* 1935: 6.

[33] See, for example, N.R. Sarkar, 5 February 1932, *PT Papers*, press clippings, fl. 11; G.D. Birla to Keynes, 28 May 1932, *PT Papers*, fl. 107, pt II; M.R. Parikh of Bombay Bullion Exchange, FICCI, *A.R.* 1933: 42; confidential letter of FICCI to member bodies, 30 July 1936, FICCI, *Corresp.*, 1936: 104–06; C.B. Mehta, FICCI, *A.R.* 1938: 46–50.

[34] N.R. Sarkar, 5 February 1932, *PT Papers*, press clippings, fl. 11; M.R. Parikh, FICCI, *A.R.* 1933: 42; Kasturbhai Lalbhai, FICCI, *A.R.* 1935: 6; Resolution in FICCI, *A.R.* 1939: 19.

[35] A.D. Shroff in FICCI, *A.R.* 1935: 589 and FICCI, *Proc. of EC*, 1936: 55.

[36] Walchand Hirachand, President, FICCI, *A.R.* 1933: 5; C.B. Mehta and M.R. Parikh, FICCI, *A.R.* 1933: 423; N.R. Sarkar, 5 February 1932, *PT Papers*, press clippings, fl. 11; Purshotamdas, 5 May 1934, *PT Papers*, fl. 76.

[37] BNCC Presidential Speech, 5 February 1932, *PT Papers*, press clippings, fl. 11.

[58] L/PO 321. For a detailed account of the unusually strong difference between

Osborne Smith and the Government of India, especially the Finance Member, James Grigg, where Smith ended up calling the Viceroy a 'weak ass, terrified of failure' and Grigg 'a liar, undercover slanderer and mongrel . . . a dirty scurrilous swine', etc., see exchange of telegrams between the Secretary of State and the Viceroy, September–October 1936, L/PO 321, and Osborne Smith to Purshotamdas, 16 November and 24 October 1936, *PT Papers*, fl. 105.

[39] Presidential Speech, 5 February 1932, *PT Papers*, press clippings, fl.11.

[40] Purshotamdas in *Advance*, 6 January 1932, *PT Papers*, press clippings, fl. 13.

[41] FICCI, *Proc. of EC*, 1934, A.R. 1934: 55, A.R. 1933: 27ff., and N.R. Sarkar, 5 February 1932, *PT Papers*, press clippings, fl. 11.

[42] See, for example, FICCI telegram to Finance Member, 12 October 1931, FICCI, *Proc. of Ec*, 1931: 16; Speech of President, FICCI, *A.R.* 1932: 7; and Resolutions passed on this subject in FICCI, *A.R.* 1932, 1934, 1935 and 1936.

[43] Resolutions in FICCI, *A.R.* 1932: 9, *A.R.* 1933: 22ff. N.R. Sarkar, 5 February 1932 in *PT Papers*, press clippings, fl. 11, and FICCI, *A.R.* 1933; Purshotamdas in Joint Select Committee of the Round Table Conference (RTC), 26 May 1933, *PT Papers*, fl. 138.

[44] Jamal Mahomed, President, FICCI, *A.R.* 1932: 7, and G.D. Birla to Lord Lothian, 4 August 1932, *PT Papers*, fl. 126.

[45] April 1932 (?), *PT Papers*, fl. 42, pt VI.

[46] Purshotamdas to Montagu, 10 October 1932, *PT Papers*, press clippings, fl. 11, and Purshotamdas in *Times of India*, 24 March 1933.

[47] Speech, 5 February 1932, *PT Papers*, press clippings, fl. 11.

[48] See Purshotamdas to A.R. Smith, 9 February 1929, *PT Papers*, press clippings, fl. 11.

[49] Kasturbhai Lalbhai, President of FICCI, accused the government of reducing their public-work expenditure by as much as 50 per cent. FICCI, *A.R.* 1935: 13–14. B.R. Tomlinson estimates a much sharper drop with the government outlay on capital expenditure declining from an average of Rs 27 crore between 1920–30 to an average of Rs 6 crore between 1931–39; see Tomlinson (1979: 91).

[50] Bagchi (1975). Quite significantly, Purshotamdas refused an invitation by Schuster in May 1931 to be a member of the retrenchment committee. The main argument he gave for his refusal was that he felt that there was a need for a basic change in government policy regarding the expenditure of military and other departments. Mere tinkering would not do. See Purshotamdas to Willingdon, 4 June 1931, *PT Papers*, fl. 106.

[51] The information and arguments in this and the following two paragraphs are taken from the following sources except where otherwise indicated. They are cited together as there is a considerable degree of overlap. G.D. Birla, FICCI, *A.R.* 1930: 13; Sri Ram, President, FICCI, *A.R.* 1931: 7; Purshotamdas to Willingdon, 4 June 1931, *PT Papers*, fl. 106; Jamal Mahomed, 5 February 1932, *PT Papers*, press clippings, fl. 11; Jamal

Mahomed, President, FICCI, *A.R.* 1932: 8; Presidential speech by Walchand Hirachand and Resolution on salaries of government servants, FICCI, *A.R.* 1933; Resolution on Military Expenditure, FICCI, *Proc. of E.C.*, 1934; Resolution on Budget Proposals, FICCI, *Proc. of EC*, 1936: 51; FICCI to Government of India, Finance Department, 2 March 1938, FICCI, *Proc. of EC*, 1937: 43–45.

[52] Walchand Hirachand to Schuster, 9 September 1931, *WH Papers*, fl. 8, pt II.

[53] Note circulated by Purshotamdas to members of the Sub Committee on Defence Expenditure, Round Table Conference, 7 July 1933, *PT Papers*, fl. 139.

[54] 7 July 1933, *PT Papers*, fl. 139.

[55] Report on the Financial Obligations between Great Britain and India, by a select committee appointed by the AICC Working Committee, sd. K.T. Shah, Bhulabhai Desai and D.N. Bahadurji, July 1931, *Bhulabhai Desai Papers*, fl. 12, Nehru Memorial Museum and Library. The report made out a case for India transferring her public debt to England.

[56] FICCI, *A.R.* 1932: 27, and G.D. Birla to Purshotamdas, 14 January 1932, *PT Papers*, fl. 42, pt VII.

[57] See, for example, FICCI to Finance Department, Government of India, 13 July and 4 September 1942, regarding the financial adjustment between Her Majesty's Government and the Government of India with reference to the defence expenditure of India, FICCI, *Corresp.*, 1942: 133–46; FICCI, Assistant Secretary N.G. Abhyankar's note on India's defence expenditure and its allocation between India and Britain, September 1941, *PT Papers*, fl. 254. Also see the strong position taken by N.R. Sarkar and H.P. Mody, members of the Viceroy's Executive Council, on this question, in Viceroy to Secretary of State, 7 December 1942, L/PO 325.

[58] Jamal Mahomed, President, FICCI, *A.R.* 1932: 8, and Resolution on Government Tax and Military Expenditure in FICCI, *Proc. of EC*, 1934 and *A.R.* 1936.

[59] FICCI to Government of India, Commerce Department, 26 April 1937, FICCI, *Corresp.*, 1937: 238–40; N.R. Sarkar, President's Speech, FICCI, *A.R.* 1934.

[60] Purshotamdas to D.P. Khaitan, 19 May 1936, and attached FICCI draft letter to Finance Department on Otto Niemeyer Report, *PT Papers*, fl. 175, pt I. It may be noted that the FICCI draft does demand cuts in railway expenditure though on the grounds that its management was costly and bureaucratic leading to its not being able to contribute to the general revenues of the country.

[61] 26 April 1937, *Economic and Overseas Dept.*, L/E/9/1149, IOR, London.

[62] It was pointed out that the USA decided to have a deficit budget of $9,000 million, while Japan and the USA raised huge loans of 811 million yens and $3 billion respectively. See Sarkar and Birla in FICCI, *A.R.* 1934: 11 and 175 respectively.

[63] G.D. Birla, FICCI, *A.R.* 1934: 159–60. It is important to note that Birla

particularly emphasized the 'rural areas' because he argued that it was in this sphere (along with trade) that the impact of the depression was felt most severely and also it involved the vast majority of the population. Industry, he pointed out, in many areas such as cotton, jute and steel was not doing so badly due to a combination of monopoly and protection. Besides, industry, he said, employed 'no more than 35 lakhs of men, viz., just one per cent of the total population'. Birla, FICCI, *A.R.* 1934: 150–64. See also, Kasturbhai Lalbhai, Presidential Speech, FICCI, *A.R.* 1935: 13–14.

[64] N.R. Sarkar, President, FICCI, *A.R.* 1934: 14 and Resolution on capital expenditure by government, FICCI, *Proc. of EC,* 1934.

[65] This is an aspect I have described in considerable detail in 'Indian Capitalist Class and Congress on National Planning and Public Sector, 1930–47', *Economic and Political Weekly,* XIII, 35, 2 September 1978; reprinted in Panikkar (1980: 45–79), and in *Imperialism, Nationalism and the Making of the Indian Capitalist Class 1927–1947,* chapters 1 and 11 (forthcoming).

References

Bagchi, A.K., 1975, *Private Investment in India 1900–39,* Madras.

Bannerji, A.K., 1965, *India's Baance of Payments,* Bombay.

Birla, G.D., 1944, *Indian Currency in Retrospect,* Allahabad.

Federation of Indian Chambers of Commerce and Industry, *Annual Report* (FICCI, A.R.), New Delhi.

Grover, V. and R. Arora (eds), 1994, *Development of Politics and Government in India,* New Delhi.

Mukherjee, Aditya, 1978, 'Indian Capitalist Class and Congress on National Planning and Public Sector, 1930–47', *Economic and Political Weekly,* XIII, 35, September.

———, 1989, 'The Rupee Question, 1926–28: Rupee–Sterling Ratio and the Gold Standard', *Studies in History,* V, I, new series.

———, 1990, 'Indo-British Finance: The Controversy over India's Sterling Balances, 1939–47', *Studies in History,* VI, 2, new series.

———, 1992, 'Controversy over Formation of Reserve Bank of India, 1927–35', *Economic and Political Weekly,* XXVII.

Panikkar, K.N. (ed.), 1980, *National and Left Movements in India,* New Delhi.

Secretary of States' Private Office Papers (L/PO), India Office Library and Records (IOR), London.

Subramanian and Homfray, 1946, *Recent Social and Economic Trends in India,* New Delhi: Government of India.

Thomas, P.J., 1939, *The Growth of Federal Finance,* London.

Tomlinson, B.R., 1979, *Political Economy of the Raj, 1914–47,* London.

Reforming Rural Credit
Experience under the
Fazlul Huq Ministry in Bengal

Manzur Ahsan

Abul Mansur Ahmed has written:

> Debt Settlement Boards, the Bengal Tenancy Act and the Money-
> lenders law inaugurated a welcome note in lives of tenant-*proja* and
> peasant debtors of Bengal. In effect they were saved from imminent
> death. Consequently the two three years of Huq Ministry could be
> regarded as golden age for the Ministers in general and peasants and
> debtor peasants in particular. (Ahmed 1969: 176)

Fazlul Huq himself, recounting his achievement in giving
relief to the debtor, declared, 'I stand here and say that not a single
province in India has been able to achieve even one-tenth of what we
have done here' (*Proceedings* 1938: 112–13). This essay is an attempt to
evaluate Fazlul Huq's contribution in alleviating the debt burden of
the peasantry. Before we proceed to the main discussion, we may take
a general view of the credit system as it stood before the coming to
power of the Fazlul Huq ministry.

Credit Relations
During the settlement operations the British officials were
struck by two contradictory phenomena in the agrarian sector, low
rent and high incidence of debt. Ascoli, the settlement officer of Dacca
district, noted that the cultivator's 'payment to his landlord in rent,
premiums and *abwabs*' formed a small percentage of his earnings,
while 'his burden of debt and the consequent domination of the money
lenders' (*Dacca RSS*: 50) formed the most prominent features of
peasants' lives. Ascoli, making a conservative estimate, calculated that
the average indebtedness per family in Dacca was Rs 122, the figure
per indebted family would be Rs 250. An average rate of interest of 45

per cent necessitated an annual payment of Rs 2,14,20,000 to the moneylenders, which was approximately a fifth of the total produce of the soil and five-and-a half times the total amount paid as rent to the landlords. Every person supported by agriculture, while having to make an average payment of Rs 2.50 as rent, was expected to make an annual payment of Rs 12 or slightly less than a quarter of his average share in the produce as interest (*Dacca RSS: 47*). The settlement officer in Mymensingh in his report (1919) doubted whether the situation in his district was as bad as in Dacca, but acknowledged that

> interest is so high in this country that its payment constitutes a severe drain on the resources of the agricultural population, especially as only a small fraction of total indebtedness can be considered as capital employed productively. Apparently it has jumped from an insignificant sum to its present proportions in the last thirty years. (*Mymensingh RSS*: 27)

The officer also believed that the *ryots*' rents and *abwabs* were lower (ibid.: 25) The settlement officer in Pabna also noted 'widespread and crushing' indebtedness.[1] Obviously, debt and interest formed the bulk channel through which the meagre surplus generated from agriculture was siphoned off. The settlement officer in Bankura wrote:

> The average cultivator is heavily in debt. He hands over the greater part of his harvest to his mahajan to meet existing obligations and, as he is usually unable to maintain himself with the balance till the next harvest, he has to borrow again a few months after. He pursues his career of borrowing and repaying from year's to year's end, always adding to his burden and never making any advance towards release. (*Bankura RSS*: 17)

The Bengal Provincial Banking Enquiry Committee in 1929 tried to give an all-Bengal estimation of debt. Its estimate of the debt figure stood at Rs 100 crore, with an average of Rs 160 per agriculturist family (Government of Bengal 1929–30: 69–70). The Bengal Board of Economic Enquiry calculated a figure of Rs 97 crore as the total debt in 1933, the average being Rs 187 per family (Bengal Board of Economic Enquiry 1935: 5–6).

Why was indebtedness so endemic in Bengal? A number of hypotheses have been put forward by observers and research scholars to explain the phenomenon. Marxist and nationalist historians argued that indebtedness was a consequence of colonial rule. The British introduced exorbitantly high land revenue to be paid in cash, which in turn compelled the peasants to produce for cash crops. Since the farmers increasingly became dependent upon the sale of their products in the market, moneylenders appeared on the scene to cater to the peasants' need for regular supplies of credit. R.K. Roy writes, 'Money-lending operation within village society set in motion the broader outflow of resources from the colony to metropolitan country. Through the operations of the rural credit system agricultural produce and raw materials were extracted from Bengal's village at abnormally low prices for ultimate transfer out of the country' (Roy 1973: 271).

A number of British officials blamed the litigious habits and extravagance of the peasants for indebtedness. But serious British analysts thought otherwise. They argued that low productivity and stagnation of agriculture was the main reason for the pervasive debt problem. The Bengal Banking Enquiry Committee held that 'there is a kind of poverty which, while not amounting to insolvency, nevertheless, makes for precarious and uncertain living. It is this latter class of poverty which is the real cause of indebtedness among agriculturists in Bengal' (Government of Bengal 1929–30: 71). In recent times this theory has received reformulation among the Cambridge historians. M.M. Islam has argued that the problem of indebtedness became acute under the colonial rule because of the lack of full commercialization of agriculture. He also writes:

> the problem of debt was the result of the low level of income of the vast majority of the peasants. . . . Since production for meeting subsistence needs was the dominant pattern and cultivators borrowed mainly for special needs arising at times of crop failure, illness, weddings and funerals, the supply of credit was scarce and the risk of default high. (Islam 1980: 41–42)

Sugata Bose has combined the low productivity thesis with a Marxist rationale. He argues:

> Faced with a rapidly diminishing holding that could not sustain a family with subsistence crops, the peasant smallholder switched to the cultivation of a high-value and labour-intensive cash crop, exposing himself in the process to the volatility of international price movements. Rendered subservient to the forces of the world

capitalist economy, the peasant family economy was perpetuated and impoverished through the operation of merchant and usury capital. The credit network served as the crucial link between the export sector and the more self-contained sectors of the agrarian economy, making insulation from the shock waves of the international economy exceedingly difficult. (Bose 1987: 36)

All these various explanations reveal interesting insights into the complex problem of indebtedness, but these touch only, symptoms of the problem rather than the root cause. Any economic problem in colonial Bengal needs to be addressed within the broader context of the colonial economic structure. In the usual capitalistic road to development historically it was observed that government always supported private property and stood behind landlords and capitalists. What happened in Bengal was far from the usual model of relationship between the state and propertied classes in western Europe. Here, foreign trade was monopolized by the British. The British de-industrialized and kept the country as a raw-material appendage of Britain. Since agriculture and industry enjoys a symbiotic relationship, the agricultural sector became stagnant because of stifled industrial growth. After 1859, the British, by a number of tenancy amendments, made important curtailments in the power and privileges of the *zamindars*. Against the backdrop of increasing tension between the *zamindars* and peasants, the British thought that that the fury of peasants against the *zamindars* might be directed against them too. They might also have been conscious of the grim reality that industrial–urban development was not vibrant enough to absorb the mass of appropriated and evicted tenants. Therefore they made an unprecedented move from political considerations. They decided to appease the peasants and give them some rights *vis-à-vis* the landlords. The *zamindari* system was not abolished but it was kept on in an attenuated form. At the same time, however, the tenants were not given full property rights but they were given a stake on the land that they had under their possession. Thus a conflict situation was created in the rural scenario whereby the *zamindars* were faced with recalcitrant tenants on the question of rent, and the picture was hardly encouraging for the *zamindars* in terms of incentive to improve the productivity of their lands because the ownership was made fuzzy by a number of British-made encasements.

In Bengal the *zamindars* could not play any role in commercialization because they were denied the right incentives. Rather, the colonialists held that the peasants should act as a catalyst to commercialization in Bengal. Peasants with meagre resources and tiny plots under their possession were expected to produce cash crops for raw materials for industries in Dundee or New York. The Bengal peasants were integrated with the world market before integrating with the domestic market. This worked well for some time, particularly when there was growing demand for the products of Bengal. Though the surplus from commercialization, instead of being recycled into domestic economy, went out of the country for serving the interests of the metropolis, some prosperity did trickle down to the peasants. The peasants needed money to grow cash crops and moneylenders came forward to cater to the needs of finance. The *zamindars*, finding income from land ever-decreasing and having no alternative avenues for investment, turned towards the burgeoning moneylending business. So long as the boom continued, everybody, from moneylenders to peasants, involved in cash crops enjoyed the benefit. But in 1930, when the depression set in, the whole system collapsed and the debt crisis acquired a nightmarish magnitude. A landlord entrepreneur having enough resources at his disposal could have been in a better position to absorb the shock coming from the international vagaries of economic crisis, but a peasant working on an atomistic and tiny holding had no means to cope with the problem. If the British had created full private ownership for the peasants, some peasants could have risen above the others through a process of accumulation and creation of large-scale farming, and they could have faced the challenge characteristic of capitalistic growth. Since the peasants were not given the right of full property ownership, they lacked the incentive to go through the hazards of making investments in the land and enjoying the rewards of higher production. Thus the problem of debt was a built-in-phenomenon of the colonial economic structure.

The depression of the 1930s might seem bizarre to a layman but not to a perceptive observer. However, the catastrophe boded ill for all involved in the rural landscape. A government report observed in 1932:

> for the second and third years in succession few landlords were able to collect as much as 50 per cent of their current demand amicably. The Zamindars found themselves in danger of having their estates

sold up for failure to pay their revenue and they were obliged to press hard for collection from tenants who had themselves collected practically nothing from their subtenants. (*Report of Land Revenue Administration* 1931–32: 201)

There were endemic sales of immovable properties in civil and revenue courts. In many cases, bidders were not forthcoming and the decree-holders were hesitant to purchase owing to difficulties of re-settlement with any advantage (*Report of Land Revenue Administration* 1933–34: 1). With the decline in prices of agricultural products, there was a corresponding rise in prices in everyday necessities. The bewildered peasants, so long used to easy credit, found it hard to meet their obligations and necessities of life as the moneylenders became shy of making advances. They could with difficulty realize the money they had lent and they had little cash to spare. The government was also very perturbed; the peasants' inability to pay their rent heightened government anxiety of depleted revenue income from the *zamindars*. The government perceived a political problem in it. There was a serious anti-*mahajan* riot in Mymensingh in 1930 (Bose 1982: 463–91), and though similar disturbances did not spread to other parts of Bengal, the government was apprehensive that local recalcitrance may be connected with a wider movement. The colonial authority, always conscious of its tenuous hold in the *mofussil* areas, tended to find a political overtone in it. The Civil Disobedience movement, with its thrust in the rural areas, only reinforced their anxiety. The government became increasingly convinced that non-payment of rent among the peasants was 'at first due to sheer inability to pay but has now become the result of an unwillingness to recognize any duty to pay'.[2] The government had additional reasons to be ruffled about the Muslims of eastern Bengal, who had to bear the brunt of low agricultural prices as a result of the depression and might switch their allegiance to leaders inimical to the British interest. Azizul Huq, a Minister in 1936, voiced the government's fears when he wrote:

> The average Bengal agriculturist is much too conservative, spiritual and resigned to his fate to be easily amenable to socialistic and communist preaching. . . . Rural indebtedness condemns the agriculturist to the position of a slave and the cultivator and his children have to be immediately saved from perpetual serfdom. Release the cultivator from the bonds of indebtedness, help him to

make agriculture pay and the country will be saved from some of the dangers of communism. (Huque 1939: 151)

The government opted to play the role of saviour of the peasantry. In western Europe the government had backed the financial capitalists but here, on the contrary, very similar to their strategy towards the landlords and the peasants, they wanted to protect the debtors. The government probably thought if they sided with the financial capitalists they could be the target of peasant wrath. Therefore, it was politically prudent to side with the debtors, the major segment of the population, and to win the sympathy and goodwill of the peasants as their best protector. The government, in 1933, passed the Bengal Moneylenders Act, curbing the interest rates. The Bengal Agricultural Debtors (BAD) Act of 1935 was passed because, in the words of a confidential official record, 'The agriculturists of Bengal, particularly of its fertile and previously most thriving districts, have become involved in debt far beyond their power to repay, and unless a remedy is provided, the consequences may be disastrous to the province.'[3] Fazlul Huq became the Premier in 1937 under the provincial autonomy introduced by the Act of 1935. He extended the operation of debt settlement boards which had been operating since 1935–36 in a limited sense throughout the province and passed another Moneylenders Act.

Debt Settlement Boards

Under this Act, the debt settlement boards were to be established to give relief to debtors and creditors by way of scaling down their outstanding debts. The boards would induce the creditors to reduce the total debt to an amount which the debtors could repay in ten or fifteen instalments. There were to be two types of boards, ordinary and special. The ordinary board would consist of five members to be nominated by the Collector from among the 'influential men of the locality'. The special board, also consisting of five members but chaired by a government official, would deal with cases referred to it by the ordinary board. These were given power to exercise compulsion in settling the debts of creditors who would unreasonably refuse to settle debts amicably. Ordinary boards were generally given jurisdiction over one, two or three *chowkidari* unions but special boards had jurisdiction over a whole *chowkidari* circle or a whole sub-division, such jurisdiction of the two being always concurrent. A debtor or any of his creditors could submit applications for settlement of debts by depositing twelve *annas* with the board within whose jurisdiction he lived. After considering the application, the board would issue a notice giving one month's time for filing a statement of debt by the creditor or the debtor. At the same time, if the board found that a case or an executive or certificate proceeding was pending before a civil or revenue court with respect to any debt for which application had been filed, the board would issue a stay order on the proceedings. The next step would be to state the amount of debt due to different creditors and also ascertain the income and expenditure of the debtor and the surplus amount payable for each instalment. After this the award would be made. The property of the debtor would act as surety for the payment of the amount payable under the award. Proceedings before the boards were to be conducted by the parties themselves or by their agents: legal practitioners were not to have access to the boards.

The performance of the debt settlement boards did not speak of a success story. Till 1943, out of the total applications submitted to the boards for settlement, only 31 per cent were settled either partially or wholly, 29 per cent were pending, and 40 per cent were transferred and dismissed.[4] There were a number of reasons for such a poor performance. Success of mutual settlement of debts depended on the mutual willingness of both the debtors and creditors to settle their obligations. But this was hardly forthcoming, particularly from the debtors. Most of the peasants were living at subsistence level, with little surplus, and their miserable life was aggravated further because of the continuous fall in prices of their products during the depression years. In the cases where the boards appeared to be successful in making amicable settlements, there was the chronic problem of debtors' inability to keep the instalments going smoothly. The Collector of Mymensingh rightly observed:

> Very few cultivators have substantial 'surplus' income. Even if the crops are slightly below normal or some of the earning members fall ill during part of the year, the so-called surplus is turned into deficit. Hence most creditors have little faith that debtors would be able to pay according to the terms of the award.[5]

The inability of the peasants was not the sole reason for the poor performance of the boards. Many peasants took advantage of the

Act to evade immediate threat from the creditors and prolonged their obligation as long as possible. If cases were filed in the civil courts against the debtors they would rush to the settlement boards, receive stay orders requesting stay of proceedings, after which they would show no interest in the case filed. It often happened that when a landlord secured a certificate decree after spending time and money against a defaulting tenant, on the sale date the tenant would appear 'triumphantly brandishing a *parwana* printed on a yellow paper staying the sale'.[6]

If a debtor failed to comply with the board's notice, it would dismiss his application; the effect of dismissal would disqualify him from having any benefit of the law for good. The government was however conscious that this warning would not induce many to respond to the board's call. Therefore, much against the spirit of the mutual debt settlement, the Act provided (section 16) that a board would have the power to coerce the parties to ensure attendance by the issue of summons, warrants of arrest and to use section 174 of Indian Penal Code if it became absolutely necessary. To show success, many boards in Faridpur, Maymensingh and Rajshahi issued warrants against debtors to compel them to appear and submit statements in creditors' cases. The government was reluctant to use coercion, as it would go against the spirit of the Act. The Cooperative Credit and Rural Indebtedness Department, in a circular issued on 28 October 1940, strongly expressed its repugnance against such measures. It stated unequivocally, 'Government are of opinion that instead of arrest, propaganda achieves better result.'[7] The result was not satisfactory; as the Collector of Rajshahi pointed out, 'persuasive measures and propaganda sound well in theory but have proved almost futile in the matter of ensuring attendance of parties'. He also noted that government abhorrence of punitive measures 'has had the effect of making debtors somewhat indolent about their attendance despite all sorts of persuasion, specially when they become engaged in their agricultural pursuits'.[8] By late 1942 exasperation among the higher officials because of endemic absence of parties reached high levels; they felt that 'non appearance of the parties, and the consequent dismissal of the cases prevents the conciliation of the debts and thereby largely frustrates the object of the B.A.D. Act'. All the district officials were directed to take action to see that the parties were compelled to attend.[9] The joint secretary justified the order. He emphasized, 'I think it was contemplated that coercive action should be taken against the parties for compelling attendance when all other methods fail, though the idea was that such steps should not be taken ordinarily.'[10]

The success of the debt settlement board depended on the eagerness and interest of the members who composed it. The selected members showed initial enthusiasm in the novelty of the work, but their euphoria was to soon vanish. Many members did not attend meetings; there were frequent stoppages of work because there was no quorum. The work was honorary and it could not be expected that the members would attend in spite of their private and domestic affairs. In view of the bleak scenario as to the success of the boards, the officials of local governments had the idea that if honorary members were replaced with stipendiary officials, things might improve. J.A. Dash, Commissioner of Rajshahi Division, was so pessimistic as to the 'prospect of recovery of loans and arrears of rent' that, in a confidential circular, he mooted the suggestion for stipendiary officers 'armed with ample powers to dispose summarily of all cases coming up or pending from that area'.[11] When opinions were sought, most of the local Collectors lent their support to the idea. During the Conference of Divisional Commissioners at Darjeeling in October 1941, the idea of stipendiary officers was brought before the Minister for Cooperative and Rural Indebtedness. The Minister quashed the idea on the ground that stipendiary officers were engaged in the Punjab and the experience was not a happy one.[12]

Debt settlement operations are frequently conducted by outside agencies when such crises develop in developing countries. But while debt settlement in these cases are sometimes taken, avowedly at least, with a welfare motive, the British viewed the project more from political motivations than with welfare objectives in mind. For example, by 1942 despondency about the work of the debt settlement boards had reached its height among local officials. They insisted that the boards be wound up. The Commissioner of the Presidency Division was the most outspoken advocate for the closure of the boards. He argued:

> The Act was passed to deal with a particular crisis: there was a danger of serious disturbances in some Eastern Bengal districts and it was believed that if there were legislation, debtors would be persuaded not to resort to violence; this object of the Act was achieved and

having served its main purpose it may be discarded now. In other respects, except in a few districts, the Act has done harm. It has destroyed the rural credit and it has encouraged the belief that it was a proper thing to evade payment of rent as well as to cheat creditors from whom loans have been taken.[13]

The Commissioner of Rajshahi Division also supported the proposal. The joint secretary did not allow the proposal to be put before the forthcoming conference of the Divisional Commissioners with the Minister as 'it was against the present policy of the Government'.[14] The debt settlement boards, launched in 1936, had a term of five years. Because of war and famine, their term was extended for two years. They were abolished in 1944.

Moneylenders Act

Moneylenders were an essential feature of rural economic life. As the Royal Commission on Agriculture noted:

> in the present state of India, he is a necessary and, that being so, his calling will not be abolished by making it illegal. He alone is in a position to provide the bulk of the capital required for current agricultural needs and, on a recurrence of severe distress, he will continue, as in the past, to support the people by timely loans. (Royal Commission on Agriculture 1928: 433)

The settlement officer in Mymensingh noted in 1919 that 'the *ryot* is not inclined to regard the *mahajan* as his enemy. As long as he can pay the interest, he is in no hurry to pay off the capital, and he has not fear of being sold up' (*Mymensingh RSS*: 27). But in the 1930s moneylenders earned the image of 'a bloodthirsty monster sucking the life blood of the borrowers' (Huque 1939: 162). There were instances of excesses committed by the moneylenders. The government was no less responsible for the draconian image of the moneylenders, overlooking the economically necessary functions performed by them. It was probably the Bengal Banking Enquiry Commission that tried to paint an evil picture of the moneylenders. They pointed out that the moneylenders charged exorbitant interest rates that ranged from 10 per cent to 300 per cent per annum (*Bengal Banking Enquiry Commission Report*: 198). Demand and supply and the degree of risk involved generally determine the interest rate. It can be called 'high' if the lending agency enjoyed a monopoly position. Since a myriad group of people, who included professional moneylenders as well as *zamindar* moneylenders, operated in the lending market, it could be said that Bengal moneylenders exacted excessive interest rates. They often lent money to the peasants without any security at all. The *krishak* associations that came up in the 1930s took up the crusade against the moneylenders and started to voice the demand that the moneylenders should be brought under government regulation.

It was in these circumstances that the Huq Ministry passed the Bengal Moneylenders Act of 1940. The important provisions of the Bill were:

> Every moneylender should furnish the borrower a statement of accounts showing the amount of principal, interest, amount advanced and payment received from the borrower.
>
> The sum total of the interest calculated could never exceed the original principal that was borrowed.
>
> If any borrower molests a debtor for the purpose of recovery of a debt, he would be punished.
>
> No moneylender should carry on the business of money lending unless he held an effective license.
>
> The Act provided that the rate of interest should be 10 per cent per annum in case of unsecured loan or 8 per cent in case of secured loan. (Das 1940)

Communal Question

During the debate in the Legislative Assembly the Congress took a neutral attitude to the Moneylenders Bill. The Congress had many 'wild men',[15] preventing them from taking an unabashedly pro-moneylenders stance. Sarat Bose declared:

> I entirely support the provisions of the Bill which relate to registration of moneylenders with a view to regulating their business but at the same time we have expressed the view that some of the provisions which have been enacted are so replete with penal provisions that almost wear the appearance of the Penal Code itself. (Provincial Bengal Legislative Assembly, 27 June 1939: 182)

But Hindu opinion was very much perturbed by the legislation against indebtedness. In fact at this time, when the Congress became marginal in the *bhadralok* political life of Bengal, it was the Hindu Mahasabha which came to dominate Hindu opinion. In the nationalist press, the BAD Act of 1935 was termed a 'Bad Act' (*Amrit Bazar Patrika*, 8 November 1937, Editorial). The legislation against indebtedness was suspected as a sinister design for destroying the 'Hindu' influence. The *Amrit Bazar Patrika* wrote:

> After cutting off their source of income the Huq Government are seeking to usurp their savings also by the Moneylenders Bill. The BAD and the B.T.A Acts have already crushed the loan companies which represented the savings of this class of people and the Moneylenders Bill is designed to destroy what might be left. (ibid.)

It was also alleged that 'the overwhelming majority of members of these boards . . . have been selected on communal considerations' (*Amrit Bazar Patrika*, 22 May 1939, Editorial). There were charges from Noakhali that there was 'absolute loss of Hindu capital of one crores of rupees at Noakhali alone during the regime of the present ministry of Bengal' (Chowdhuri 1940: 123–24). The Hindu Mahasabha took up the cause of the plight of 'Hindu capital'. A meeting organized at the Calcutta Town Hall by S.P. Mookherjee, in a resolution, condemned the 'legislative measures' which 'wipes out Hindu capital without any corresponding benefit to agriculturists' (ibid.: 124–25).

It is very difficult to say whether the debt settlement boards were packed with Muslim members or not, because there is no documentary evidence available to verify this claim. In 1939 the Ministry decided to issue instructions to district officers that they should not nominate persons to local bodies who were actively hostile to the Ministry.[16] Though no such instructions regarding the settlement boards is available, it is possible that many local officers who were the sole authority to recommend the formation of the boards and suggest the names of the members might, on their volition, have picked up a majority of Muslim members, as the debtors were mostly from the Muslim community. Since the Hindu community in general was aligned with the Congress, it is also possible that many officials would have had an aversion to pick up Hindu members. One interesting feature of this communal tirade regarding debt legislation was that it tended to put all the blame on the Fazlul Huq Ministry, notwithstanding the fact that a Moneylenders Act was passed in 1933 and the

BAD Act was passed in 1935, much before Fazlul Huq came to the power. The Hindu Mahasabha's attention was directed against the Muslims, not against the architect of the measures (the British government) or against the financial capitalists. But the impact of the legislation had the consequence of intensifying ill-feeling and hatred between the two communities. The anguish and hatred that spread at this time turned into the communal holocaust of 1946.

The British wanted to get political mileage on several scores under the cover of anti-moneylender measures. First, they wanted to get the message across that it was the government who understood the peasants best and their rights could be best guaranteed by it; therefore, the peasants should not respond to leaders inimical to government interest. Secondly, by projecting the moneylenders as the enemy, the British tried to shield themselves from peasant fury. They in fact wanted a conflict situation whereby the Hindu moneylenders would get involved in internecine warfare against the Muslim peasants. Finally, since the mid-nineteenth century, they had initiated a process of making the *zamindars* a crippled class; now, in the 1940s, by another stroke, they wrote the death warrant of Bengal's financial capitalists. These two groups were the lynchpins of the nationalist movement in Bengal.

The peasants were the worst sufferers in the process. The credit market where they could get easy loans dried up completely. Fazlul Huq could hardly understand the British mechanism; rather, he tried to gain easy popularity by adopting British-sponsored measures which were rhetorically attractive but contained no real solutions.

Notes

[1] *RSS* Pabna and Bogra, cited in Bose (1987: 107).

[2] Home Confidential (Poll) 873/33 (1) of 1933, cited in Sarkar (1987: 155).

[3] *Proceedings of the Government of Bengal. Judicial and Legislative Depts., Legislative, for the quarter ending September, 1937* (1938).

[4] Government of Bengal, B-Proceedings, Cooperative Credit and Rural Indebtedness (henceforth CCRI), Rural Indebtedness (heneforth RI), June 1943, Progs. Nos 334–409.

[5] Collector of Mymensingh to the Commissioner of Dacca Division, 29 July 1941. Government of Bengal, B-Progs., CCRI, RI, Bundle 9, September 1942, Progs. Nos 77–78.

[6] Reply by Kalipada Maitra, manager of the estate of the Nawab of Murshidabad, *Report of the Land Revenue Commission, Bengal* (1940: 82).

[7] Assistant Secretary, Government of Bengal, CCRI, RI, the Collector of

Rajshahi, 28 October 1940. Government of Bengal, B-Progs., Bundle 4, February 1941, Progs., Nos 560–61.

[8] Collector of Rajsahi to the Commissioner of Rajshahi Division, 4 June 1941, Bundle 7.

[9] Assistant Secretary CCRI to the district officer, 10 October 1942. Government of Bengal, B-Progs., CCRI, RI, Bundle 9, Progs., No. 50.

[10] Joint Secretaries note, 2.9, 1942. Progs., Nos 50–51.

[11] Confidential note by A.J. Dash, Commissioner of Rajshahi, to joint secretary, 7 July 1941. Progs., Nos. 69–70.

[12] Confidential Proceedings of the Conference of Commissioners held at Darjeeling, 11 October 1942.

[13] The Commissioner of the Presidency Division to the Joint Secretary, CCRI, 9 July 1942. Government of Bengal, B-Progs., CCRI, RI, Bundle 9, May 1943, Progs. No. 262.

[14] Joint Secretary CCRI, Note, 14.7.1942. Ibid. Progs. Nos 242–74.

[15] Reid to Linlithgow, 19 April 1939, Linlithgow Collection.

[16] Reid to Linlithgow, 5 April 1939, Linlithgow Collection.

References

Abul Mansur Ahmed, 1969, *Amar Dhekha Rajnitir Panchas Bachar*, Dhaka: Nowroz Kitabistan.

Azizul Huque, 1939, *The Man Behind the Plough*, Calcutta: Boom Company.

Bankura Survey and Settlement Report.

Bengal Board of Economic Enquiry: Preliminary Report on Rural Indebtedness, 1935, Calcutta: B.G. Press.

Bose, Sugata, 1937, *Agrarian Bengal: Economy, Social Structure and Politics 1919–47*, Cambridge: Cambridge University Press.

———, 1982, 'The Roots of Communal Violence in Rural Bengal: A Study of the Kisoreganj Riots', *Modern Asian Studies*, 16, 3.

Chowdhuri, Manoranjan, 1940, in the *Financial Times*, July, cited in *The Modern Review*, Vol. LXIII, No. 2, August 1940.

Dacca Survey and Settlement Report, referred in the text as *Dacca RSS.*

Das, Girish Chandra, 1940, *The Bengal Moneylender Act*, Dacca: Ashutosh Press.

Government of Bengal, *Report of the Bengal Provincial Banking Enquiry Committee, 1929–30*, Vol. I.

Islam, M.M., 1980, 'Problems of Agricultural Indebtedness in British India: Some Traditional Views Reconsidered', *Calcutta Historical Journal*, Vol. IV, No. 2.

Mymensingh Survey and Settlement Report.

Proceedings Bengal Legislative Assembly, fourth session, 10 August 1938, Vol. LIII, No. 2.

Proceedings of the Government of Bengal: Judicial and Legislative Departments, Legislative, for the quarter ending September, 1937, Calcutta: B.G. Press.

Report of the Land Revenue Commission, Bengal, 1940, Vol. V, Alipore: B.G. Press.

Report of the Land Revenue Administration of Bengal, 1931–32, Calcutta: B.G. Press.

Reforming Rural Credit

Roy, R.K., 1973, 'The Crisis of Bengal Agriculture 1890–1977: The Dynamics of Immobility', *Indian Economic and Social History Review*, X, No. 2.

Royal Commission on Agriculture in India, Abridged Report, 1928, Bombay: Government Central Press.

Sarkar, Tanika, 1987, *Bengal 1928–34: The Politics of Protest*, New Delhi: Oxford University Press.

185

Money and Finance in the Periphery

A Tool of Expropriation in Colonial India

Sunanda Sen

Introduction

Amidst today's clamour about Free Trade, privatization, open market, globalization, etc., it is a fact often forgotten that India had technically the full benefits of these wonderful phenomena for a whole century or more of colonial rule. And yet nothing singular took place as far as India's growth as an industrial country is concerned. The real question that is avoided in many of the discussions of the economic history of the colonial period is that the Free-Trade mechanism served, and surely still serves, the dominant partner(s) in the economic relationships. The story is of how money and finance were controlled by the colonial power, within an ostensible system of unrestrained market mechanism, and made to serve the interests of the colonial power alone to the great detriment of India's own economic interests. A reading of this has, therefore, wider theoretical significance than an ordinary exercise in the study of Indian economic theory.

Currency and Exchange Rate Movements

It was never possible for India under colonial rule to choose either the medium of currency or the exchange rate in the national interest. Examples of British dominance on related matters include the choice of silver as the medium of Indian currency[1] and its pegging to British sterling during 1893 to 1917, and later in 1925, at overvalued rates as compared to the market price of silver. From the beginning of the fixed rate of the rupee in 1893, when silver prices were falling in world markets, the goal was to de-link the rupee from depreciating silver prices. During the 1890s the India government was defending the ongoing policy of monetary contraction in the domestic economy, on account of the need to prevent the rupee from sliding

186

below the official rate at 1s., 4d. Even before the rupee rate was officially pegged to sterling in 1893, the steady decline in silver prices
which started in the 1870s caused a considerable amount of financial
strain for the India government which had to meet its sterling liabilities in England. The government wanted to avoid further inroads into
the fiscal revenue to meet sterling liabilities abroad, notably including
the Home Charges, if the rupee were to depreciate with falling rupee
prices. Also, a depreciating rupee affected the interests of the resident
Europeans in India as the sterling value of their remittances started
declining. The official policy was in conformity to what was recommended by the Herschell Committee on Indian Currency and
Finance in 1893. According to a private estimate, about Rs 525 million worth of Indian currency was actually melted and thus demone-
tized between 1893 and 1898. No fresh coin was minted during the
period. While the measures proved convenient to the government as
well as the European community in India, domestic business suffered, both with the monetary stringency at home and with the adverse
competitive position in overseas markets as the rupee in effect was
overvalued in relation to other silver currencies of countries like
China. In particular, the growing size of sterling reserves maintained
by India in England as deposits with banks and as sterling securities
caused considerable resentment in India, especially with increasing
credit shortages experienced within the country. By the time the Royal
Commission report on Indian Currency was released under the chairmanship of Henry Fowler, the Indian as well as European merchants
(for example, Allan Arthur) were already complaining about the
exorbitantly high interest rates on credit advanced during the busy
season within the country.[2] Influential merchants like Montague P.
Webb demanded access to official reserves in England and suggested
that those might be used to advance credit within the country at rates
lower than what was prevailing at the moment. Even the European
bankers, like the Governor of the Bank of Bengal, Martin Lindsay,
recommended the use of reserves at the bank to alleviate the ongoing
credit shortage. The debate continued along with credit stringency in
the face of rising official reserves of India in England till there was a
collapse of the old system of currency and exchange with the beginning of World War I in 1914. However, the Government of India as
well as the India Office officials (including J.M. Keynes[3]) in England
paid little attention to the complaints of the Indian public.

With the onset of World War I, the fixed exchange rate of the rupee gave way to fluctuating rates. The rate was delinked from sterling in August 1917 as it was no longer possible to manage the pre-war official peg at 1s., 4d. By 1919 the war had ended, while the rising silver prices in world markets and the fall in the exchange value of sterling pushed up the rupee rate to 2s., 5d. Thus the exchange rate of the rupee moved *up* from 1s., 4d. to 2s., 5d. during 1917–19. The movement was consistent with the rise in silver prices during the period. Interestingly, despite such appreciations in the exchange rate of the rupee, India's trade balance did *not* worsen during the period. As for exports, these responded favourably to rupee appreciation, while imports did not drop much. As for an explanation, it is not possible to interpret such improvements in India's trade balance in the face of the appreciating rupee by price movements alone. (Wholesale prices in India rose by an annual 8 per cent during 1913–20.) Non-price factors, which included the war-time controls on resource allocation in the economy, probably had a stronger influence on the improved trade balance during the period. Imports of gold and silver fell considerably as well, the latter with reduced coinage of silver coins in the country.[4] The upward trend in the overvalued rupee, however, was reversed within a few years after the war as official attempts to maintain the rate at 2s. proved unsuccessful and the rupee floated again under the pressure of falling silver prices. The rate fell to 1s., 3d. by 1921–22. The exchange rate of the rupee was soon to become an issue of national debate, especially with its expected rise as the British government was trying to push it up by reducing money supply. By June 1925 Government of India came up with the open announcement that the rupee needs to be fixed at an exchange rate vis-a-vis sterling of 1s. 6d., a rate higher than the pre-war rate of 1s. 4d. This coincided with Britain's return to gold at pre-war parity in 1925. At this point of time silver prices had already started falling in the market and the rupee rate was again *higher* than what was warranted by its metallic content at the falling silver prices in world market. The minting of rupee coins was discouraged by temporarily withholding in England the sales of Council Bills which were the medium of exchange to settle the payments for exports from India. Such measures avoided, to some extent, the increased cost and difficulties of silver procurements during the war years. Along with the official move to mop up savings in India by issuing rupee bonds, the steps had adverse effects on credit available for local business during the war as well as in the post-war years, as was recognized by Schuster, the Finance Member, much later in the 1930s. European purchases of rupee bonds at the high exchange value of rupee during 1917–21 turned out to be quite profitable, thus providing incentives to the Government of India to continue with the overvalued rupee even when the drop in silver prices was reversed during the inter-war years. The rupee rate continued to be fixed at 1s., 6d. till the end of 1946, just before the end of colonial rule.

A major reason for the reluctance of the British rulers to let India choose its own medium of currency and to manage its exchange rate in terms of gold sterling was the need it felt to cater to the financial interests of the City of London which had already evolved as the hub of financial centres in the industrial area.[5] Thus, despite the continuous surpluses in commodity trade which the country continued to earn over almost the entire history of British rule in India (other than during exceptional years like the Indian famines of the late nineteenth century or the Great Depression of the 1930s[6]), the rupee never had the opportunity either to have a gold content or to have a parity with the mighty sovereign at levels which could be consistent with one or the other the following: (a) the market price of its silver content; (b) the purchasing power parity; (c) the rising sterling assets India acquired and maintained even after using the commodity trade surpluses for the purchase of silver and payment of the Home Charges.[7]

To narrate some of the specific details, fixing the rupee at 1s., 4d., by a decree in 1893, was an act on the part of the British rulers to create a fiat-money in India and save the exchequer from the rising rupee cost of servicing the Home Charges fixed in sterling. This was done while paying the least attention to protests on the part of the Indian exporters, who were facing stiff competition from China with a silver currency that was depreciating along with the depreciating metal.[8] Managing the rupee also generated profits for silver merchants in the City which had close contacts with the India Office. The latter was keen to retain and exercise a monopoly over the huge contingent of silver imports for coinage in India.[9] The floating of the rupee during the war years of 1914–17 did imply, once again, that it was not possible for India to pitch the exchange rate of the rupee at levels which were consistent to the market and/or in the national interest. Reversals in the silver market as started with the onset of World War I in 1914 and, again, at its end in 1918 severed the rupee from its fixed peg with sterling.[10] The pattern of exchange rate management as described above, however, continued.

It is revealing to observe the official concerns on the rising rupee rate during the war, which touched 2s., 4d. by 1919. It was argued that the rise would jeopardize the flow of Home Charges.[11] Concerns as above brought a temporary halt to the float and the rupee was temporarily fixed to sterling at 2s. in 1919, as was later recommended by the Babington-Smith Committee on Indian Currency and Finance (1926). No attention , however, was paid to the other recommendations, both of the 1926 Committee and earlier than that, of Fowler's Committee on Indian Currency (1898) for having a gold standard in India. Once again, the fixed rate of the rupee at 2s. in 1919 was not consistent to what was warranted by the prevailing market value of its metallic content. Within a few years the market witnessed further drops in silver price, and Indian business magnates like Purushottam Thakurdas were disgruntled at the fixed peg of 2s. which greatly overvalued the rupee in terms of its metallic content. Falling silver prices finally forced the rupee to float again to find its level at 1s., 3d. in 1921, causing concern in official circles about the future of the 'fallen rupee', especially with the related fiscal burden of providing for Home Charges in sterling. Measures were taken to stop the slide with contractionary fiscal-monetary measures, the details of which are provided later in this paper. However, as it has been pointed out earlier, England's return to gold at pre-war parity in 1925 brought back the rupee to a fixed parity at 1s., 6d. with sterling, which was in line with the suggestions of the Hilton Young Committee (1931). The rate, once again, was considered too high by Indian businessmen in terms of export competitiveness. Unlike what happened with an overvalued rupee during the war years, the exchange rate did have an adverse effect on India's trade balance over the next few years. The slump in world commodity markets, which came at the end of the war, also contributed adversely to India's exports. The disparity between the market and official price of the two metals even led to flights of capital from joint stock companies in India which wanted to fetch better prices abroad for gold. In the meantime the government announced a 'special' price for sovereign in India set at Rs 15, a price that was higher than its exchange rate at 1s., 6d. This encouraged, for a change, the inflow of gold sovereigns into India. At the same time, the special price prevented gold from being sold in India at a premium. The move attracted imports of sovereign worth £2.5 million to India over the next two years. However, underlying the move was a systematic design to insure against possible losses to Britain through further decline in the gold value of sovereigns. Thus it was not motivated by any desire to add to the monetary reserves of the Indian government, located in India. The strategy indicated one more instance of official policies to protect the interests of the ruling country in general, and of the dominant interests of finance in the City of London in particular.

The fixed rupee–sterling rate continued even when sterling was delinked from gold parity and started floating on its own at the end of the Great Depression in 1931. The exchange rate of the rupee continued to be fixed in terms of sterling during the rest of British rule in India and even later in the post-independence period.[12]

It is evident from the above that the political subordination of India to Britain shaped the official policy concerning the rate of exchange. Recommendations by the 1898 as well as 1919 Royal Currency Commissions to link the rupee to gold, and to permit convertibility, were never taken seriously by policy makers in India. Currency policy in India, which included both the rupee rate in sterling and the location of the country's sterling and gold reserves in England (resulting in a severe monetary and credit stringency in the domestic economy), led to a political debate between the government and the Indian business classes, backed by the nationalists. Sentiments ran high in public circles, with demands to link the rupee to gold and also to permit India the use of gold accumulated by the country for coinage. Prospects of improved trade balances and opportunities for accumulation of gold were cited as grounds for such proposals. According to Thakurdas, an influential businessman in India during the period, money supply in India actually contracted sharply, by Rs 45 crores between 1920–24 and by another Rs 16–17 crores by 1927.[13] The 1s., 6d. rate which was fixed in 1925 was defended by British officials, including the Finance Secretary Cecil Kisch who was a witness before the Hilton-Young Committee of 1926 on Indian currency. He justified his argument on the ground that the rate would stop the melting of the currency if silver prices were to move up again. He also pointed out that a switch to the gold standard in India was likely to cause disruptions in the world market for gold and silver, causing the latter to fall in terms of gold. However, he supported an eventual changeover of Indian currency to gold, an argument supported by the influential

Finance Member in India, Basil Blackett, as well, in his evidence to the Hilton Young Committee. Neither of the two, however, disputed the official position on the rate at 1s., 6d., which was also approved by the European Chamber of Commerce.[14] Anticipating the adverse impact of the overvalued rupee rate on India's exports, Victor Sassoon, a major cotton merchant, protested along with other businessmen. Expectations of a falling rupee rate also led joint-stock companies to pull out capital from India, as was alleged by Dalal, a prominent businessman in India.[15]

Flow of Transfers from Colonial India

As the Charter of the East India Company came to an end in 1833 it was the direct responsibility of the India government to ensure a steady flow of annual transfers from India, thus marking the beginning of what has been described as 'Tribute' in the literature. Financial transfers from colonial India can be identified in the magnitude of the trade surplus which rose by more than five times between the quinquennium 1866-70 and 1911–15. The uptrend in trade continued till the onset of the global depression during the 1930s. But for the years of the Great Depression when India was exporting gold, the country generally was a net importer of gold as well as silver, the latter used as a medium of coinage. However, the imports of silver for coinage were often restricted by the British officials and were at levels much below the demand for coinage in India. Despite these low inflows of precious metal, the country maintained, on a net basis, steady surpluses in commodity trade, which resulted not only in the payment of Home Charges but also the accumulation of sterling reserves in England. Since payments under Home Charges were in the nature of tribute, while the sterling assets maintained by India in London were hardly used as monetary reserves for the country, one can treat the flow of trade surpluses as financial transfers from India.[16]

From the beginning of the British rule in 1833, the Government of India was entrusted by Britain to ensure a steady transfer of its export surpluses to Britain to meet the payments towards Home Charges, and a mechanism had to be devised to effect the transfer. This came about in 1851 with the formal launching of Council Bills in England, which were in the nature of trade bills sold to exchange banks wanting to remit funds to India. The Bills were cashed in rupees as those were presented to the Treasury in India, which in turn made arrangements for those payments by utilizing funds earmarked as 'Expenditure Abroad' in the budget. This completed the two-stage transfer process, by using India's export surpluses, to meet the Home Charges in England. We mention below some other uses of the remittance device *via* the Council Bills, which explain the growing interest of the India Office as well as the Bank of England in the City in these transfers.

(a) Purchases of silver for coinage in India were made out of the proceeds of the Council Bills sold in England, thus avoiding gold shipments from India. The proceeds also financed the purchase of sovereigns in transit, settled through telegraphic transfers.

(b) It was possible to use the proceeds of the sales of Council Bills to meet the capital expenditure of the India Office in England, thus meeting expenses under the head of public works and railways in India, and reducing the need to borrow in England.

(c) The sterling proceeds from sales of the Council Bills could also be used to transfer gold to India government's Gold Standard Reserve (GSR), which could be used to invest in sterling securities without any fiduciary reserve.

(d) Finally, the proceeds of Council Bills could also be maintained as bank deposits in the City.

Proceeds of sales of the Council Bills in sterling enabled the India Office to build up a sizeable stock of reserves in England, which included its treasury balances, short-term bank deposits and sterling securities purchased out of the GSR. While gold reserves were notionally the best possible means of monetary expansion in India, the stock, maintained with the currency reserves in London was hardly used as base for the country's currency system. Instead, these resources were deployed as deposits in the City, and intermediated by the latter for British investments abroad. With acute monetary and credit stringency in India, the accumulation of these large stocks of sterling assets with India Office soon became a matter of public debate.[17]

Despite the uncertainties during the war years, sterling reserves continued to grow in England and were around £20 million by 1920. During the war years Government of India advanced a substantial sum to England. As can be judged from the archives of the War Office of the Government over 1921–23, the sum could be of the order of £35.8 million. However, despite such payments, the India Office was not short of liquidity, a fact which is explained by cuts in sales of Council Bills during the war years when only exporters of strategic war materials were paid through this means.[18] The situation at the end of World War II, however, was a little different as the India Office began temporarily borrowing sterling in the City. India's sterling assets in England went up during the World War II period, from £53.2 million in 1939 to £1038.7 million by 1945. By July 1944 the value of these sterling assets in the form of sterling bills and sterling securities was £828 million, thus making India the largest creditor nation vis-a-vis Britain when the war ended in 1945. The procedure of extracting financial surpluses from India to meet expenses of the India Office and to build up sterling assets which provided sources of liquidity to the City (rather than to India) thus continued without much interruption during the long period of British rule between 1833 to 1946.

Fiscal-Monetary Developments

As with the currency arrangements, India under colonial rule continued to have its fiscal policies moulded in favour of the ruling country. As mentioned above, the domestic budget in India continued to provide for expenditure abroad to meet the India Office's expenditure in England and other sterling liabilities. In effect, the above amounted to a continual expropriation of surpluses in India by Britain.[19]

The well-designed move on the part of the colonial rulers to transfer funds to England resulted in a shortage of credit in India. Moreover, the accumulation of sterling assets with the help of the country's net export proceeds and the budgetary devices to earmark expenditure abroad created a situation which in effect denuded the country of its net revenue from trade. In standard macroeconomic jargon this amounts to a negative multiplier, the trade surplus working as a leakage rather than an expansionary factor for the country's gross domestic product (GDP).

It is possible in this context to document systematic efforts on the part of Government of India to cut back its expenses on famine relief even when famines were officially acknowledged. By the recommendations of the Select Committee of the British Parliament in 1867, all expenses of the Government of India on public works expenditure were to be met by fresh official borrowings from the London money market.[20] However, in reality, provisions were made for public expenditure in the revenue account of the Indian budget, at least until the onset of World War I. Again, in terms of the recommendations of the same Select Committee, Government of India could use these funds to cancel the outstanding loans under unproductive heads. In effect, the procedure amounted to the use of current revenue not only to amortise unproductive loans, but also to meet interest payments on productive loans, most of which were contracted in the process of the conversion of unproductive to productive debt as implicit in the Select Committee's recommendations.[21] The process implied a substantial freezing of revenue, amounting to £11 million by 1913, as interest payments on productive loans (which were 60 per cent of the annual Home Charges at £18 million). The analysis reveals a certain degree of camouflaging in what is recorded as official statistics on productive debt. The finances in reality serviced unproductive debts (say, to fight the Afghan War) and related expenses, much of which, as was rightly claimed by the nationalists, had a political origin.

With the onset of the Great Depression in 1929, fiscal problems for the Government of India became rather acute. The problems were compounded by the drop in commodity exports which was sought to be compensated by large values of gold exported by India, often with distress sales of jewellery by the public. Earlier the government had made it a practice, during the inter-war years, to overcome fiscal problems by entering into the domestic market as a borrower. Thus the rupee debt of the government went up steadily, from Rs 4.5 billion to Rs 6.8 billion between 1917–18 to 1922–23.[22] The move was needed as possibilities of raising loans in sterling were limited in London and the India Office also was facing a financial squeeze. Fresh rupee borrowings by the Government of India in local markets contributed further to credit stringencies in India.

Fiscal policy during the inter-war years was one of ad-hocism, tuned to the financial interests of the City. A steady fall in revenues, from an annual average of Rs 940 million during 1914–20 to Rs 855 million during 1921–29, was compensated by steady declines in public expenditure, especially during 1923–33,[23] which was matched by occasional public borrowings.[24] Rather paradoxically, the canons of sound finance, often advocated by policy-makers in England, were hardly operative in India with frequent budget deficits and public borrowings.

As for monetary policy, the impact was felt in terms of restrictions on money supply and availability of credit, once again in the interests of the British government and the dominant financial interests in the City. During the 1890s, Rs 525 million worth of rupee coins were melted while minting of fresh coins were altogether stopped during the years 1893–98. The measures were supposed to help in stabilizing the overvalued rupee rate in terms of sterling to which it had been pegged in 1893.[25]

The use of Council Bills for remittances aggravated the seasonal stringency in the money market. The sale of the Bills during October–March (the busy season) was on an average 44 per cent higher than that between April–September. This was true for the period 1893–1914. Thus the government was forced to maintain a margin of liquidity in the treasury which had to be higher in the busy season, in order that the bills be met. The treasury in turn had to withdraw its reserves from the three Presidency banks, thus further aggravating the seasonal stringencies of credit.[26] Credit shortages were quite common in India, especially during the harvesting season between October to March, when interest rates charged by the three Presidency Banks reached newer heights, causing an adverse impact on the entire credit market. Again, financial stringency in London and the related shortages at the India Office at the end of World War I in 1918 led to a renewed phase of currency contractions in India, with a near-total withdrawal of the remittances of export earnings via Council Bills, the sale of which was restricted. The measures aggravated sharply the credit and monetary shortages in India during the immediate post-World War I years.

As mentioned earlier, the supply of rupee coins in India was further constrained by the official policy to procure silver in London, often from approved sources, which defied all norms of a free market. The silver trade was controlled by a London group which even had alliances with the India Office officials, with consequences often detrimental to the availability of silver for coinage.[27]

The fiscal system in colonial India, as with the currency arrangements, was thus geared to the trading and financial interests of Britain. These continued to influence the duties on products including imports and, more importantly, to modulate the level of public borrowings. It is also possible to document a systematic effort on the part of Government of India to cut back expenditure under the head of famine relief despite the frequency of famines during the second half of the nineteenth century. All the productive expenses of the government (which covered public works of various sorts), in terms of the recommendations of the British Parliament's Select Committee in 1867, could be financed by loans, often raised in the City. However, in reality, heads of public expenditure provided for in the revenue account of the budget could be diverted to alternate heads like cancellation of unproductive loans. The practice was in accord with the Select Committee's recommendations. The device in effect used the current revenue not only to amortise unproductive loans, but in effect converted the latter to productive ones which had their origin in war and other political activities in the past.

Fiscal measures geared to Britain's economic gains also affected the public debt policy in India. The government in India was found to be borrowing heavily from the local money market around 1917 when the official finances were already fully stretched with war commitments. While this crowded out others in the private credit market, the Europeans were encouraged to hold these rupee debts at an all-time high of the Indian currency of around 2s., 4d. Government of India collected large sums as war loans, an indirect estimate of which, as mentioned above, was about £35.8 million. The needs of the India Office finances clearly got priority over Indian finances, as can be seen from the stopping of Council Bill sales by the former during 1921–22, and virtually no sales took place in the next couple of years. The move was to avoid further depletion of India Office's balances which had already run down, and also to avoid silver purchases by the former at the high post-war prices. With expenses beyond control during the war years, the India Office was thus short of cash, despite its depletion of sterling currency reserves located in London, large borrowings in the City at the end of the war to the tune of £68.6 billion (at about 40 per cent of its expenses in London) during 1921/22 to 1923/24, and also the repayment of war loans by Britain at the end of the war in 1919. The Imperial war effort remained a channel of drainage for India, and war loans were much in use both during the World War I and World War II, with the latter leaving behind a stock of sterling reserve for India at around £1.5 billion in 1939, which was used later to settle the claims of the sterling companies in India. On the whole the canons of 'sound finance' as preached in British economic theory and policy had thus very little to do with the ad-hocism which could be identified in Indian fiscal policy, especially with public borrowing and lending.

The paradox – of trade surpluses and large reserves along with monetary squeeze in the country – testifies, once more, the dominance of the ruling state, in support of its own finance and industry and against the national interests of the colony in the periphery.

Conclusion

The experience of India during the colonial period matches well with the state of other nations in the periphery which faced similar situations. The process, however, did not end with the end of political rule in the periphery. This is amply evident even with the experiences of India, which has achieved a level of industrialization since independence that compares favourably with that of many other nations in South Asia, the Middle East and Africa. We have already cited the problems in fixing the exchange rate in the national interest as multinational finance capital assumes a dominant position with international integration of financial markets. The need to import capital on the part of these countries is seen to grow both with a greater degree of import dependence and rising capital account liabilities, with capital inflows at stiffer terms and an added degree of speculative swings. The residual finance that is left for real sector growth on a long-term basis is often too thin for the purpose. It is no longer possible to manage fiscal and monetary policy without complying with the pressures of liberalization which include the package of structural adjustments and stabilization policies including decontrol, liberalization of trade and industry, privatization, financial liberalization, fiscal cuts on the social sector, and an end to direct and indirect subsidies to the priority sectors including exports and agriculture. With debates still challenging the benefits of being a small open economy in the unequal process of exchange in the world economy, the periphery still looks back to the prospects, however unattainable, of following a path of autonomous growth in a world which is more equal.

Notes

1. Sen (1992), pp. 89–91, 197–98.
2. *Report on Indian Currency and Finance*, 1914 (Chamberlain Commission Report), Appendix VII, pp. 203, 540; *Report on Indian Currency and Finance*, 1898 (Fowler Committee), p. 552. See also Sen (1992), pp. 25–27, 72–77; Banerjee (1999).
3. See for the rather negative attitude of Keynes, Letter dated 17 October 1913, India Office Records/L/F/220 collection 224.
4. See K.N. Chaudhuri, in Kumar, ed. (1982); Goldsmith (1983).
5. See Sen (1992).
6. See Banerjee (1999).
7. Sen (1992), pp. 89–91, 23–28.
8. Ibid.
9. Ibid.
10. Ibid.
11. *Royal Commission on Indian Currency*, 1926.
12. *Royal Commission on Indian Currency*, 1931.
13. Mukherjee (1990).
14. Evidence by Cecil Kisch and Basil Blackett to Hilton Young Commission, *Report on Indian Currency and Finance*, 1926.
15. Mukherjee (1990).
16. See for details of the arrangement of the financial transfer and the use of Council Bills for the purpose, Sen (1992), Chapter 2.
17. See ibid., Chapter 3.
18. *Report of the Royal Commission*(Hilton Young Committee), 1926, Appendix 74.
19. Sen (1992), Chapter 2.
20. Select Committee Report to the British Parliament, cited in *Final Report of the Royal Commission on Expenditure in India* (Welby Commission), 1900, pp. 44–45, 71.
21. See Sen (1992), pp. 31–32, for an elucidation of the underlying logic.
22. Goldsmith (1983), p. 140.
23. Dharma Kumar, in Kumar, ed. (1982), p. 940.
24. Goldsmith (1983), p. 112.
25. *Report on Indian Currency and Finance*, 1914, Appendix VII, pp. 203, 540.
26. Ibid., p. 233.
27. Keynes Papers (Box 53 A7 item 8), Marshall Library, Cambridge. See in particular the unofficial correspondence between Felix Schuster of the India Office and the silver merchant Samuel Montague and Co., dated 9 January 1912 and 13 November 1912. Also see India Office records, IOR / l/f/7/214 Financial Coll. No. 24, files 1–7.

References

Bagchi, A.K., 1989, *The Presidency Banks and the Indian Economy 1876–1914*, Oxford University Press, Calcutta.

Balachandran, G., 1996, *John Bullion's Empire*, London, Curzon Press, London.

Banerjee, Debdas, 1999, *Colonialism in Action*, Orient Longman.

de Cecco, M., 1974, *Money and Empire: The International Gold Standard 1890–1914*, Blackwell, Oxford.

Goldsmith, Raymond W., 1983, *The Financial Development of India 1860–1977*, Oxford University Press, Delhi.

Hariss, S.E., 1931, *Monetary Problems of British India*, New York.

Indian Currency Commission Reports, 1893, 1898, 1914, 1926.

Keynes, J.M., 1913, *Indian Currency and Finance*, Macmillan, London.

Kumar, Dharma, ed., 1982, *The Cambridge Economic History of India c. 1857–1970*, Vol 2, Cambridge University Press; papers by Dharma Kumar and K.N. Chaudhuri.

Mukherjee, Aditya, 1990, 'Indo-British Finances: The Controversy over Sterling Balances 1939-47', *Studies in History*, January–June.

Rothermund, Dietmar, 1996, *The Great Depression: 1929–39* , Routledge.

Sen, Sunanda, 1992, *Colonies and the Empire: India 1890–1914*, Orient Longman, Hyderabad.

Sen, Sunanda, 2000, *Trade and Dependence*, Sage, New Delhi.

B.K. Dutt: A Development Banker from Bengal

Indrajit Mallick

In the context of developing economics, the banking system has historically played a bigger and a more fundamental part than the capital markets in financing industrialization. In the early stages it was a combination of the government and the banking system, and it is generally recognized now that the latter has certain advantages in this task.[1] In this context, the banker with market power plays a special role. He chooses the degree of risk-taking in the industrial economy, the smoothing of income in risky agriculture, and proivdes local savers with liquid secutities. In each important geographical zone the banker with market power is required so that he can take risks in finance with adequate safety cushion, and lubricate the wheel of industry and commerce. This market power directly and primarily derives from a certain degree of protection that the financial and monetary authorities bestow on the banking sector (for maintaining stability in the financial sector, and to sustain the power and rent-seeking structure of the modern industrial economy). Two other important reasons are the presence of increasing returns in banking and the asymmetric structure of information in the credit market. However, despite the presence of market power, one must concede that, without the ability of the banker to guide his bank through initial birth-pangs and the inherently risky path of its youth, and finally to stablize its growth in maturity, one would hardly see banks making their mark over time. Such a role played by the captains of the financial industry is a necessary condition for significant growth in trade and production, let alone innovation and technological progress in industry. If the captains cannot play this role, the scope of development of industry and markets in a poor economy would be completely shut down. This special entrepreneurial talent in finance has often been neglected by the development literature, and it is time to integrate the experience of economic history with the theory of economic development and the theory of financial intermediation to rectify this unhappy oversight. In this essay we take this interdisciplinary path to study an entrepreneurial banker emerging in eastern India a few decades before independence and to study the dynamics of his story. Before we embark on that ambitious path, one must reflect a little on the nature of entrepreneurship.

Market conditions always leave roon for the talented entrepreneur to exploit and even change them at times. The question is whether entrepreneurial skill is present and what are the preconditions for its successful exploitation. The acute scarcity of this particular type of skill (as witnessed by the high degree of frequency of failures of start-ups in any industry) with respect to its demand frequently makes us think there can be no theory of an entrepreneur in terms of how he develops, how he reacts to economic opportunities and problems, as well as how he breaks through formidable entry barriers present in industry. An entrepreneur (unlike the standard wage earner or financial investor) is thus viewed as an exception rather than a rule, despite the pervasive influence of economics in our lives. Therefore, so the argument goes, given its statistically residual nature, what can one hypothesize about entrepreneurial behaviour? To the extent that wealth, attitude and talent permits, some people will be entrepreneurs and there is not much to theorize beyond that (given that the firm has a distinct legal as well as economic identity of its own, it is not to be equated with the entrepreneur). In other words, one cannot write a textbook on how to be a successful entrepreneur as one could write a theory of optimal managerial behaviour in textbook form. The primary diffuclty lies in the fact that entrepreneurship is an art that has multidimensional behavioural requirements and involves complex dynamics in its implementation and planning which no single academic discipline can handle alone. It is a talent at the end of the day, and you either have it or do not. However, one can at least lay down the conditions under which the probability of entrepreneurial experiments may increase at certain stages of socio-economic development, and the conditions under which such experiments may produce a critical mass of successful and active entrepreneurs with significant impact on technological innovation, growth, trade and risk-bearing. Historians have long recognized that social and intellectual revolution, political protection and economic freedom typically throw up a number of entrepreneurs, as does the influence of family business or education. Given these conditions, the (potential) entrepreneur looks at a product, market and industry, and asks: 'is there another, more efficient way of doing things here?' The ability to ask a provocative question is positively correlated with the capability to answer it and implement the solution in practice. The purpose of this essay is to see a financial entrepreneur from this point of view while keeping in mind the challenges, as well as the qualitative and quantitative changes faced by the banking industry in the task of managing at a critical stage of development of the Indian economy.

India in the early twentieth century faced the task of financial development as a necessary step to mobilize savings at a significantly higher rate, and of channelling savings to investment, to allocate resources efficiently across projects and to share risks in economic activity in an efficient manner. Though the government was seen as the indisputable leading player as well as the maker of the rules of the game on the financial landscape, it still had to rely on an efficient banking system which was decentralized to a large extent. The general challenge for these banks was to carve out their niche in the private sector, and to play their required part in government finance through investment in treasury securities of different maturities and risks. They also had to coexist with the informal financial sector which still dominated agriculture finance and rural–urban commerce. Regional idiosyncracies made the development of banks more specifically tied up with regional comparative advantages and relative scarcities of economic goods and services. One need not recount economic and financial history from regional perspectives in any significant detail. However, one comment is pertinent. Western and southern India have had the major share of pioneering individuals in finance, and, with the increasing industrial importance of these regions, these individuals played a significant role in terms of command of resources and growth in their local economies and further strengthened growth in these regions. The eastern part of the country, on the other hand, saw trade and industry diminish in importance relative to the former regions since the latter half of the twentieth century and the trend became the market in the last three decades. Financing, therefore, was more of a challenge to upcoming bankers in places like Bengal, Bihar, Orissa and Assam, despite some traditional businesses like tea finance, coal finance, financing of chemicals, potteries, etc., being there. Therefore, when comparing the financial industry leaders of different regions, this should be kept in mind.[2] To what extent the relative lack of financial entrepreneurs in the eastern region explains a part of the relative decline remains an interesting question. In this paper we shall focus on an individual who played an important part in the development of banking in India – especially eastern and north-eastern India – and who had a significant impact on the socio-economic development of the latter region. The protagonist of our story is Bata Krishna (B.K.) Dutt, a banker from Bengal, whose life spanned a substantive part of this century. There are three major contributions which make it imperative to study his life and achievements: first and foremost, he was instrumental in building up a large bank which served the various economic needs of the region in its development phase; second, he was one of the key personalities who was instrumental in the development of banking as an institution during the decolonization of India's financial system; and third, he was one of the pioneers of the idea of a social and developmental role for banking in the country.

Before we begin, a brief personal introduction of our subject and an attempt to locate him in the socio-cultural space of the country's early twentieth-century history are perhaps necessary. The emergence of entrepreneurs like B.K. Dutt was no accident. With the Swadeshi movement, the Bengali *bhadralok* were inspired to take to business and history with a different justification. Indigenous industry was required to fight the British rulers in commercial terms. Further, this was an era of emerging modernity in India. To the entrepreneurs of this era, it was a matter of marrying individual enterprise, education and scientificity with money matters. This coincided with the Bengal renaissance which saw towering personalities who were not only superior intellects, but also socio-economic visionaries who could start and build enterprises of their won. P.C. Ray of Bengal Chemicals was a teacher of chemistry and an experimental scientist, as was Jogesh Chandra Ghosh of Sadhana Aushadhalay – while Ramesh Sen, who set up a factory for making socks and vests in Mymensingh, was a lawyer. By 1907–08, the emphasis of nationalist enterprise in Bengal had shifted from industrial production to commerical services like banking and insurance. The need for formal indigenous institutions which could finance the trade and commerce of Indian industry was increasingly felt, and the new financial entrepreneurs began to take advantage of the opportunity with a sense of social responsibility. Bengal, again, led by example, with eminent men like Dwarakanath Tagore going into banking and reputed lawyers in different towns making finance a more formal institution especially with regard to agriculture and small-scale industry.

Our story begins in the town of Comilla in Bangladesh. Bata Krishna Dutt was born in Comilla in 1910.

> Comilla was an interesting location – on the one hand, adjacent to the 'tribal' interiors of Tripura, on the other hand, to the sprawl-ing tea estates in North Bengal and Assam. In a way, a less structred society, which could boast of cultural icons like Ustad Alauddin Khan, Himanshu Datta, Sachin Deb Burman and others. This was an area which in 1930–31 would become famous for its revolu-tionary terrorist movement. (Dutt 1994)

This was also known as an area of 'banks and tanks', financial entre-preneurs and builders of *swadeshi* insitutions. B.K. Dutt's father Narendra was a social reformer and entrepreneur who took to devel-opment banking in 1914 by giving up his lucrative law practice. These qualities moulded the character of most of his children, of whom B.K. Dutt was the eldest. After completing his studies and on his return to Comilla, B.K. Dutt joined the bank to work as a trainee.

Building Up the Institution

Within a few weeks after B.K. Dutt's joining Comilla Banking Corporation, Narendra told him that if he did not like working with his bank, he could establish a bank of his own and prove that he could make it. It was clear that Narendra had confidence in the ability of his son and wanted him to be as independent as he himself was when he started Comilla Banking Corporation. In 1930, the son took over the defunct Comilla Rice and Oil Mills Ltd. (a company owned by his father) and converted it into the New Standard Bank of India Ltd. The initial paid-up capital was about Rs 30,000. Dutt ran his bank with very little overheads, like the traditional loan companies. This was an exception to the rule that you need quite a bit of own capital to start a financial insitution. In Dutt's case it was his reputational capital and the goodwill his family enjoyed that allowed him to cross the entry barrier. The bank was housed in Mahesh Bhattacharya's garage, from where also ran the Mantala Tea Co., managed by his father's company. Between 8 and 10 in the morning, the bank would finish its office work in the garage, and then Datta and his co-workers would travel around on their bicycles as a veritable mobile bank. They would then set up shop in the balcony of the bar-library at the district court, servicing the financial transactions of the numerous lawyers, clients, peasants, *jotedars* and *talukdars* who would regularly visit the court from all over the district. Soon the Chief Justice allowed him to set up an iron shed for his bank within the court premises. As its capital increased gradually, the New Standard Bank included tea estates in the list of its customers. Soon the Comilla Banking Corporation and New Standard Bank were doing business in Calcutta as well. By 1946 it became obvious that the stage had come when it was mutually profitable for the two banks to merge, and at Governor Deshmukh's suggestion, New Standard transferred its assets to Comilla Banking Corporation. The institution of inter-bank deposits creates the necessity of cooperation even among the most bitter competitors in banking, and Dutt was quick to leverage this to secure cooperation from all the banks which were bankers to his bank. Economic theory explains the relative scarcity of entrepreneurs, especially in less developed countries, in terms of the large set-up costs of business and imperfect capital markets. But financial entrepreneurs have the advantage that they can rely mainly on deposits. Certainly this seems to have been the case here. However, there arises a problem with an evolution based on high deposit to own capital ratio: with too little own capital and too much of other people's money, the banker becomes prone to taking excessive risks. In fact, this is precisely what happened in Bengal in the early twentieth century (see Bagchi 1987; Bannerjee 2000). But our protagonist exhibited commitment, discipline and banker's prudence, and ensured that his bank would follow a different path. Here we have an example of history and future both playing a role. The expectations of and ambitions about the future led to a certain pattern of restrained behaviour, on the one hand, and on the other, the socio-cultural qualities embedded in him by historical circumstances reinforced the behaviour pattern.

The banking crisis of 1946–50 brought the large banks of Bengal like Comilla Union and Bengal Central in contact with the Dutts. They started discussing a merger which finally took place in 1950, creating the United Bank of India (UBI) – a large bank which could cater to the whole of the eastern region. At that time there was hardly any precedent in Indian banking so far as large-scale mergers were concerned – thorny legal and financial problems aside, there was the unenviable task of negotiating with different stakeholders including other banks who were to be potential partners, conducting due diligence, and administering and managing the process of change. The fact that the merger was successful is sufficient testimony to Dutt's growing skills as a banker. Not only did he benefit his bank and the depositor community, but he also created a vital precedence for a spate of amalgamations that followed after independence. The image of the large bank and the collective strength of the most influential bankers getting together ensured that bank-runs stopped, and a severe confidence crisis on a much larger scale was thus averted. The next step was to create enough reserves and capital, restructure, and expand througout the country to diversify against region-specific risks. In all this B.K. Dutt showed unmatched dexterity, and both deposits and advances grew at a fast rate of about 20 per cent. The domination of UBI in the east and the north-east was prominent. Also, Dutt's expertise in tea enabled the bank to become specialized in tea financing and to be a leading banker in this sector. Yet, at the same time, he carefully chose a well-diversified basket which consisted of coal accounts, wholesale trade, cotton textiles, etc. He kept a close watch over the industries and would prevent problems from developing by credit rationing whenever he foresaw demand and ensuing cash-flow problems in those industries.

However, what was most impressive was how Dutt enabled UBI to become a prominent bank at the national level, starting from the humble stature of a regional bank. Various schemes were adopted by him to penetrate the national market. His advisor, Laughland, set up a scheme for lending money to Multani bankers.[3] UBI took to this not only beccause it was a very good business without any risk, but also because it was a useful system to lend money to small businessmen. In the matter of the bill rediscounting facility provided by the Reserve Bank of India to banks, the officials of the Reserve Bank pointed out that UBI had large and well-known customers on its books. Special efforts were initiated by Dutt to get large and well-known accounts in Madras, Bombay, Ahmedabad and elsewhere with great success. In Bombay, Dutt's growing influence in various financial committees set up by the government led to his interaction with persons like A.D. Shroff and Morarji Vaidya (introduced by a local businessman to Dutt), which in turn helped UBI in securing, for the first time, ties with the Tatas and Birlas. During the days of the Shroff Committee, on one of

Dutt's visits to Bombay, for the first time UBI made a loan to a textile unit belonging to the Tata group. Vaidya also transferred some other companies to Voltas (a Tata group company) and UBI being a banker to these companies, relations with the Tatas were further strengthened. United Bank went to Ahmedabad with the good wishes of B.K. Shah of New India Insurance Company Ltd. B.K. Dutt and his managers got to know Kasturbhai, Arvindbhai, Rohitbhai and others who brought in a good number of accounts. Subsequently Dutt became a Director of the Industrial Credit and Investment Corporation of India (ICICI) at the instance of Kasturbhai and K.L. Mitha, and became close to M.T. Parekh, then General Manager of ICICI. UBI had a branch in Madras which was the only one in the south. It was not bringing in substantial influence and business, and Dutt was thinking of closing it. At this time, he met C.M. Kothari of Madras who opposed the idea of closure and offered to introduce Dutt to the business community in Madras. Althogh his efforts did not take UBI far enough, further help was obtained from C.R. Srinivasan, a Director of the Reserve Bank who liked Dutt and organized a local committee of the bank in Madras, comprising Kasturi Srinivasan of *The Hindu*, T.S. Santhanam of the TVS group and others. Thus UBI rose in status and acquired some influence in the city. Its relations with the TVS group has persisted and grown over time. In Delhi, it had good connections all over. Uttam Singh Dugal developed a close relationship with the bank. Dutt developed a relationship with M.S. Oberoi and helped to build up his hotel chain. This was the beginning of a long-standing relationship with a very good industrial client and brought UBI continuous business. Dutt was very helput to the Oberoi group and personally stood by Oberoi in many difficult situations.

In Calcutta, Dutt demonstrated the wisdom of forming long-term relationships with innovative entrepreneurs who were beginning to get a fair market share. It must be mentioned that substantial discretion is required in maintaning and managing a relationship with a big borrower. Dutt used this discretionary and flexible approach in lending to good effect. Soon his borrowers were unwilling to switch to competitors even at advantageous terms. Closeness of ties allowed Dutt to cross-sell other products to borrowers. Further, the information generated from relationship banking, and trust and reputation factors, kept adverse selection and moral hazard problems at bay (see Boot and Thakor 2000). Bengal Chemical was a pioneer industry financed by

UBI. Bengal Enamel, East India Pharmaceuticals and Bengal Immunity were some others. A close relationship developed with East India Pharmaceuticals which was founded by Ashok Kumar Sen. Hirendra Nath Dutta Gupta, Sen's brother-in-law, knew Dutt and this started the relationship. Initially the firm had no overdraft requirements but later reliance on the bank increased and the bank became the lead banker to the firm. In the media field, the bank financed Saraswati Press and later the Ananda Bazar group. Foundries in Howrah and cold storage units (especially for potato cultivation) were financed. The big industrial groups also got their due share of attention. Oberoi, Goenka and Badri Poddar were some of the renowned clients. B.K. Dutt specially mentions in his diary his ties with the Oberoi group: 'M.S. Oberoi and his hotel chain were built with UBI assistance and the personal help of the author: I personally stood by him in difficult situations. He is a very capable hotelier with international status.' S.B. Roy of the Oberoi group used to handle the transactions with UBI. He remembers the beginning of this important relationship: 'It was the year 1962 when we approached UBI and got Rs 5 lakhs sanctioned from the comptroller of advances Rajenbabu.' Initially the group had hotels in Calcutta and Srinagar. Later they started to build hotels in other cities as well and UBI used to help with construction finance. According to S.B. Roy, B.K. Dutt had a weakness for Raibahadur M.S. Oberoi because, like his father N.C. Dutta, the Raibahadur was a self-made man and he reminded him of his father. He carefully nurtured the relationship and soon all the banking business requirements of the group came to be handled exclusively poised for growth due to the emphasis of the plans for heavy industry. After the merger, Martin Burn became a client. The President of Martin Burn came on to the bank's Board. This enchanced the image of the bank substantially and was an event worth celebrating, recalls Ranjit Dutta (interview with author). IISCO was another firm which had UBI as one of its bankers.

Developing Banking as an Institution

No doubt Dutt became a role model to emulate for all banking entrepreneurs in Bengal in the post-independence period. But more important were his contributions to setting proper rules of the game for the development of banking in India. The three areas he focused on were necessary banking legislation, mechanisms to avoid a banking crisis and structural changes in banking.

He argued for legislation enabling speedy and easy mergers between troubled banks as early as 1946. Section 44A of the Banking Companies Act dates from this time. After B.K. Dutt started his fight for a special provision in the law for merger of banks, section 44A of the Banking Companies Act was inserted in the statute on banking, making it possible for the Governor to sign the order of the merger without reference to the court or winding up of the bank. Interestingly, United Bank of India was the first bank under the merger provision.

In order to avoid a banking crisis, Dutt proposed mergers and deposit insurance. Mergers had to be initiated by the banks themselves though the law and the state would play an important role. But deposit insurance required a change in the regulatory policy. Anticipating that it would not come about easily, he took recourse to merger during the banking panic. However he considered deposit insurance a superior mechanism to mergers. Dutt emphasized that many of the banks which failed during this time were not unviable in size and structure – some could maintain a liquidity ratio of over 55 per cent, some had only 35 per cent of their capital locked in advances and some could in fact pay out 70 per cent of their liabilities before they closed. Again, using the hindsight drawn from contemporary theory of banking, we know today that crisis would not have beset these banks had deposit insurance and bank-runs became self-fulfilling prophecies (Diamond and Dybvig 1983), since when all depositors simultaneously run on a bank, then, under a fractional reserve system of banking, the bank is bound to go insolvent even if not bankrupt. Moreover, the history of banking panics throughout the world testifies to the fact that when bad banks suspend payments they exert a negative externality on the otherwise viable ones by spreading false rumours and causing insolvency. Therefore deposit insurance was necessary to safeguard against these dangers. Conservatives might argue that deposit insurance can lead to complacency and excessive risk-taking by banks unless the insurance premiums can be suitably adjusted to risk (a difficult job for the insuring agency), as the recent financial crises reveal. It is difficult to infer whether Dutt realized that there was a 'moral hazard' problem with the insurance concept (Stiglitz and Weiss 1981). He argued that amalgamation might lead to a great rise in operational costs, without engendering the expected economics of scale. (Here too we find Dutt on the right side of a very contemporary debate in banking: Berger *et al.*

210

2000.) But above all, amalgamation eliminated local competition and created monopolies, which harmed the public because banking was a service which should thrive in the context of competition. According to Dutt amalgamation as a method gained legitimacy in India because of its success in the United Kingdom.

> Very few realized how different the institutional contexts were in the two nations. In U.K., most mergers happened because banking houses were sold in the market to corporate buyers, the banks being mostly family or partnership businesses which could not anyway have operated in perpetuity like joint-stock banks with limited liability, as was the case in India. In the United States, however, when more than 6000 banks crashed in 1931, it was not followed by amalgamation but other methods like insurance. And in Germany in recent years, banking consolidation had been carried out not through mergers but through an actual division of larger banks into a number of smaller banks, which were supposed to assist regional development. (Bannerjee 1999)

Amalgamating banks that had become weak and vulnerable was not a sufficient condition for restoring the health of the financial system unless an adequate supply and distribution of fresh capital was forthcoming. But which shareholder would trust banks with capital in the middle of a financial crisis? If the problem was of trust and confidence, then there was only one proper remedy and that was deposit insurance. To the extent that this insitutional innovation took time to come into fruition, mergers would be a weak substituting principle, and it was a viable strategy as long as recourse to it was taken before a serious shortfall of capital and liquid reserves had developed. The individual banks who formed UBI were lucky that their management reacted quickly to the bank-runs and pooled enough surviving capital to make their depositors confident. This stopped the run on them, but this was an exception in those trying circumstances and not a rule. Dutt's appeal to the policy makers to insure bank deposits thus had impeccable logic and a keen historical insight which would make many modern finance theorists and economic historians proud. However, those belonging to the school of thought started by Bagehot would not agree (Bagehot 1873). Saving imprudent bankers would be a mistake which would make history repeat itself, they argued. Modern iconoclasts in the world of theoretical finance like Douglas Gale and Franklin

Allen would see optimality in bank-runs (Allen and Gale: 1999), and tell the policy makers to allow runs because things 'would get worse otherwise' (a concept foreign to even a free marketeer like Milton Friedman: Friedmann and Schwartz 1963). Fortunately, for the banker on the street there exist some counter-arguments on these issues. Since differentiating between the prudent and not so prudent ones would not be a favourite job for the hard-pressed monetary authorities, their real dilemma would be whether to save all at the cost of keeping a few irresponsible ones alive or to allow some of the risk-averse but unfortunate ones to die in order to keep the banking society free of risk lovers. Dutt, for one, pointed out that closure of banks *en masse* would not only cause a gaping lack of credit services in all the regions, but also cause widespread unemployment, disrupt local economic activities including trade in agricultural produce, and ultimately have a large effect on all sectors of the Indian economy. On the welfare aspect of crises, one can argue that liquidation of banks would be costly to society when the problem is not with 'fundamentals'[4] but with the 'state of the mind of the depositors'. One would be inclined to think that this was the reason why Dutt also argued for a Rehabilitation Finance Corporation as an institution complementing the Deposit Insurance Scheme.

On the structural aspects of banking, Dutt argued for the opening of small 'unit banks' all over the country, even though some argued that, in the face of the popular idea of the time of reduction in the number of banks through amalgamation, such unit banks were 'primitive' institutions. Dutt argued that in place of the vertical expansion of banking institutions operating on centralized norms and terms, a horizontal expansion could make banking as an institution sensitive to local and specific industrial and employment needs (speech on 'Reorganization of the Banking Structure: Need for Rural Banks in Rural Areas', undated, probably between 1949–51.) In fact, at the insistence of the Bengal National Chamber of Commerce, Dutt wrote up a detailed scheme for the system of such unit banks, which was submitted to the Rural Banking Enquiry Committee appointed by the Government of India in November 1949, under the chairmanship of Purushottamdas Thakurdas. It was a novel document which carefully analysed the agency problems that can arise in branch banking and how rural unit banks would be a superior alternative. He also painstakingly showed how small-sized unit banks had the natural advantage of mobilizing resources for investment at a faster rate without having to take excessive risks, and how a little community participation could make them viable organizations. However, his plan was silent on allowing competition between banks which branching permits and which raises the quality of banking service. Surely he could have learnt a Smithian lesson (Gale 1993) or two on this issue, but, having said that, one must not forget to add that many banks have retained their local and regional nature despite free inter-state banking in today's democracies.

Ideas on the Social and Development Role of Banks

Within a decade or so after independence, it was becoming clear that if anything, the banking sector was becoming more and more constricted in comparison to the early years of small, provincial banks, and hardly creating the spread of banking habits that would be necessary in the context of any reasonable social welfare function. It was widely felt that certain dominant sectors of the economy, with their presence ensured in the Boards of Directors of banking institutions, were channelizing much of the resources towards themselves, at the cost of agriculture and small-scale industry. Dutt was quick to point out the inadequacies of the system and regretted that the question of the general expansion of banking resources still remained unaddressed (Chairman's speech, UBI Ltd., 1968). In another speech, Dutt pointed out that at the end of 1968, the cities of Bombay, Calcutta, Madras and Ahmedabad contributed deposits to the tune of Rs 1597 crores, while their share in bank credit amounted to Rs 1804 crores. If account was taken of liquidity requirements against deposits, the imbalance between advances and deposits assumed further significance. On the other hand, while the non-metropolitan areas contributed deposits to the tune of Rs 2451 crores, bank advances amounted to only Rs 1110 crores. Clearly, resources were being diverted from non-metropolitan centres to metropolitan centres. Distributive trade and instalment credit were being ignored in the countryside (Dutt, 'Responsibilities of Business towards Banks', address to FICCI, New Delhi, 12 April 1971, pp. 4–5). All this implied that the state had to ensure an equitable and growth-oriented expansion of banking services.

Let us go back to theory again briefly. Neoclassical economic theory implicitly states that banks play an egalitarian role by allowing people to save and obtain a reasonable rate of return and thus accu-

213

mulate wealth (Stiglitz 1969); recent theoretical models of income distribution based on information economics have highlighted the fact that credit markets are typically imperfect and consequently convergence to equality may be extremely slow and poverty traps might still persist (Banerjee and Newman 1991). Recent developments in the theory of development of financial markets has argued, on the other hand, that with an increase in aggregate savings, the set-up costs of starting a financial intermediary could be met by a sufficient number of entrepreneurs, which would enable efficient risk-bearing to take place through financial intermediaries. This in turn would lead to greater income and a lower level of income inequality (Greenwood and Jovanovich 1990). Thus savings affects the growth pattern of an economy in this way. But raising savings requires an autonomous mechanism before banks can develop adequately. This is where the economic vision of the policy maker comes into play. In Dutt's mind the mechanism was the socialization of banks. The fundamental need, he pointed out, is that each bank's future should directly be tied up with the economic development of a zone in which it operates. It would then be under structural pressure to leave no stone unturned to develop the zone of its operation, in so far as imagination and appropriate objectivity, along with the provision of finance can achieve such development. It is therefore necessary to bring about a system which will confine the area of operation of a bank to a designated banking zone. If this could not be done, then forced nationalization was the only option in his mind.

This was Dutt's mission and vision statement in a nutshell. There is something of the Gandhian idea of development reflected here, and it also has a relation with the community participation literature in economics and sociology in light of recent experiences of less developed countries. From the modern viewpoint of information economics one can say that usage of local resources where information is better available creates efficiency gains, but there may be limits to it. Dutt's ideas on community participation in banking and group-lending schemes, and emphasis on small borrowers were based on equity considerations rather than efficiency gains. What is missing is appreciation of the free rider problem which pervades the provision of public goods. Perhaps one cannot blame Dutt on this issue, for those were days of valour and self-sacrifice. Sadly, things have changed and

214

some of those ideas can only be called unrealistic ideals in today's maximizing and opportunistic society.

Personally, Dutt was against excessive regulation and intervention by government or the Reserve Bank of India in banking matters, but neither did he subscribe to the profit-maximizing role of the banker. He and his senior managers at UBI persistently argued that the business community should take up social responsibilities, rather than asking the state to take over the running and restructuring of the economy. While they often differed with some of the government policies regarding banking, they at the same time campaigned with entrepreneurs to develop a certain social attitude if they wished to prevent direct nationalization of banking institutions.

Conclusion

B.K. Dutt was shaped by the economic compulsions and aspirations of life, as well as the spirit of idealism shaped by our culture and national history. To what extent he represented the average banker of his period may be debated. Perhaps he was too progressive and too special to be a representative example, and this is also precisely why he had a large influence on banking policy, the financial community and his clients. But his management of the bank seems to emerge from modern textbooks on banking and economics (Frexias and Rochet 2008).

I am indebted to Saugata Mukherjee, Amiya Bagchi and Sugata Marjit for encouraging me to write this paper. The usual disclaimer applies.

Notes

[1] Of course, the government has a special role in mobilizing capital as well as directing its use in less developed countries, but the attendant risk of misallocation of resources through incentive and information problems of planning and conflict of objectives at the political centres has proved this to be at best a necessary and not a sufficient condition for economic development.

[2] It is true that banks could in principal hold diversified portfolios which cut across regional boundaries, but the socio-economic barriers to branching in this land of diversity ensured that there would be limits to regional financial integration. Some communities like the Marwaris have defied these barriers with considerable success, but in general community migration and dispersion throughout the country have been an exception rather

than a rule. Banks, therefore, have been by and large community banks, much to the lamentation of the neoclassical economist and the euphoria of the sociologist.

[3] The phrase came to be associated with a number of families which originally hailed from Multan in Sind but subsequently settled in Bombay. They had devised their own system of lending money with controlled risk and without any security. Generally they lent Rs 5000 to a party, though a number of Multani bankers could together lend a few lakhs of rupees to a borrower. These bills were discounted by the Imperial Bank and other banks.

[4] Conditions under which, as long as depositors do not all simultaneously run on the banks, every financial claim is paid, is known as a situation of sound fundamentals in banking industry (Tobin 1969).

References

Allen, F. and D. Gale, 1999, 'Optimal Financial Crises', *Journal of Finance*, LIII (4), August.

Bagchi, Amiya Kumar, 1987, *Evolution of the State Bank of India, Parts I and II*, Oxford University Press, Bombay.

Bagehot, W., 1873, *Lombard Street: A Description of the Money Market*, H.S. King, London.

Banerjee, A. and A. Newman, 1991, 'Risk Bearing and a Theory of Income Distribution', *Review of Economic Studies*, Vol. 58, pp. 211–35.

Bannerjee, Prathama, 1999, 'Notes on UBI Merger', unpublished manuscript, Centre for Studies in Social Sciences, Calcutta.

Bannerjee, Prathama, 2000, 'A Social History of Banking in Bengal', unpublished manuscript, Centre for Studies in Social Sciences, Calcutta.

Berger, A.N., S.D. Bonime, L.G. Goldberg and L.J. White, 2000, 'The dynamics of market entry: The effects of mergers and acquisitions on *de novo* entry and customer service', Working Paper, Wharton School of Management, University of Pennsylvania.

Boot, A. and A.V. Thakor, 2000, 'Can relationship banking survive competition?', *Journal of Finance*, Vol. 55, pp. 679–713.

Diamond, D. and P. Dybvig, 1983, 'Bank runs, deposit insurance and liquidity', *Journal of Political Economy*, Vol. 91, pp. 401–19.

Dutt, B.K., 1994, *Pages from a Banker's Diary*, B.K. Dutt Trust, Kolkata.

Frexias, X. and J-C Rochet, 2008, *Microeconomics of Banking*, second edition, MIT Press, Cambridge, MA.

Friedman, M. and A. Schwartz, 1963, *A Monetary History of the United States, 1867–1960*, Princeton University Press, Princeton, NJ.

Gale, Douglas, 1993, 'Unit Banking versus Branch Banking', Boston University Working Paper, Boston, MA.

Greenwood, J. and B. Jovanovitch, 1993, 'Financial Development, Growth and Distribution of Income', *Journal of Political Economy*, 98 (5), pp. 1076–1107.

Stiglitz, J., 1969, 'Distribution of Income and Wealth among Individuals', *Econometrica*, 37 (3), pp. 382–97.

Stiglitz, J. and A. Weiss, 1981, 'Credit Rationing with Imperfect Information', *American Economic Review,* Vol. 71, pp. 393–410.

Tobin, J., 1969, 'A general equilibrium approach to monetary theory', *Journal of Money Credit and Banking,* 1 (1), pp. 15–29.

Contributors

KRISHNA MOHAN SHRIMALI. Professor of History, Delhi University, Delhi.

OM PRAKASH. Professor of Economic History, Delhi School of Economics, Delhi University, Delhi.

NAJAF HAIDER. Lecturer in History, Delhi University, Delhi.

SHIREEN MOOSVI. Professor of History, Aligarh Muslim University, Aligarh.

A.R. KULKARNI. Former Professor of History, Pune University, Pune.

RAJAT KANTA RAY. Professor of History, Presidency College, Kolkata.

DWIJENDRA TRIPATHI. Former Professor of Business, Indian Institute of Management, Ahmedabad.

ADITYA MUKHERJEE. Professor of Contemporary Indian History, Centre for Historical Studies, Jawaharlal Nehru University, New Delhi.

MANZUR AHSAN. Reader in History, Jahangirnagar University, Dhaka, Bangladesh.

SUNANDA SEN. Former Professor of Economics, Centre for Economic Studies and Planning, Jawaharlal Nehru University, New Delhi.

INDRAJIT MALLICK. State Bank of India, Kolkata.

219

Index

Index

Index

John of Julfa, 68

Kabul, 4
Kadapah (Cuddapah), 21
Kalanju coinage, 14
Kale, D.V. 101
Kallikatti (south Karnataka), 19
kamavisdars, 97, 112
Karimis, 8
karjapati (levy), 112
Karja Rokha (documents), 109
Karnul (Kurnool), 21
Karori, 67
Kasindra hoard, 6, 26
Kasturbhai Lalbhai, 208
Kasturi, Srinivasan (*The Hindu*), 208
Kayika, 20
Keynes, J.M., 152, 187
Khan, Subahdar Azam, 51
khar muhra, 62
Khare, G.H., 100
khazana, 70
Khurran (Jahangir), 67
Kisch, Cecil, 191
Kolhapur stone inscription of Bhoja II, 19
Kolhapur stone inscription of Gandar-
    aditya, 24
Konkan, 13
Kothari, C.M., of Madras, 209
Ksatrapas, 21
Kstrapa coins, 7
Kulkarni, A.R., 93, 109
Kulke, Hermann, 13
Kunbi, 106
Kushana gold coins, 22
Kushanas, 9
krishak, 181

Lakhumana Ghaisasa, 20
Lakshman Appaji, 97
Lakshmi-type, 3
Lalbhai Kalinbhai Zaveri, 140
landlords, 11
laris (silver coin), 94
Legislative Assembly, 154, 181
Lekhadhipati, 18

Lindsay, Martin, 187
Living without Silver, 7, 21
Lowick, N.M., 8
London, 72, 149, 189, 191, 192, 193, 194,
    195, 196, 197
Lord Curzon, 135

Madhavrao, Gosavi, 95
Madhya Pradesh, 6
Madras, 207, 208, 213
Magha, 21
mahajans, 59, 64
Maharashtra, 6, 12, 93
Maharaja, 134, 135, 137, 143
Mahavira temple (at Arasans), 19
Mahmudis (Gujarati), 101
Mahuli fort (Satara fistrict), 94
major banking houses of Maratha, Tul-
    shibagwale, Chiplunkar, Khasgi-
    wale, Biwalkar, Dixit Patwardhan
    and Vaidya, 105
Malabar, 46
Malacca, 15
Malay peninsula (Krabi), 17
Malda, 52
Maldives, 62
Mamluck, 8
managaram, 12
Mandu, 67
mansabdars, 64
Mantala Tea Company, 205
masters of the mint, Anikar and Vatkar, 98
Marathas, 93, 99
Maratha chiefs, Pant-Sachiv of Bhor,
    Pratinidhi of Andhra, Patwardhan
    of Sangali and Miraj, 115
Maratha court of Thanjavur, 118
Marco Polo, 13
market towns, Agra, Hathros, Khurza, 127
Marshall Plan in Europe, 188
Martin, Burn, 209
Marwadi Chamber of Commerce, 121
Marwaris, 120
Masulipatnam, 49, 72, 85
matha, 26
medieval England, 18

Index